"*Spiritual Healing from Sexual Violence* approaches healing from sexual violence from an intersectional perspective that brings forth the voices of people with BOTH lived experience and professional training. It is also an act of antiracism in that contributing authors are from BIPOC communities. Additionally, it integrates religion and spirituality and helps the reader grapple with the complexities of our intersectional social identities and the ways in which those inform our experiences and approaches to intervention with and support of survivors."

Tammy Hatfield, PhD, *professor in the School of Social and Behavioral Sciences at the University of the Cumberlands, Kentucky, USA*

"*Spiritual Healing from Sexual Violence* encompasses spirituality as both a destructive and healing means. For many this will make the book more appealing and broad reaching. This book, I believe, will resonate with some survivors for whom more traditional talk therapy has not proved as effective."

Miriam Duignan, *head of communication at the Wijngaards Institute for Catholic Research, UK*

"What's fascinating for readers about using *Spiritual Healing from Sexual Violence* is the intersectional, interdisciplinary ways of thinking. There is so much about which readers can become more curious when the various themes touch their humanity from different perspectives. The themes chosen for each chapter in this book are engaging, and each chapter turns the prism of understanding."

Marge Kloos, *pastoral care professor emeritus, University of Mount St. Joseph, Ohio, USA*

Spiritual Healing from Sexual Violence

Spiritual Healing from Sexual Violence: An Intersectional Guide is a collection of essays from survivors, scholars, activists, spiritual leaders, and social justice practitioners that offers numerous intersectional and culturally competent options for women, men, and nonbinary conforming adults to create their own safe healing conditions and establish pathways for recovery. These chapters provide a wide range of survival stories that raise awareness of the issues involved in healing after sexual assault and also provide inspiration for reforming negative societal issues and patterns. In a classroom setting, these chapters deliver both the culturally grounded knowledge and the skillsets necessary for recovery.

This book is a vital guide for students and practitioners in counseling, social work, theology, and gender studies.

Debra Meyers, PhD, is a professor of history, gender studies, and religious studies at Northern Kentucky University.

Rev. Mary Sue Barnett is a priest (ARCWP), founder of the Louisville Coalition for CEDAW (Convention on the Elimination of all Forms of Discrimination Against Women), and a mental health hospital chaplain.

Spiritual Healing from Sexual Violence

An Intersectional Guide

Edited by Debra Meyers and
Mary Sue Barnett

NEW YORK AND LONDON

Cover image by Kimberly C. Rhyan

First published 2023
by Routledge
605 Third Avenue, New York, NY 10158

and by Routledge
4 Park Square, Milton Park, Abingdon, Oxon, OX14 4RN

Routledge is an imprint of the Taylor & Francis Group, an informa business

© 2023 selection and editorial matter, Debra Meyers and Mary Sue Barnett; individual chapters, the contributors

The right of Debra Meyers and Mary Sue Barnett to be identified as the authors of the editorial material, and of the authors for their individual chapters, has been asserted in accordance with sections 77 and 78 of the Copyright, Designs and Patents Act 1988.

All rights reserved. No part of this book may be reprinted or reproduced or utilised in any form or by any electronic, mechanical, or other means, now known or hereafter invented, including photocopying and recording, or in any information storage or retrieval system, without permission in writing from the publishers.

Trademark notice: Product or corporate names may be trademarks or registered trademarks, and are used only for identification and explanation without intent to infringe.

Library of Congress Cataloging-in-Publication Data
Names: Meyers, Debra, 1956– editor. | Barnett, Mary Sue, editor.
Title: Spiritual healing from sexual violence : an intersectional guide / edited by Debra Meyers and Mary Sue Barnett.
Description: New York, NY : Routledge, 2023. | Includes bibliographical references and index.
Identifiers: LCCN 2022049707 (print) | LCCN 2022049708 (ebook) | ISBN 9781032334998 (hbk) |
ISBN 9781032334950 (pbk) | ISBN 9781003323631 (ebk)
Subjects: LCSH: Spiritual healing. | Sex crimes.
Classification: LCC BT732.5 .S6666 2023 (print) |
LCC BT732.5 (ebook) | DDC 261.8/3272—dc23/eng/20230223
LC record available at https://lccn.loc.gov/2022049707
LC ebook record available at https://lccn.loc.gov/2022049708

ISBN: 978-1-032-33499-8 (hbk)
ISBN: 978-1-032-33495-0 (pbk)
ISBN: 978-1-003-32363-1 (ebk)

DOI: 10.4324/9781003323631

Typeset in Sabon
by Apex CoVantage, LLC

Contents

List of Figures		ix
About the Contributors		x
My Survivor Story in 750 Words		xiv
BY KIMBERLY C. RHYAN		
Introduction		1
DEBRA MEYERS		
1	A Sacred Trust: The Spiritual Community's Duty	5
	LAUREN D. SAWYER	
2	Empowering Prayer for Healing	23
	ABBY KING-KAISER	
3	Clergy Abuse and Students' Moral Injury	42
	ASHLEY THEURING AND ANNE K. FULLER	
4	Healing with God's Nonlinear Nonbinary Love	60
	PAUL A. TENKOTTE	
5	Somatic Spirituality for the Traumatized	80
	HYE HYUN HAN	
6	Deconstruction and Reclamation: A Healing	97
	ANNETTE WILLIAMS	
7	A Spiritual Being Having a Human Experience	116
	QUANITA ROBERSON	

8 Ancestral Releasing of Trauma Through Ritual SANDRA SAUCEDO	127
9 Healing with Maa: A Shakti Bhaktic Approach RACHELLE ELIZABETH	141
10 Nature as Muse MARION GAIL DUMONT	159
11 The Healing Power of Divine Intimacy MARY SUE BARNETT	175
12 Reclaiming the Divine on the Road to Recovery DEBRA MEYERS	195
Index	212

Figures

10.1	Raven and the Rose: Pyrography on fungus	164
10.2	Woodland Talisman Pendant: Red Cedar	164
10.3	Drawings and Watercolor	168
10.4	Madness of Mis Shawl: Wool fiber, rabbit fur, and turkey feathers	169
10.5	Betrayal: Vessel made of copper and silk taffeta	169
10.6	Changing Tides: Oyster shell, gold leaf, Moonstone, and Douglas fir	170
11.1	Woman Christ, Raped on Campus by Julie Tallent	186

About the Contributors

Rev. Mary Sue Barnett is a priest, ordained by the Association of Roman Catholic Women Priests. She is founder of the Louisville Coalition for CEDAW (Convention on the Elimination of All Forms of Discrimination Against Women) a grassroots nongovernmental organization that seeks to implement the rights and principles of this United Nations women's treaty on the local level. She has advocated for women and girls at the United Nations in New York City and Geneva, has assisted victims during rape kit exams, and has created feminist liturgies for the spiritual support of survivors. She also serves as a chaplain at psychiatric and Level 1 Trauma hospitals. Barnett recently published *Hating Girls: An Intersectional Survey of Misogyny* (2021).

Marion Gail Dumont, RN, PhD, completed a Bachelor of Science from Seattle Pacific University focusing on maternal-child nursing. In 2013 she earned a doctorate degree from the California Institute of Integral Studies in Philosophy and Religion with a specialization in women's spirituality and a particular focus on women's mysteries, sacred arts, and healing. Over the course of her career, she has received training in other healing modalities including Therapeutic Touch and Reiki. As a writer, artist, nurse, and practitioner of the healing arts her work emerges out of personal experience and an understanding of the interconnectedness of nature, art, and spirituality.

Rachelle Elizabeth is a doctoral candidate in Theology and Ethics at the Graduate Theological Union in Berkeley, California. She works and studies as a scholar-practitioner of (Hindu) Shakta Bhakti philosophy as it relates to healing after trauma and the creation of an eco-praxis that engages decolonial theory, interfaith dialogue, aesthetics, and social justice. Elizabeth is also a Minnesota Master Naturalist and the co-founder of Northwoods Shakta, a Shakti Bhakti community focused on ecological healing in the Minnesota Northwoods.

Anne K. Fuller, PhD, is an assistant professor in the School of Psychology at Xavier University in Cincinnati, Ohio. She received her PhD in

Clinical Psychology from Loyola University Chicago, with a focus on children and families. Her research focuses on factors that promote risk and resilience regarding mental health and well-being among children and adolescents as well as community-based research. She has also conducted research related to trauma and has received training in trauma-focused interventions for children and adolescents.

Hye Hyun Han is a PhD candidate focusing on Christian Spirituality at the Graduate Theological Union in Berkeley, California. Her research focuses on the areas of human objectification, including the theological objectification of women in Christianity, sexual objectification of the female body in the continuing wars in Korea, and somatic spirituality for people traumatized by such objectification. She recently published articles titled, "The Body as the Space in which Power Operates: Sexual Violence of Clergymen in the Korean Church" and "Art-Based Spiritual Practice for the Victims of Human Objectification." She is also an ordained minister of the Korean Methodist Church.

Rev. Abby King-Kaiser is a Presbyterian pastor who has spent most of her career as a campus minister. A MDiv graduate of the Pacific School of Religion in Berkley, California, she is the Director of the Dorothy Day Center for Faith and Justice at Xavier University in Cincinnati, Ohio. Her first role at Xavier invited her to provide spiritual growth and support for all the non-Catholic students, including starting a Protestant Worship Service.

Debra Meyers, PhD, is professor of history, gender studies, and religious studies at Northern Kentucky University. Meyers received her PhD from the University of Rochester and has published numerous books as a professor at Northern Kentucky University including *Hating Girls: An Intersectional Survey of Misogyny* (2021). Meyers was recognized for her achievements with NKU's 2019 Frank Sinton Milburn Outstanding Professor Award, which honors a faculty member who has demonstrated excellence in teaching, scholarship, and service over the course of her/his career.

Kimberly C. Rhyan is a soul-inspired educator, advocate, artist, speaker, and survivor. She is a creative who seeks to enact social change through her art and writing. She is a dedicated advocate for foster youth and mental health awareness. She speaks nationally and presents workshops, utilizing her story, resiliency practices, and the creative arts. She earned her bachelor's degree in Fine Art and master's degree in Creative Art Therapy. Her personal story of reconciliation and resiliency focuses on moving from hurt to healing through empowerment and self-care. This mindset influences her creative journey, and she hopes that her art nurtures growth and healing for others.

About the Contributors

Quanita Roberson is the executive director of Nzuzu Consulting, author, and shaman dedicated to addressing embedded trauma. Roberson is a spiritual teacher, speaker, author, life coach, and a storyteller focused in the areas of healing, initiation, grief, leadership, diversity, and inclusion. Her education includes organizational management and development with a concentration in integral theory. She has published three books: *Soul Growing: Wisdom for 13-year-old boys from men around the world*; *Soul Growing II: Wisdom for 13-year-old girls from women around the world*; and *The InnerGround Railroad: A 40 Day Journey to Remembering Soul and Spirit*.

Sandra Saucedo, PhD, earned her doctorate in philosophy and religion with a concentration in women's spirituality, as well as a master's in integral health studies from the California Institute of Integral Studies, San Francisco, California. Born in La Paz, Bolivia, she is an artist, healer, nutritionist, sexologist, and life coach with a shamanic lens from the Tiwanaku (Aymara) people of Bolivia.

Lauren D. Sawyer, PhD, is an educator and ethicist living in Seattle, Washington. In her role as program manager for FaithTrust Institute, she developed trainings and curriculum for a variety of spiritual communities and participated in investigating allegations of clergy misconduct. Lauren's expertise includes feminist sexual ethics, white evangelical purity culture, and trauma-informed responses to gender-based violence. Lauren received her PhD in Christian social ethics from Drew University and teaches at Seattle School of Theology and Psychology.

Paul A. Tenkotte, PhD, has extensive publishing experience, including authoring/editing ten books and four researcher guides, writing chapters and entries for thirteen additional books, and authoring/editing hundreds of articles for a wide range of media. He also has participated in twenty television documentaries. His weekly column, *Our Rich History* www.nkytribune.com/category/our-rich-history, is read nationally for its insightful series and articles on Ohio Valley heritage. An award-winning teacher, he serves as professor of history and gender studies at Northern Kentucky University (NKU) in metropolitan Cincinnati.

Ashley Theuring is an assistant professor in theology, specializing in constructive and practical theologies. She completed her doctorate at the Boston University School of Theology in the Practical Theology program. Her theological research is informed by her past work at a rape, crisis, and abuse center, Women Helping Women of Hamilton County, where she was an advocate and educator. Her research continues to be informed by contemporary communities of trauma survivors and focuses on exploring religious practices, meaning making, and survival in response to trauma.

Annette Williams, PhD, is an associate professor and chair of the Women's Spirituality Department at the California Institute of Integral Studies. She holds a doctorate in philosophy and religion with specialization in women's spirituality. Her research interests have centered on soul healing from sexual trauma, and the theme of women's spiritual power and agency within the Yorùbá *Ifá* tradition, with specific reference to the primordial feminine authority of *àjẹ́*. A recent offering is "Wisdom of the Primordial Feminine, Wisdom of Women: Odù Ifá and Yoruba Religious Tradition," in *Philo-Sophia: Wisdom Goddess Traditions*, edited by Debashish Banerji and Robert McDermott.

My Survivor Story in 750 Words

Kimberly C. Rhyan

My parents divorced when I was a baby
And between 12 months and 5 years old,
I experienced all but one of the ACEs
Those are called Adverse Childhood Experiences—
I experienced abuse and neglect
I witnessed violence in my home
I had a family member attempt suicide
I had parents with substance abuse and addiction problems
I had a parent with mental health disorders
I suffered instability due to parental separation—

At age 2,
I witnessed and experienced domestic violence
And became a helpless victim
During those formative years,
I cannot remember outright,
But my body remembers,
My heart still hurts,
The aftershocks
Haunt my spirit.
My mother's love was vacant
A father was AWOL
And I was unsure,
If I would ever feel safe—

As a pre-teen to an adolescent,
from age 11 to 14,
I was molested and sexually abused—
Every morning and evening,
I squeezed my legs tightly together
To keep him out
but he succeeded

and I always held back tears,
As he violated my trust,
made excuses for his abuse,
And threatened my existence—
Every day, every month and for too many years,
I questioned my self-worth,
And wished I had never been born.
The fear alone, was paralyzing,
As I summoned the strength
To survive just one more day—
I was just a kid
I wish someone taught me
that my body belonged to me
And I was unsure,
If I would ever feel safe.

I finally spoke my truth at 14,
My mother chose the date and time,
When she cornered and confronted me,
She pulled a piece of paper from her purse,
One of countless notes,
I hid in my room for years—
I wrote for help,
I wrote to be heard,
I wrote to be rescued,
Instead, I felt betrayed—
I collapsed and cried on the kitchen floor.
My mother's disbelief was difficult to endure,
Their abuse was more than unfair,
my mother never left my abuser's side
She chose him over me
My mother didn't stand up for me
She said, "don't make me choose,
Because I will always choose my husband"
She called me a bitch and sent me back to foster care—
Until I aged out,
just like 1,000s of Ohio's foster youth—
And
I was unsure,
If I would ever feel safe.

In my 20s
I was hurt by what I hoped was real love
I became an empty shell

Living as a ghost
I never once believed
I was lovable—
And I was unsure,
If I would ever feel safe.

In my 30s I was raped,
And believed it was my fault.
Years later, I was also assaulted on a first date
when I declined dinner and left the date early.
He followed me and hit my car.
Instead of running, I stood up to him,
But he punched me and put his arms around my neck
And slammed me against the wall.
I did not ask for it,
nor did I deserve what happened to me.
Yet, I know, what happened to me,
happens to countless women each day—
And I was unsure,
If we would ever feel safe.

In my 40s, I have guarded my heart
And strived to stay clear of love
I clearly distance myself,
To protect myself from being hurt
I avoid long-term relationships—
Life just makes more sense this way—
What my married friends think of as a lifestyle,
I believe, isn't much of a life at all—
Because I do want more
My survivor story doesn't erase my desires and dreams—
But I have always seemed unsure,
If I would ever feel safe.

I endured years of abuse while anxiety creeped into my veins.

I am Resilient.

I will continue to find ways to thrive and arrive, as I overcome triggers, anxiety, and depression.

I am Not my PTSD.

Painting and writing are my healing practices.

I am a Creative.

I find ways to cope and keep on keeping on, despite setbacks and roadblocks.

I am Not a Statistic.

I've learned to overcome past shadows.

I am Stronger than my Mother—

I walk my journey to express determination to persist and succeed.

I refuse to give up.

Every day is a new beginning,
My experiences do not define me,
They refine me and redesign my purpose,
I am a resilient—not silent—Survivor.
And this is my soul-inspired message for you—
Never give up on yourself because your story matters—
Just pick up the pen and begin to heal.

Introduction

Debra Meyers

According to the RAINN (Rape, Abuse & Incest National Network) website (rain.org), sexual predators assault victims in the United States *every 68 seconds*. For most females, the assailant was someone they knew and trusted. Researchers estimate that between 20 and 45 percent of females have been sexually assaulted as children—approximately half of which were incest.[1] There are many organizations providing physical and mental assistance to victims, such as Zero Abuse Project and Sexual Assault Response Teams (SART). However, in addition to physical and mental trauma many victims suffer spiritual damage as well. Victims deeply steeped in religious dogma often experience a terrifying fear of falling from God's grace or the spiritual questioning of their religious belief in God's fairness. And when the perpetrator is a religious leader that the victim trusted and respected, the trauma may paralyze them and send them into a downward spiral that prevents any type of healing. While the substantial research into the impact of sexual abuse on spirituality is immense, few secular organizations deal with the spiritual trauma these victims face. And the organizations set up to address spiritual trauma are far more difficult to identify for victims and/or their parents.

Typically, social service providers overlook the cultural and spiritual resources that could be deployed in a victim's struggle to heal. With the overwhelming number of victims, most financially strapped assistance programs must focus on housing, counseling, peer support, skill-set building, and healthcare. But ignoring the spiritual needs of these victims may further traumatize them.

Most faith traditions do not offer ministers adequate training in pastoral care specifically dealing with sexual violence. Indeed, many religious leaders compound the trauma by participating in silencing victims using "theological justifications, particularly the sanctity of the family, to justify its silencing" of victims. These ministers have been "in unquestioning collusion with patriarchy in terms of assuming the normativity (and believability) of males."[2] The underlying theology of Christianity today idealizes qualities (especially for women) "those of a victim: sacrificial love, passive acceptance of suffering, humility, meekness, etc. Since these are the qualities idealized in Jesus 'who died for our sins,' his functioning as a model reinforces the scapegoat syndrome for women."[3] Worse yet, children are often presented with a terrifying image of the divine as a father who would welcome the death of his own son on the cross.[4] Given the theological challenges, most ministers provide little real support for sexual assault victims.

Adding to this vacuity of support are the many religious leaders who commit sexual assaults on their flock. These perpetrators often use religious teachings to justify sexual violence and silence the victims. Theological issues related to suffering, forgiveness, authority, and sexuality can be used to distort a victim's perspective in the aftermath of an assault. Ministers may employ this inculcated vulnerability to suppress a victim's call for help. Perpetrators may use religious texts and teachings to exonerate themselves and further subjugate the victim into cooperating. Even faith leaders with good intentions *without proper training* can exacerbate the pain and suffering of a sexual assault victim. Harmful language that blames the victim or faith-based justification of the perpetrator may be so ingrained in the good-faith minister that they do not realize how they are adding to the suffering of the victim. This often leads to victims blaming themselves for the sexual assault and viewing their situation as God's will.

With the overwhelming numbers of sexual assault victims with deep religious convictions, we need to address their spiritual recovery as well as their mental and physical healing. And given the increasing diversity in the United States, sexual assault victim services must address the needs of survivors from specific cultural communities. Culturally competent programs are required to integrate resources, including spiritual ones, that will meet the needs of sociocultural identities of marginalized populations. Thus, there is a tremendous unmet demand for this intersectional and interdisciplinary book as a pathway to recovery for many victims of sexual assault to be used in college classrooms, in faith-based recovery programs, as well as secular victim assistance organizations.

Spiritual Healing from Sexual Violence: An Intersectional Guide is a collection of essays from survivors, scholars, activist reformers, spiritual leaders, and social justice practitioners offering numerous intersectional and culturally competent options for women, men, and nonbinary conforming adults to explore as a means to create their own safe healing conditions and establish pathways for recovery. These chapters provide many culturally unique survival stories that can raise awareness of the issues involved in healing after sexual assault while influencing society's values and belief systems that currently hinder a victim's ability to heal. In a classroom setting, these chapters deliver both the culturally grounded knowledge and the skillsets necessary for recovery.

We begin the book with a survivor's poem from Kimberly Rhyan that summarizes the trauma, pain, grief, and many obstructions victims face before creating a personalized pathway to spiritual recovery. There is no easy fix or simple steps that everyone can adopt. Instead, this book offers a diverse and intersectional collection of possible pathways forward. Chapters 1 to 5 provide suggestions for healing in group or organizational structures. Lauren D. Sawyer, in Chapter 1, reminds us that religious organizations can sometimes provide a hospitable environment for predators and because of this fact, religious communities have a moral obligation to provide the effective healing practices that FaithTrust has developed over the years. Similarly, Abby King-Kaiser in Chapter 2 outlines a practical and empowering strategy for ecumenical healing implemented in a university setting while Ashley Theuring and Anne Fuller investigate the serious moral and spiritual impacts the Roman Catholic clergy sexual abuse crisis has had on university students in Chapter 3. In Chapter 4, Paul Tenkotte unpacks the LGBTQIA+ community's struggle with sexual abuse trauma in the context of the community's liminal social status. Hye Hyun Han, in Chapter 5 dives deeply into the relationships between and among our bodies, sexual assault, and spirituality as they relate to our rape culture that objectifies victims' bodies.

Chapters 6 to 12 provide personal stories of trauma and recovery. Annette Williams, in Chapter 6, examines childhood sexual abuse from a Black woman's perspective using a heuristic research paradigm to restore her personal power. Also rooted in African traditions, Shaman Quanita Roberson offers a different set of options for spiritual healing while finding her place in her community after being forced to live with her perpetrator even after his conviction in the court system in Chapter 7. Life coach, Sandra Saucedo, addresses the healing pathways taken by Latina women after migrating to the United States in Chapter 8 while Rachelle Elizabeth offers readers unique practices from the Shakti bhakti tradition that have helped many women embrace the Divine Mother in Chapter 9. Marion Gail Dumont's personal spiritual journey is explored in Chapter 10 where she details practical ways in which nature and art can be used to find wholeness after trauma. In Chapter 11, hospital chaplain, Mary Sue Barnett offers suggestions for recovery based on her personal experience as well, by locating the Divine within a victim's own body to alleviate suffering when faith communities abandon victims. Similarly in Chapter 12, Debra Meyers describes her own spiritual healing process that also centers on locating the Divine within when traditional religious dogma left her feeling like God had abandoned her. For many of our contributors, reconceptualizing the Divine and its relationship to victims offers many supportive pathways toward spiritual healing. Collectively, these chapters in *Spiritual Healing from Sexual Violence* outline diverse, intersectional recovery steps for gender-based violence while exposing some of the destructive beliefs and practices of our current rape culture.

Notes

1 Dianne Herman, "The Rape Culture," in *Women: A Feminist Perspective*, 3rd ed., ed. Jo Freeman (Palo Alto, Calif.: Mayfield, 1984) 32.
2 Christie Cozad Neuger, *Counseling Women: A Narrative, Pastoral Approach* (Minneapolis: Fortress Press, 2001) 95.
3 Mary Daly, *Beyond God the Father: Toward a Philosophy of Women's Liberation* (Boston: Beacon, 1973) 77.
4 Annie Imbens and Ineke Jonker, *Christianity and Incest*, trans. Patricia McVay (Minneapolis: Fortress Press, 1992) 212. See also Black, Basile, Breiding, Smith, Walters, Merrick, Chen, and Stevens, National Intimate Partner and Sexual Violence Survey, www.cdc.gov/ViolencePrevention/pdf/NISVS_Report2010-a.pdf.

Bibliography

Black, Basile, Breiding, Smith, Walters, Merrick, Chen, and Stevens, National Intimate Partner and Sexual Violence Survey, www.cdc.gov/ViolencePrevention/pdf/NISVS_Report2010-a.pdf.

Daly, Mary. *Beyond God the Father: Toward a Philosophy of Women's Liberation* (Boston: Beacon, 1973).

Herman, Dianne. "The Rape Culture," in Women: A Feminist Perspective, 3rd ed., ed. Jo Freeman (Palo Alto, Calif.: Mayfield, 1984).

Imbens, Annie and Ineke Jonker. *Christianity and Incest*, trans. Patricia McVay (Minneapolis: Fortress Press, 1992).

Neuger, Christie Cozad. *Counseling Women: A Narrative, Pastoral Approach* (Minneapolis: Fortress Press, 2001).

Chapter 1

A Sacred Trust
The Spiritual Community's Duty

Lauren D. Sawyer

Background

Spiritual communities have a moral responsibility and sacred duty to care for the vulnerable in their midst and therefore ought to prepare for allegations of sexual abuse, especially when the perpetrator is a leader or member of the community. What we have seen instead, however, are spiritual communities doubling down on protecting perpetrators over and against the spiritual, emotional, and physical safety of victim-survivors.

This chapter leverages the 40-plus years of experience and insights of FaithTrust Institute, a multifaith organization that provides training, resources, and consultation to spiritual communities that are addressing gender-based violence and abuse (both domestic violence and spiritual leader misconduct).[1] Founded by feminist ethicist and United Church of Christ clergywoman Rev. Dr. Marie Fortune in 1977, FaithTrust Institute has been at the forefront of the movement to prevent and respond to sexual abuse and misconduct within religious organizations. For over 15 years, FaithTrust has worked closely with primarily Protestant Christian denominations and Buddhist communities to develop safe church/sangha policies, provide healthy boundaries training for leaders and board members, and consult on and investigate allegations of misconduct. Central to FaithTrust Institute's theological and ethical approach to its work is understanding that spiritual communities can either be a resource or a roadblock to victim-survivors. That is, spiritual communities can either facilitate the healing process (resource) or hinder it (roadblock). This article works to unpack common roadblocks—through composite case studies adapted from real-life examples—and provides concrete ways spiritual communities can be better resources to victim-survivors through what we call the *justice-making agenda*.

Laying the Groundwork

Upon receiving credentials, ordination, transmission, or installation, spiritual leaders are given the sacred task to care for the congregants, students, clients, or practitioners in their community. Formally, we say that spiritual leaders have a fiduciary responsibility for the assets—the people—in their care.[2] A power imbalance exists between those in the role of the spiritual leader and those who look to them for spiritual guidance. "Ministerial relationships are asymmetrical," writes Christian ethicist Darryl W. Stephens, "the pastor is there to serve the needs of the parishioner (fiduciary duty), not the other way around."[3] This is true whether the spiritual leader is wearing her robes or collar, whether she is in the pulpit, on the cushion, or on social media. "When a clergyperson interacts with a person in her congregation, she represents more than herself." She acts as a representative of the congregation or sacred community, the profession of clergy or spiritual teacher, the religion itself, and God/the Divine.[4]

Consistent with liberal feminist thought,[5] we at FaithTrust teach that power is a neutral category—it is about having more or fewer resources than another person within a specific context. A spiritual leader typically has more resources than the congregant, student, client, or practitioner in their care, and they can use those resources to help or harm them.[6] A congregant, student, client, or practitioner, then, typically has fewer resources than their spiritual leader and is vulnerable to being helped or harmed by their leader. A rabbi could use her title and credentials (power) to speak publicly about reproductive rights for Jewish women. A member of the synagogue, who in counseling shares her story of an abortion with her rabbi (vulnerability), could be harmed if the rabbi publicly shares the member's story without her consent. Because of the power of the rabbinate, people look to the rabbi as an authority—indeed, a stand-in for God. She can use that power and authority to either help or harm those in her care.

There are certain contexts in which a congregant, client, student, or practitioner may have more social resources based on privileges associated with wealth, gender, race, or physical resources related to strength or ability. They may use those resources to help or harm peers or their spiritual leader. For instance, a 300-pound male parishioner could use his strength (power) to corner his petite female pastor (vulnerability) in her office and sexually assault her. Or, a white yoga practitioner could use her race (power) to propagate racial stereotypes, causing practitioners of color (vulnerability) to no longer attend the yoga center. However, much of the power dynamics a spiritual leader will be confronted with in their vocation will be related to their power inherent to their role in relation to the vulnerability of those whom they are called to serve.

The Hebrew Bible provides a memorable example of power, vulnerability, and fiduciary duty in the prophet Ezekiel's censure against the *false shepherds*:

> The word of the Lord came to me: Mortal, prophesy against the shepherds of Israel; prophesy and say to them: To the shepherds—thus says the Lord God: Woe, you shepherds of Israel who have been feeding yourselves! Should not shepherds feed the sheep? You eat the fat; you clothe yourselves with the wool; you slaughter the fatted calves, but you do not feed the sheep. You have not strengthened the weak; you have not healed the sick; you have not bound up the injured; you have not brought back the strays; you have not sought the lost, but with force and harshness you have ruled them. So they were scattered because there was no shepherd, and scattered they became food for all the wild animals.[7]

In this story, the shepherds have a sacred duty to care for their flock. But rather than doing so, the shepherds use their power over the vulnerable sheep to meet their needs. Instead of "strengthen[ing] the weak and heal[ing] the sick . . . [binding] up the injured . . . [bringing] back the strays . . . [seeking] the lost," the shepherds clothe themselves in their sheep's wool and feed themselves from their sheep's fat. While of course shepherds need to be fed and need to be clothed, they are meant to do so outside of their flock; their responsibility to *this flock* is compassionate care. By taking advantage of their power over the flock, these shepherds—like abusive spiritual leaders—betray the sacred trust of their flock.[8]

Psychologists Carly Parnitzke Smith and Jennifer J. Freyd describe this betrayal of sacred trust as *betrayal trauma*. Congregants, students, clients, and practitioners have a reasonable expectation that the professionals that they seek spiritual advice or counseling from will seek to do no harm. They trust them, often with very intimate details of their lives. Yet, like the shepherds in the Hebrew text, some leaders use their power—intentionally and unintentionally—to harm those they are obligated to serve. When this happens, the impact may be "more harmful than abuse perpetrated by strangers." Smith and Freyd write that this is "because of the violation of trust within a necessary relationship."[9] They suggest that the reason for this higher impact is because of the coping mechanism such a betrayal of trust requires: "blindness" or "extended unawareness."[10] The victimized person needs to maintain the relationship with the person who betrayed them, and they cannot do so if they confront the reality of the violence enacted upon them.

Smith and Freyd's work expands beyond the interpersonal experience of betrayal by a trusted professional to the institutions that house them. Institutional betrayal describes the ways in which institutions—sanghas, churches, temples, retreat centers, gurdwaras, etc.— "exacerbate the impact of traumatic experiences."[11] When a member of one of these communities experiences trauma such as sexual violation, they trust that their institution will provide care and they often depend solely on these institutions to do so. Womanist ethicist Stephanie M. Crumpton writes that the church is often the first place Black women will seek help when experiencing sexual violence.[12] Particularly for those in marginalized communities, people will call the spiritual community before law enforcement.[13] And yet, faith communities are often ill-equipped to respond effectively to disclosures of violence, especially by those perpetrated in the community.[14] Indeed, some victim-survivors may intentionally avoid going to their spiritual home for help, knowing them to be inept at responding[15] in trauma-informed ways.[16]

Are our communities safe, especially for victim-survivors of sexual violence? "In many corners of the world the Christian family is considered sacred. It may be sacred—but is it *safe*?"[17] We can ask this question of all of our faith families, whether Muslim, Jewish, Sikh, Baha'i, Buddhist, or Wiccan. With this foundational understanding of fiduciary responsibility, power and vulnerability, and institutional betrayal, we now turn to three case studies, exemplifying failures by spiritual communities in addressing violence perpetrated by and against its own members. Then we will turn to the justice-making agenda—a way to ensure that our communities are, indeed, safe.

Case Studies and Analysis

Case studies provide a helpful way to illustrate complex, real-life situations in a "bounded" way.[18] They allow readers to narrow in on the specific issues being raised without further exposing real victim-survivors to re-traumatization. Here we provide three case studies that represent present-day challenges we have seen spiritual communities face in trying to (and failing to) provide trauma-informed care to victim-survivors. These three composite stories are adapted from recent cases that we have consulted on or investigated. They are all based in the United States. Note that in all three stories, the faith tradition of the victim-survivor has been changed as a way to emphasize that the concerns raised in each story could happen anywhere, and indeed, they do. After each case study, we will provide analysis of the primary roadblocks the spiritual communities faced in responding to sexual violence.

Case Study 1: Myoyu

After an investigation substantiated the abusive behavior of a beloved dharma teacher, an urban Zen center hosts a community-wide conversation on how to work toward becoming a safer place for female students of the dharma. A young cisgender woman named Myoyu comes forward and says that she does not believe that the roshi abused women as the report alleged. 'Women are *not* victims because they have agency. I learned that from my teachers here,' she says. 'If those women slept with Roshi, they did so by choice.'

This first case study opens with a positive example of a spiritual community taking accountability for the betrayal of its members. While we do not know what further steps the sangha is taking to ensure that victim-survivors are safe beyond this community-wide conversation, it is worth noting that their approach is not one of secrecy, but of transparency and truth-telling. This sense of communal camaraderie is disrupted by Myoyu's statement of disbelief. She does not believe that the roshi could have behaved in such a way. He was always honorable in her interactions with him, and she does not believe that these women were truly victims.

In a society where women are socialized to be victims and not sexual agents,[19] it is commendable that Myoyu would take such a stance on women's bodily autonomy and choice. However, she is missing a key piece in understanding Roshi's abuse and the women's vulnerability, and that is power. Myoyu believes that the female students willfully had sex with their teacher and are, perhaps, now seeking revenge for something they chose to engage in. But because of the power differential between the spiritual teacher and his students, there can be no meaningful consent. "Consent to sexual activity, in order to be authentic, must take place in a context of mutuality, choice, full knowledge, and equal power, and in the absence of coercion or fear."[20] Students—or congregants or clients—cannot freely say no to a teacher's advances without fear of punishment. That punishment could be in the form of being ostracized by the beloved community, losing access to a favored relationship, or losing access to the spiritual teacher's insights. Sometimes victim-survivors acquiesce to abuse, even for years, in order to maintain a relationship with the abuser or community.[21] This is a form of betrayal *blindness* described above.

In this story, spiritual teaching functions as a roadblock for Myoyu understanding and effectively responding to the victim-survivors in her community. The teaching itself—that women are sexual agents—is a good and important lesson on its own. But in the context of spiritual leader misconduct and abuse, a belief in women as agents can be misconstrued to mean they willfully chose to be violated. All people are, in certain contexts, vulnerable to being victims of violence. In this case, the victim-survivors were not victims because they were women, though perhaps their gender contributed to their being singled out by Roshi. These women were victimized because they were students who trusted their teacher, and the sexual violation they experienced was also a spiritual betrayal.

Case Study 2: Jasleen

> Jasleen is a South Asian Sikh woman who was sexually assaulted by her teacher. Afraid to go to the police, Jasleen goes to the leaders at her gurdwara, asking that they ban him from teaching for her safety and the safety of others. The leaders tell Jasleen they cannot do that without sufficient evidence. When Jasleen emailed the leaders with a full account of her story, citing her evidence, they stopped responding to her. Stonewalled by her spiritual leaders, Jasleen decides to make her story public by posting a YouTube video of her testimony. In it, she calls out the leaders of her gurdwara by name. Once her video spread throughout the Sikh community, Jasleen began receiving emails from strangers: some telling her she is crazy and others blaming her for the assault. When the teacher is eventually arrested for another assault, and more victim-survivors come forward, the gurdwara decides to hire a third-party organization to investigate. Jasleen tells the investigators that worse than the assault itself was the community's dismissal of her account and their support for her abuser.

Of the many troubling aspects of this case study, perhaps the most concerning is the community's minimizing of Jasleen's abuse. Not taking Jasleen's concerns seriously, the spiritual leaders demanded evidence, and community members spewed hateful and victim-blaming accusations at her. In Christian communities, we might see the language of sin used to minimize the behaviors of perpetrators: 'They committed sexual sin' is used to describe rape, and therefore atonement for the *sin* is just between God and the accused. In Sikh and Buddhist communities, guru devotion may be used to minimize abuse; if the guru is believed to be a "sacred conduit through which the power and blessings of the tradition are transmitted to the student," the student may be told that anything the guru does (including sexual violence) is for her benefit.[22]

In understanding the dynamics of this case study, and in responding to violence in our own communities, it is important to have an intersectional lens, that is, an awareness of the overlapping identities that can contribute to Jasleen's "unique experiences of oppression and marginalization."[23] People within and outside of the gurdwara refused to believe Jasleen's story as credible, calling her *crazy*. The term *crazy* is often used against women as a way to discount their experiences.

But what may have seemed crazy or irrational to people on the outside was a natural progression for the traumatized Jasleen who needed her story to be heard.[24]

There is an unrealistic expectation that victim-survivors fit a certain profile; pastoral theologian Kristen Leslie calls this the "Myth of the Virgin Mary Survivor."[25] They must exhibit certain emotions, wear certain kinds of clothing, be reserved and not too loud, all in order to be believed by their community and the general public. But no person perfectly fits this profile, certainly not women of color. We know that white women are more likely to be believed than women of color because the former are perceived to be more innocent.[26] Black feminist ethicist Traci C. West writes of the culturally constructed "moral hierarchy" of sexual abuse, where some forms of abuse are considered "morally worse than others" because of who is being abused.[27] For example, a child is considered more innocent than a white woman and a white woman more innocent than a woman of color. This makes it especially hard for an adult woman of color like Jasleen to be heard and cared for.

The leaders of the gurdwara may have also turned against her as a means of protecting not only the institution but protecting the perception of Sikhs in the United States. As Jasleen's story gains traction, the leaders may fear racist backlash from the broader community. This is particularly common in marginalized racial and religious communities in North America who seek to protect themselves against dominant white (Christian) culture.[28]

Unlike Myoyu's story above, Jasleen's spiritual community does not commit itself to transparency and accountability. It is not until the offending teacher was arrested that the organization chose to take responsibility—likely in fear of a lawsuit.[29] An institution's instinctual response will always be to protect itself, but in doing so, it leads to collateral damage.[30] Many more victim-survivors came forward once news of the arrest spread. Jasleen felt that the experience of disbelief by her community was worse than the sexual assault itself. This is consistent in Smith and Freyd's work in institutional betrayal, in what they call a "second assault" when a victim-survivor is "further blamed or stigmatized when they seek help."[31]

Case Study 3: Jax

> Jax is a transgender nonbinary person who has been attending a progressive mainline church off-and-on for months. First only occasionally, then almost every Sunday Jax was in attendance, a cis male member of the church made lewd comments about Jax's body and clothing choices during the passing of the peace. Jax stopped

attending. When the pastor noticed Jax was no longer at Sunday services, she reached out and Jax told her what happened. The pastor said she would address it. Not sure what to do, the pastor arranged to talk with the man one-on-one about his behavior. He apologized profusely, citing a misunderstanding. Weeks later, Jax returned to church only to see the offending man in his typical pew. Jax left immediately and subsequently ignored the pastor's many phone calls.

In this case study, we have several complexities that do not exist in the previous two case studies. The primary concern of this case study is the peer-to-peer sexual harassment of Jax by a cisgender male member of the community.[32] Though Jax and their harasser are peers in terms of their role (i.e., they are not clergy), they have different degrees of social power. The cis man is a significant financial contributor and a member known by others in the community more so than Jax who only attends sporadically. As a member, he may also be protected by a church constitution, and depending on the institutional structure, he may be a voting member unlike a visitor like Jax. The man is also directly targeting Jax's trans body and nonbinary gender identity, thus using his power as a cisgender man to exert power over a marginalized person. Trans people are often harassed for not being "normal" compared to cisgender folks or are considered overly sexual and thus deserving of lewd remarks.[33] In a study by National Center for Transgender Equality, 48 percent of transgender people who responded to their survey "reported being denied equal treatment, verbally harassed, and/or physically attacked in the past year because of being transgender."[34] Trans folks of color experienced compounding levels of violence against them.[35]

According to the United States federal government, sexual harassment is "any repeated or unwanted verbal or physical sexual advances; sexually explicit derogatory statements; or sexually discriminating remarks made by someone in the workplace which are offensive or objectionable to the recipient, give discomfort or humiliation, or interfere with the recipient's job performance."[36] Sexual harassment includes lewd comments on one's body, as seen in this story, but can also be more subtle actions (i.e., sexual propositions or "salacious" comments) if both unwanted and prolonged.[37] However, because neither Jax nor the offending man are employees of the church, there are no federal laws that protect Jax against sexual harassment in this particular context. And while there may be church policies that protect members from harassment, there are probably guiding faith tenets expressed in a constitution or covenant that members agree to abide by. These constitutions or covenants may emphasize the importance of treating others with respect, including language on inclusivity, or guiding teachings like the Golden Rule. Whether sexual harassment is a violation of a law or organization policy, it is morally wrong and ought to be thoroughly addressed by spiritual communities.

In this story, we see a disconnect between the pastor's promising that she will "address" the harassment and providing protection for Jax, the vulnerable party. We do not know if the church had a sexual harassment policy or not. Was the pastor unaware of the proper procedure in addressing an instance of sexual harassment?[38] Or does the policy only cover clergy or staff sexual harassment? Instead of reporting the sexual harassment to the proper party (a bishop or judicatory leader, say), the pastor tried to handle the situation herself. She treated the situation as conflict management—meeting with the offending person as if he were an employee with a habit of showing up late, not someone actively sexually harassing someone in the community. The minister's response was not commensurate with the severity of the situation.

As soon as the offending man apologized for his harassing behavior and claimed a misunderstanding, the pastor was quick to forgive him. We do not know how exactly the pastor responded in their one-on-one meeting, but we know that the man was in his same pew the next time Jax attended, as though nothing had happened. This was likely very scary for Jax, and it makes sense that they would not want to communicate with the pastor after that betrayal of trust. Once again, we have an apt example of Smith and Freyd's betrayal trauma. Quick forgiveness is often used in Christian communities—and other traditions where forgiveness is a key value—to silence victim-survivors. This is particularly inappropriate as the offender was not willing to take full accountability for his behavior and the pastor made the choice to forgive him on behalf of Jax who was not given a voice.[39]

All three of these case studies illustrate a failure of spiritual leaders to adhere to a sacred calling to serve their communities. We see leaders misuse their power by minimizing abuse, perpetuating abuse, and attempting to resolve an issue quickly. We also see the ways in which theology or spiritual teachings inhibit communities from listening to victim-survivors and taking seriously the extent of their pain. Where theology and spiritual teaching could be a resource, they have become a roadblock to victim-survivors' healing. Thus, to the question, the spiritual community "may be sacred—but is it *safe*?" the answer for Jax, Jasleen, and the women in Myoyu's sangha is a resounding *no*.

Spiritual communities *can* provide safety and a pathway of healing for victim-survivors, however. As much as the institution and their leaders can, and do, betray its most vulnerable, they also have the means to ensure justice. In the next section, we will walk through some of the elements of a justice-making agenda and how spiritual communities can commit to a trauma-informed, victim-centric response to sexual violence.

The Justice-Making Agenda

In *Is Nothing Sacred?* Marie M. Fortune outlines the seven elements of justice-making in response to the nefarious abuse of a Presbyterian pastor, Peter Donovan. These seven elements are truth-telling, acknowledgment of the violation, compassion, protection of the vulnerable, accountability, restitution, and vindication.[40] Though Fortune's book is decades old, these ethical standards have proved both relevant and timeless in Faith-Trust's work developing and testing community policies. The elements of justice-making, which we will unpack shortly, contribute to a community's commitment to what we call the justice-making agenda. Rather than prioritizing protecting the institution—the natural first response of an institution under attack—the justice-making agenda prioritizes the needs of the victim-survivor.[41] The justice-making agenda reflects the conscious action of a community to ground itself in its teachings, to take victim-survivors seriously, to care for them, and to hold the perpetrators accountable for their actions and institutions accountable for their policies. No longer will theologies and teachings be roadblocks, but they will be resources unto healing for victim-survivors.

What would it look like for Myoyu's, Jasleen's, and Jax's spiritual communities to enact a justice-making agenda? Truth-telling is the first element of justice-making. "Truth-telling is not merely a rendering of the facts; it is giving voice to a reality," writes Fortune.[42] All of the victim-survivors in these three case studies were silenced, not given space to speak their truth. For Jasleen, the gurdwara leaders could have enacted the justice-making agenda by listening to her when she first came to them. They could have helped her file a police report and physically joined her at the police station if she was afraid to interact with law enforcement herself. Had Jasleen not wanted to go to the police even with moral and physical support, the leaders of the gurdwara still had a fiduciary responsibility to do an internal investigation into the allegations. They should have barred the roshi from teaching at the sangha until the police investigation, and an internal investigation, were complete. After truth-telling comes acknowledging the violation—Jasleen's leaders could have named the extent of the harm done to her and, had the first half of the story remained true, acknowledged the harm done to her through the investigation process. If Jasleen experienced re-traumatization from the gurdwara's investigation, they needed to acknowledge that as well.

Compassion describes "the willingness to 'suffer with' another person coupled with the desire to alleviate the suffering."[43] Myoyu did not show compassion for victim-survivors because she did not understand the abused women as victims. Her compassion extended only to the perpetrating roshi. Being victim-centric means putting the needs of the vulnerable party (the victim-survivor) before the more powerful party (the perpetrator); it means listening to them, believing them, and protecting them from further abuse. However, this does not mean you must demonize the perpetrator. Victim-survivor and advocate in the Buddhist community, Lama Willa Bythe Baker, asserts that you can hold a perpetrator accountable while still showing compassion to them. "If we are going to live the ethics of *ahimsa* (non-harm) and compassion, it is time for communities to rise above hate," she writes. "It is possible to challenge a perpetrator, hold them accountable, and heal a community with love."[44] While we ought to also show compassion to Myoyu as a member of the sangha, not a leader, the community-wide conversation would have been a good opportunity for the leaders to educate her and the rest of the community on the impact of abuse on a person's sense of choice as well as common trauma responses. Through this education, the sangha leaders could be protecting the vulnerable in the community from further abuse, the fourth element of justice-making. In this way, compassion for victim-survivors and protecting them goes hand-in-hand.

Accountability is the fifth element of justice-making. The perpetrator in Jax's story was not held accountable by the pastor but was allowed to continue attending church as if nothing had happened. The pastor confronted the perpetrator—a good first step—but forgave him quickly instead of holding him accountable for his behaviors. She needed to involve her supervisors and keep close record of his behaviors, while keeping Jax abreast of the situation.[45] If the church had a policy in place that addressed member-to-member harassment, there could be a formal internal investigation into the man's behavior. During the investigation, the pastor could directly care for Jax, including providing an advocate or support person to help Jax through the process. However, without a policy, the pastor cannot bar the member from the church or initiate an investigation into his behavior. She could use this opportunity to educate the community on what sexual harassment is and what behaviors are against their shared covenant as people of faith. She could provide other means of protection for Jax, including helping Jax search for a more suitable church.

If there were a member-to-member harassment policy, investigation, and the allegations of harassment were substantiated, the institution ought to provide restitution to Jax. Restitution, the sixth element of justice-making, may be reached in terms of covering therapy costs for Jax, though not specifying who their therapist must be. Restitution could also be symbolic: had the perpetrator, and the pastor, acknowledged the harm they caused and taken responsibility for it, Jax may have felt safe enough to return to church.

Finally, the seventh element of justice-making involves *setting free* the victim or providing vindication.[46] This ought to be victim-led, as no one can force someone to be set-free from the pain and harm caused by an abusive spiritual leader or community member. What would vindication look like for Jax, Jasleen, and the women in Myoyu's community? Perhaps it is the ability to practice their faith where and how they want to without fear of harm. Perhaps it is the freedom to speak about their abuse with the reassurance that they will be listened to and believed.[47]

While the elements of justice-making are ideals that spiritual communities ought to strive toward, the reality is that even the most trauma-informed community with the best policies can fail to protect its vulnerable members from harm caused by perpetrators or re-traumatization. We must seek perfect justice for victim-survivors, but we must accept that approximate justice may be the achievable reality. "We long for a place where justice will confront the corruption and oppression, where, even if we cannot prevent these [abuses], at least we can call them by name."[48] Thus we return to the importance of that first element: truth-telling. If we have failed to protect the vulnerable in our midst, can we be honest about it? Can we name the extent of the harm, and from there, seek some restitution for the victim-survivor? Can we revise our policies to make it that much harder for a perpetrator to enact violence on someone in the community? Can we speak from the pulpit, stage, or cushion about our responsibility as people of faith to stand against violence and to do no harm? Truth-telling must lie at the heart of healing.

Conclusion

By nature of their position, spiritual leaders have power that allows them to help or harm those who are more vulnerable than they are. When spiritual leaders use their power to help, they can provide tremendous care, facilitate healing and connection with the Divine, and speak as a moral authority on issues that matter. But when spiritual leaders use their power to harm, they can cause a ripple effect of harm on individuals as well as the broader community. They can use power to acutely harm others (as in Jasleen's story) or to allow perpetrators escape punishment (as in Jax's story). As representatives of a faith tradition and of God, spiritual leaders have a sacred responsibility to wield their power to serve the community in a helpful, healing way.

This chapter provided concrete examples of common responses by spiritual communities to sexual violence. In all three case studies, spiritual leaders failed to use their authority to center victim-survivors, putting the protection of the institution over the protection of the vulnerable. While the theologies and traditions of the communities in these case studies could have helped facilitate healing, they became roadblocks to it. Honoring women's agency became a way to victim-blame and forgiveness became a way to avoid holding a perpetrator accountable. In the final section, we reimagined what justice could look like in these three stories, with the recognition that perfect justice is not always attainable. As more and more denomination- and organization-wide sexual abuse cases are uncovered, we must not lose hope in achieving approximate justice. We must continue our commitment, as leaders and members of spiritual communities, to ensure the safety of the most vulnerable in our midst.

Notes

1 FaithTrust Institute is a national, multifaith, multicultural training and educational organization, www.faithtrustinstitute.org and www.facebook.com/search/top?q=faithtrust%20institute.
2 See Darryl W. Stephens, "Fiduciary Duty and Sacred Trust," in *Professional Sexual Ethics: A Holistic Ministry Approach*, eds. Patricia Beattie Jung and Darryl W. Stephens (Minneapolis: Fortress Press, 2013), 23–33.
3 Stephens, 27.
4 See Stephens, 27. Marie M. Fortune, *Is Nothing Sacred? The Story of a Pastor, the Women He Sexually Abused, and the Congregation He Nearly Destroyed* (Eugene, OR: Wipf & Stock, 2008), 110. Karen Lebacqz and Ronald G. Barton, *Sex in the Parish* (Louisville: Westminster/John Knox, 1991), 105.
5 See, for example, Iris Marion Young, *Justice and the Politics of Difference* (Princeton: Princeton University Press, 1990).
6 Marie M. Fortune, "Understanding Power and Vulnerability," *Healthy Boundaries 201 – Beyond Basics* (Seattle, WA: FaithTrust Institute, 2012), 27–28. See also Marie M. Fortune, *Love Does No Harm: Sexual Ethics for the Rest of Us* (New York: Continuum, 1998), 41–42.
7 Ezekiel 34:1–5, New Revised Standard Version Updated Edition.
8 See Marie M. Fortune, "Commentary on What the Sheep Teach Us," *Healthy Boundaries 201 – Beyond Basics*, 20–21.
9 Carly Parnitzke Smith and Jennifer J. Freyd, "Institutional Betrayal," *American Psychologist* 69, no. 6 (September 2014): 577.
10 Smith and Freyd, 577. See also Freyd's articulation of "adaptive blindness" in Jennifer J. Freyd, "Violations of Power, Adaptive Blindness and Betrayal Trauma Theory," *Feminism & Psychology* 7, no. 1 (1997): 22–32.
11 Smith and Freyd, 577.
12 Stephanie M. Crumpton, *A Womanist Pastoral Theology against Intimate and Cultural Violence* (New York: Palgrave MacMillan, 2014), 2. See also Tameka L. Gillum, "The Benefits of a Culturally Specific Intimate Partner Violence Intervention for African American Survivors." *Violence Against Women* 14, no. 8 (2008): 917–943, https://doi.org/10.1177/1077801208321982. Hillary Potter, "Battered Black Women's Use of Religious Services and Spirituality for Assistance in Leaving Abusive Relationships," *Violence Against Women* 13, no. 3 (March 2007): 262–84. doi: 10.1177/1077801206297438.
13 The National Resource Center on Domestic Violence provides resources on the relationship between marginalized communities and law enforcement. See National Resource Center on Domestic Violence, "Working with

Marginalized Communities," VAWnet, 2021, accessed June 3, 2022, https://vawnet.org/sc/identifying-and-preventing-gender-and-intersectional-bias-law-enforcement-responses-domestic-3.

14 See Nancy Nason-Clark and Barbara Fisher-Townsend, *Men Who Batter* (New York: Oxford University Press, 2015), 160.

15 See the study done by the Sikh Family Center: Harmit Cheema and Mallika Kaur, "Strengthening Our Roots: Listening & Learning from Survivors & Supporters," Sikh Family Center's Survivor-Centered Advocacy Project Report 2017, accessed June 3, 2022, http://sikhfamcenter.wpengine.com/wp-content/uploads/2018/04/SFC_FocusGrpReportENGFINAL-2017.pdf.

16 According to the Substance Abuse and Mental Health Services Administration, "A program, organization, or system that is trauma-informed realizes the widespread impact of trauma and understands potential paths for recovery; recognizes the signs and symptoms of trauma in clients, families, staff, and others involved with the system; and responds by fully integrating knowledge about trauma into policies, procedures, and practices, and seeks to actively resist re-traumatization" (SAMHSA's Trauma and Justice Strategic Initiative, "SAMHSA's Concept of Trauma and Guidance for a Trauma-Informed Approach," SAMHSA, July 2014, accessed June 2, 2022, https://store.samhsa.gov/sites/default/files/d7/priv/sma14-4884.pdf).

17 Catherine Clark Kroeger and Nancy Nason-Clark, *No Place for Abuse: Biblical and Practical Resources to Counteract Domestic Violence* (Downers Grove, IL: InterVarsity Press, 2001), 74.

18 Matthew B. Miles and A. Michael Huberman, *Qualitative Data Analysis: An Expanded Sourcebook* (A Thousand Oaks, CA: SAGE Publications, 1994), 25.

19 Pastoral care counselor Christie Cozad Neuger argues that how girls are socialized in the home makes them particularly vulnerable to being abused. Girls are taught to acquiesce, to consider others' feelings before their own, leading them to be chronically unsure of *what* they desire. They know by heart what they *should* want in order to be a "good" girl. She writes that this socialization may keep a girl from forcefully saying no when a trusted person tries to take advantage of her sexually, in fear of losing a friendship or being disliked, thus putting her at risk of being violated (Christie Cozad Neuger, "Premarital Preparation: Generating Resistance to Marital Violence," in *Men's Work in Preventing Violence Against Women*, eds. Christie Cozad Neuger and James Newton Poling [New York: Haworth Press, 2002], 47–48).

20 Fortune, *Is Nothing Sacred?* 38.

21 Pastoral counselor Pamela Cooper-White wisely states that "Whatever a woman chooses within such violently constrained choices—even if her choices may not look like the 'empowered' woman who fights back—must be understood as resistance, and a strategy for survival" (Pamela Cooper-White, *The Cry of Tamar: Violence against Women and the Church's Response*, 2nd ed. [Minneapolis: Fortress Press, 2012], 21).

22 Scott Edelstein, *Sex and the Spiritual Teacher: Why It Happens, When It's a Problem, and What We All Can Do* (Somerville, WA: Wisdom Publications, 2011), 117.

23 Lettie L. Lockhart and Jacquelyn Mitchell, "Cultural Competence and Intersectionality: Emerging Frameworks and Practical Approaches," in *Domestic Violence: Intersectionality and Culturally Competent Practices*, eds. Lettie L. Lockhart and Fran S. Danis (New York: Columbia University Press, 2010), 17.

24 Cooper-White, 71.

25 Kristen Leslie, *When Violence is No Stranger: Pastoral Counseling with Survivors of Acquaintance Rape* (Minneapolis: Fortress Press, 2003), 106.
26 Leslie, 19.
27 Traci C. West, "The Factor of Race/Ethnicity in Clergy Sexual Abuse of Children," *Concilium* 2004/3 (June 2004): 46–47.
28 See Toinette Eugene and James Newton Poling, *Balm for Gilead: Pastoral Care for African American Families Experiencing Abuse* (Nashville: Abingdon Press, 1998), 22. See also West, 48.
29 See Carol Merchasin, "Sexual Misconduct in Spiritual Communities: A Lawyer's Perspective" in *Responding to Spiritual Leader Misconduct: A Handbook*, edited by Lauren D. Sawyer, Emily Cohen, and Annie E. Mesaros (Seattle, WA: FaithTrust Institute, 2022).
30 See Sawyer, Cohen, and Mesaros, *Responding to Spiritual Leader Misconduct*.
31 Smith and Freyd speak specifically of the judicial system here but more broadly to other institutions in this article. Smith and Freyd, 575.
32 Some liberal/progressive communities struggle to take seriously the call to write robust policies and maintain clear grievance procedures because they believe sexual violence "would never happen here." Having women and queer folks in leadership does not guarantee that abuse will not happen in a community. This assumption of "that would never happen here" works to silence victim-survivors. But just as abuses of power happen across faith traditions, they exist across the liberal/conservative spectrum as well.
33 See Daniela Jauk, "Gender Violence Revisited: Lessons from Violent Victimization of Transgender Identified Individuals," *Sexualities* 16, no. 7 (2013): 807–825.
34 Sandy E. James, et al. "The Report of the 2015 U.S. Transgender Survey," National Center for Transgender Equality, 2015, accessed June 3, 2022, 197, https://transequality.org/sites/default/files/docs/usts/USTS%20Full%20Report%20-%20FINAL%201.6.17.pdf.
35 James et al., 203–204.
36 Judith A. Waters and Daniel Gross, "Sexual Harassment," in *The Encyclopedia of Rape*, ed. Merril D. Smith (Westport, CT: Greenwood Press, 2004), 229.
37 Waters and Daniel Gross, 230.
38 It is quite common for spiritual communities to have safeguarding policies that protect against the abuse of minors. Communities are beginning to see the necessity for policies that protect vulnerable adults as well.
39 See Margaret Arms, "When Forgiveness is Not the Issue in Forgiveness: Religious Complicity in Abuse and Privatized Forgiveness," in *Forgiveness and Abuse: Jewish and Christian Reflections*, eds. Marie M. Fortune and Joretta Marshall (Binghamton, NY: Haworth Pastoral Press, 2003), 107–128 and Sheila A. Redmond, "Christian 'Virtues' and Recovery from Child Abuse," in *Christianity, Patriarchy, and Abuse: A Feminist Critique*, eds. Joanne Carlson Brown and Carol R. Bohn (Cleveland, OH: Pilgrim Press, 1989), 70–88.
40 Fortune, *Is Nothing Sacred?* 114.
41 See Sawyer, Cohen, and Mesaros, *Responding to Spiritual Leader Misconduct*.
42 Fortune, *Is Nothing Sacred?* 114.
43 Fortune, *Is Nothing Sacred?* 115.
44 Willa Blythe Baker, "How You Can Support a Victim of Clergy Sexual Misconduct," *Lion's Roar*, May 21, 2019, accessed June 2, 2022, www.lionsroar.com/support-victim-sexual-misconduct.

45 Waters and Gross, 230.
46 Fortune, *Is Nothing Sacred?* 117.
47 See Azza Karam, "To Listen Well is to Give Breath," in *Responding to Spiritual Leader Misconduct: A Handbook*, eds. Lauren D. Sawyer, Emily Cohen, and Annie E. Mesaros (Seattle, WA: FaithTrust Institute, 2022).
48 Fortune, *Is Nothing Sacred?* 118.

Bibliography

Arms, Margaret. "When Forgiveness is Not the Issue in Forgiveness: Religious Complicity in Abuse and Privatized Forgiveness." In *Forgiveness and Abuse: Jewish and Christian Reflections*. Edited by Marie M. Fortune and Joretta Marshall 107–128. Binghamton, NY: Haworth Pastoral Press, 2003.

Baker, Willa Blythe. "How You Can Support a Victim of Clergy Sexual Misconduct." *Lion's Roar*. May 21, 2019. Accessed June 2, 2022. www.lionsroar.com/support-victim-sexual-misconduct.

Cheema, Harmit, and Mallika Kaur. "Strengthening Our Roots: Listening & Learning from Survivors & Supporters." Sikh Family Center's Survivor-Centered Advocacy Project Report 2017. Accessed June 3, 2022. http://sikhfamcenter.wpengine.com/wp-content/uploads/2018/04/SFC_FocusGrpReportENGFINAL-2017.pdf.

Cooper-White, Pamela. *The Cry of Tamar: Violence against Women and the Church's Response*. 2nd Edition. Minneapolis: Fortress Press, 2012.

Crumpton, Stephanie M. *A Womanist Pastoral Theology against Intimate and Cultural Violence*. New York: Palgrave MacMillan, 2014.

Edelstein, Scott. *Sex and the Spiritual Teacher: Why It Happens, When It's a Problem, and What We All Can Do*. Somerville, WA: Wisdom Publications, 2011.

Eugene, Toinette, and James Newton Poling. *Balm for Gilead: Pastoral Care for African American Families Experiencing Abuse*. Nashville: Abingdon Press, 1998.

Fortune, Marie M. *Love Does No Harm: Sexual Ethics for the Rest of Us*. New York: Continuum, 1998.

Fortune, Marie M. *Is Nothing Sacred? The Story of a Pastor, the Women He Sexually Abused, and the Congregation He Nearly Destroyed*. Eugene, OR: Wipf & Stock, 2008.

Fortune, Marie M. *Healthy Boundaries 201 – Beyond Basics*. Seattle, WA: FaithTrust Institute, 2012.

Freyd, Jennifer J. "Violations of Power, Adaptive Blindness and Betrayal Trauma Theory." *Feminism & Psychology* 7, no. 1 (1997): 22–32.

Gillum, Tameka L. "The Benefits of a Culturally Specific Intimate Partner Violence Intervention for African American Survivors." *Violence Against Women* 14, no. 8 (2008): 917–43. https://doi.org/10.1177/1077801208321982.

James, Sandy E., et al. "The Report of the 2015 U.S. Transgender Survey." National Center for Transgender Equality, 2015. Accessed June 3, 2022. https://transequality.org/sites/default/files/docs/usts/USTS%20Full%20Report%20-%20FINAL%201.6.17.pdf.

Jauk, Daniela. "Gender Violence Revisited: Lessons from Violent Victimization of Transgender Identified Individuals." *Sexualities* 16, no. 7 (2013): 807–825.

Karam, Azza. "To Listen Well is to Give Breath." In *Responding to Spiritual Leader Misconduct: A Handbook*, edited by Lauren D. Sawyer, Emily Cohen, and Annie E. Mesaros. Seattle, WA: FaithTrust Institute, 2022.

Kroeger, Catherine Clark, and Nancy Nason-Clark. *No Place for Abuse: Biblical and Practical Resources to Counteract Domestic Violence.* Downers Grove, IL: InterVarsity Press, 2001.

Lebacqz, Karen, and Ronald G. Barton. *Sex in the Parish.* Louisville: Westminster/John Knox, 1991.

Leslie, Kristen. *When Violence is No Stranger: Pastoral Counseling with Survivors of Acquaintance Rape.* Minneapolis: Fortress Press, 2003.

Lockhart, Lettie L., and Fran S. Danis. *Domestic Violence: Intersectionality and Culturally Competent Practices.* New York: Columbia University Press, 2010.

Merchasin, Carol. "Sexual Misconduct in Spiritual Communities: A Lawyer's Perspective." In *Responding to Spiritual Leader Misconduct: A Handbook*, edited by Lauren D. Sawyer, Emily Cohen, and Annie E. Mesaros. Seattle, WA: FaithTrust Institute, 2022.

Miles, Matthew B., and A. Michael Huberman. *Qualitative Data Analysis: An Expanded Sourcebook.* A Thousand Oaks, CA: SAGE Publications, 1994.

Nason-Clark, Nancy, and Barbara Fisher-Townsend. *Men Who Batter.* New York: Oxford University Press, 2015.

National Resource Center on Domestic Violence. "Working with Marginalized Communities." VAWnet. 2021. Accessed June 3, 2022. https://vawnet.org/sc/identifying-and-preventing-gender-and-intersectional-bias-law-enforcement-responses-domestic-3.

Neuger, Christie Cozad. "Premarital Preparation: Generating Resistance to Marital Violence." In *Men's Work in Preventing Violence Against Women.* Edited by Christie Cozad Neuger and James Newton Poling, 43–59. New York: Haworth Press, 2002.

Potter, Hillary. "Battered Black Women's Use of Religious Services and Spirituality for Assistance in Leaving Abusive Relationships." *Violence Against Women* 13, no. 3 (March 2007): 262–84. doi: 10.1177/1077801206297438.

Redmond, Sheila A. "Christian 'Virtues' and Recovery from Child Abuse." In *Christianity, Patriarchy, and Abuse: A Feminist Critique.* Edited by Joanne Carlson Brown and Carol R. Bohn, 70–88. Cleveland, OH: Pilgrim Press, 1989.

SAMHSA's Trauma and Justice Strategic Initiative. "SAMHSA's Concept of Trauma and Guidance for a Trauma-Informed Approach." SAMHSA. July 2014. Accessed June 2, 2022. https://store.samhsa.gov/sites/default/files/d7/priv/sma14-4884.pdf.

Sawyer, Lauren D., Emily Cohen, and Annie E. Mesaros. *Responding to Spiritual Leader Misconduct: A Handbook.* Seattle, WA: FaithTrust Institute, 2022.

Smith, Carly Parnitzke, and Jennifer J. Freyd. "Institutional Betrayal." *American Psychologist* 69, no. 6 (September 2014): 575–587.

Stephens, Darryl W. "Fiduciary Duty and Sacred Trust." In *Professional Sexual Ethics: A Holistic Ministry Approach*. Edited by Patricia Beattie Jung and Darryl W. Stephens, 23–33. Minneapolis: Fortress Press, 2013.

Waters, Judith A. and Daniel Gross, "Sexual Harassment." In *The Encyclopedia of Rape*. Edited by Merril D. Smith, 229–231. Westport, CT: Greenwood Press, 2004.

West, Traci C. "The Factor of Race/Ethnicity in Clergy Sexual Abuse of Children." *Concilium* 2004/3 (June 2004): 40–50.

Young, Iris Marion. *Justice and the Politics of Difference*. Princeton, NJ: Princeton University Press, 1990.

Chapter 2

Empowering Prayer for Healing

Abby King-Kaiser

Introduction

What is the relationship between the ways we pray, alone and in community, and our deepest, most intimate suffering? Faith communities everywhere are filled with people who are recently harmed, recovering from events in their distant past, wrestling with who God is in light of their trauma and more. Faith communities are also filled with people of deep faith who are not equipped to author their own prayer. As a result, prayer in the face of trauma and injustice feels hollow, ineffective, and even hypocritical. The lines between the liturgy, worship, and prayer are blurry, and we are often left feeling empty compared to other kinds of action. But access to worship and prayer spaces for survivors really can matter. Liturgy and prayer can be used to help survivors thrive if we take steps to create a healthy healing environment.

No one in our communities should suffer in silence, and no one should suffer without the resources for healing that their faith can provide. Our faith communities should accompany people in their grief and trauma, towards wholeness and healing. As we do, we will be called to create a world where this kind of harm is both unacceptable and eventually, unimaginable. How can we move, individually and collectively, from being ill-equipped and overwhelmed to become beacons of hope and healing?

For communities and individuals who want to create dynamic change, I suggest two steps:

- Nurture spiritualities that provide every member space to author their own prayers, reflections, liturgies, practices, even if only in private spaces.
- Provide public space for survivor-centered and authored prayers, reflections, liturgies, and practices to shape and heal.

When these two steps occur simultaneously and in the context of community, survivors are not further isolated by their internal processes, but instead, they are able to move towards healing in the context of their faith community. As this unfolds, faith communities will move from listening deeply to the suffering in their community, to public prayer, spiritual formation, shared leadership, and eventually action for and with survivors, working towards just communities.

Listening to a Community and its Context

In the spring of 2019, an Instagram account debuted. It was all in black and white. The majority of the feed was handwritten signs telling stories. Some of those signs were held by people who could be recognized; some showed only hands while most were hung from a cord. Each story was what someone *wished people knew about my rapist*.[1]

This student project grew out of a leadership program at Xavier University, the Jesuit Catholic university where I am a campus minister. The Arrupe Leaders Program invites seniors into a year of discernment and development that culminates in a project intended to leave a legacy for the campus. The project was intended to last a week, but as stories were told, many more stories surfaced. We added survivor resources and information to the site.

The boundaries of our faith communities are more ambiguous and permeable than we tend to assume. People do not live compartmentalized lives, and faith traditions often look for ways practices can bring different aspects of our lives together. Jesuit Catholic universities are concerned with *cura personalis* (care of the whole person). As a community, it means we are concerned for the development of the whole person, including spiritual development. I watched this Instagram account unfold as a campus minister.

As their minister, I continually reflected on the ministry. Did this student's faith and leadership in faith communities on campus impact her project? How does this project impact my ministry? How will this experience impact the care I offer students? Annie Selak reminds us that "Reading liturgy through a trauma-lens creates demands for liturgy to which theologians and ministers alike must respond."[2] This project was an important source of wisdom on suffering in our community. I wasn't being faithful to the God of love if I did not pay attention and let this project impact me as a minister, leader, educator, and person of faith.

Common Ground started in the fall of 2013, with a multi-racial and multi-denominational student leadership board. A student led, ever-evolving, liturgy band led music. Within a couple of years, students provided over half of the preaching each year. With an emphasis on hospitality and engaging prayer, the liturgy was truly the work of all the people. Younger students were recruited right away to perform tasks like reading Scripture and singing, while older students stepped into progressively more challenging and public roles such as leading prayer, designing reflection, or ultimately preaching. The role of the pastor shifted from creating and delivering liturgies to teaching students to design services, with an emphasis on encountering God. At its height before pandemic interruptions, approximately 40 students worshipped together each week, with special or themed services drawing up to 75 students.[3]

Common Ground developed in a university culture that was actively trying to improve how it supported survivors, and this effort was rooted in the university's religious identity. In an open letter to Survivors of Sexual Violence at Xavier, then President Fr. Michael Graham, S. J., said:

> It is my responsibility to share Xavier's commitment to comprehensively and compassionately address sexual violence—not just because of our requirement to do so under Title IX, but because of the mission that guides and grounds us as a Jesuit university. We must educate students, faculty and staff on what sexual violence is—your rights, options and resources—and tell you proactively how we can and will support you here. We make this commitment to every student and every survivor regardless of what paths you determine are right for you in seeking healing and recovery.[4]

In our campus context, the support and care of survivors of sexual assault and power-based violence focuses on providing opportunities for survivors to reclaim their agency, voice, and sense of control as quickly as possible. This may begin with the ability to choose if and when an investigation begins. But it grows into a campus culture where seniors who want to impact their campus create campaigns such as @whatiwishpeopleknewaboutmyrapist. As people of faith and people worshipping and ministering in this context, we had to ask ourselves how we should reflect these realities. How does liturgy come alongside the processes of investigation, support, and healing to become a tool for individuals to reclaim their voice? How can prayer contribute to a campus culture that is more just and more loving, forming young adults for healthy relationships and creating space for them to heal from both recent trauma and trauma they have carried since childhood?

In a mass or worship filled with college students, one can use simple statistics to realize that this is a pressing need. According to the Center for Disease Control and Prevention (CDC), roughly one in five women "have experienced complete or attempted rape during their lifetime" while "1 in 3 female rape victims experienced it for the first time between 11–17 years old."[5] Thus a significant number of college students are victims of sexual violence. What is the obligation of their college liturgies and faith communities when they arrive? How does that change when their college experiences unfold? Every community needs to answer similar questions for themselves in their own context. And this process begins with deep listening.

Common Ground began as a vehicle to serve a variety of Protestant students on our Catholic campus since we had a sampling of people from many religious traditions. This became a strength as students brought their own traditions with them and compassionately opened themselves to new ideas from other traditions. We used to say we were not like anyone's home church, but that it could be a home while at Xavier. Eseoghene Obrimah, the author of a prayer included later, described the community this way:

> Common Ground, for me, was the first spiritual/religious gathering where folks showed up as their full selves. And not just in an abstract sense. Like, literally, brought everything about themselves, their taste in music, their faith questions, their academic struggles and personal dilemmas to God and community. I think so much of how to understand religious spaces had to do with showing up/presenting yourself as worthy of God, whatever that means. Common Ground encouraged, in what looked like an effortless way, showing up as yourself.[6]

We created a unique place for liturgy and prayer that fostered healing and spiritual growth. This new opportunity forced me to listen carefully to the needs of the community and think about how those needs might change our worship and prayer.

Other communities will have their own challenges and contexts. Survivors will have their own stories and perhaps leaders will be survivors too. I suggest that leaders ask themselves some important questions that will assist them in serving their communities:

- How might you and your community listen carefully to stories that need to be told?
- Who might you invite into the conversation?
- Whose stories and presence are missing?
- What does it take to center those stories and let them change your community's worship and liturgy?

Praying For and With Survivors in Public

Claudio Carvalhaes offers some additional questions to ponder as communities create new healing spaces:

> How are we to pray with the unwanted of the world? How can our prayers not only address the disasters of the world and the killing of

people everywhere but also, in God's love, offer hope and actions of transformation? And in that way of praying, how do we get to the point where we can see our own vulnerability, our own incompleteness, our own frailty, and our own shakable ontological structure and impossibility to deal with life itself?[7]

Faith leaders must also be conscious of feelings of shame, victim-blaming, and other unhealthy attitudes in the community. Susan Marie Smith suggests that "In times of suffering, healing rituals can be the boat to carry someone who is languishing on his or her own to the other shore of wholeness."[8] Liturgy, public worship, and public prayer can be acts of care, even when those being cared for are entirely anonymous, unnamed, or named but not present. This act of prayer is also an act of hope towards healing. One of the Common Ground students underscored the potential of liturgy in providing support and accountability. She wrote: "people harmed can be given the resources to heal and harm doers can be held accountable and given the opportunity to learn and change while ultimately transforming the community so that sexual and power-based violence can be eradicated."[9]

Each of our faith communities are unique to their time, place, and a people. To understand the opportunities that might fit with a community, faith leaders need to examine the underlying tradition, the governance over public worship or liturgy, and look for opportunities to share responsibility for worship with those marginalized by the community, the tradition, or the larger society. Using my own tradition and context, I will demonstrate interrogating long-held tradition for graced opportunities to use public prayer for the healing and liberation of survivors.

I am ordained in the Presbyterian Church (U.S.A.), that articulates both our theology and ritual forms for worship in its constantly updated *Book of Order*. Functioning both as a binding constitution and a theological framework, the "Directory for Worship," one of the largest sections, opens with this passage:

> Christian worship gives all glory and honor, praise and thanksgiving to the holy, triune God. We are gathered in worship to glorify the God who is present and active among us—particularly through the gifts of Word and Sacrament. We are sent out in service to glorify the same God who is present and active in the world.
>
> God acts with grace; we respond with gratitude. God claims us as beloved children; we proclaim God's saving love. God redeems us from sin and death; we rejoice in the gift of human history, and everyday events—shapes all of Christian faith, life, and worship.[10]

If we come to worship a God who is active and present among us, how do we call upon that God when we have experienced trauma? If we are sent out from worship in service, how should worship reflect the deepest needs in our community that we are called to address? If we are claimed as beloved children, how do we affirm that in worship for those who have been made to feel, by the Church and by society, as if they are anything but beloved? How might worship actively offer new life to those suffering through the trauma of sexual or power-based violence? How can our rhythms of tapping into Divine action and offering a response be rhythms relevant, attuned, and healing for those who have experienced trauma?

These are complicated questions that cannot be answered so much as lived into. These are questions that shaped my ministry on campus and as a faith leader for college students. Worship and liturgy are not segregated from our real lives, but a place where encounter with the Spirit of God can break into these hardest places in unexpected ways.

It is easy for our constitutions and directories to feel like binding and limiting rules instead of liberating places to bring our deepest challenges. It is also easy as a clergyperson to think that my vows bestow upon me some kind of special power for writing liturgy. When I make these tensions visible to myself, I look differently at the "Directory for Worship." I am reminded that "every action is to glorify God and contribute to the good of the people."[11] As a worship planner, when I look at a liturgy, am I considering the real experiences of the people in the pews, sitting on the couches, or watching on Instagram live? As a campus minister, this means looking at prayers, sermons, and Scripture with the experiences of survivors in mind. Does this interpretation of Scripture implicitly support a culture that does not acknowledge sexual violence? How does prayer sound to the listener trying to recover from trauma?

Public prayer is, of course, a place where we bring the real concerns of our people and communities into worship in explicit ways. It is also a place where our silence can speak volumes. Does our congregation pray for those suffering from physical health challenges by name but avoid speaking about mental health challenges directly? Does our community address particular stressors in people's lives directly while leaving others out? Do we pray for suffering across the globe while ignoring suffering on our doorstep?

Prayer is a place where we can creatively cultivate the whole community to invite us into those deep places, even with words. Many traditions offer ways that anyone can enter dialogue with God. These are the spaces where we are invited to break open our forms for liturgy, worship, and prayer to bring in the concerns of survivors in both implicit and explicit ways. These are also the spaces where we can create that co-responsibility that builds towards empowered authorship of prayer. However, one of the Common Ground survivors reminded me that "Not every survivor is ready to go to the church or God to seek comfort and pushing that path on survivors is a great way to drive them away from the church." She suggested that "A gentle invitation through designated prayers, services, etc. is enough. Inviting members of the community to come together and acknowledge the impact and harm sexual assault and violence cause is the first step in supporting survivors in the community."[12]

So often, recognition of what weighs us down, even in broad or public ways, can be the door that needs to open in order to bridge our worst experiences to the ways that the church connects us with God's grace. When you fear praying is not enough, remember how prayer can start so much more. And then, find ways to do more than pray.

Create a Culture of Shared Responsibility for Prayer

In the New Testament, Acts 2:8 states: "How is it that each of us hears them in our native language?" The gift of Pentecost was not speaking in other languages, it was hearing other languages as if they were our own. The gift of God's Spirit is understanding. We are empowered by God's Spirit to transform our listening into understanding and action. This passage and others became the foundation for Common Ground's community and liturgy. Its first student leaders represented four fairly different traditions—Evangelical Lutheran Church in America, African Methodist Episcopal Church, Roman Catholic, and Apostolic Pentecostal. Out of Acts 2 grew a respect for the tradition of each member and how all traditions could be brought into the new liturgy. In forming their liturgies, the devotion to learning, community, communion, and prayer, from Acts 2:42 after the Pentecost, shaped the form that public worship and celebration would take. Liturgy became a shared responsibility when understood with all these facets.

A culture of shared worship was underscored in Common Ground's early years by rotating practices that continually invited the whole community to participate. When a student delivered a sermon at the front of the room, we would often stop and discuss how we heard God speaking though the sermon. During Holy Week preceding Easter students provided an artistic reflection on the Scripture that required each member's participation and pushed everyone outside of their comfort zones. Communion was not served from the front, but the elements were passed around the room and students served each other. Alone, each of these practices are minor components of the service, but cumulatively they build a culture of worship that is participatory and engaging.

At the end of every Common Ground service, before the benediction, I said "Common Ground is what it is because you show up, spending time with God and each other." Common Ground could go on without any clergy person, staff, or other professional presiding over the liturgy. Without its student leaders embracing and enacting their co-responsibility, it could not become a space where liturgy played a liberating role in the lives of survivors. "Emphasizing liturgical co-responsibility underscores the fact that synergy for solidarity depends on the faithful to translate this vision into practice."[13] This co-responsibility is what allowed students to build one prayer skill on another, and feel empowered to write, design, question, and rewrite both public liturgies for Common Ground, and then, their own private prayers. This process can be applied to other religious organizations by considering the entirety of a faith community. Faith leaders can begin by asking:

- What values are emphasized in your worship culture?
- How does your worship culture reflect the world that your faith is calling you to build?
- How is power shared, or not, and how does this impact those in your community?
- How does the culture support or challenge survivors as they seek healing?

Identify and Develop Leaders

After careful reflection on the questions above, faith leaders might begin to identify potential leaders in their communities. Student leaders formed the core of the Common Ground community, therefore much of our potential healing and growth required all students to take on leadership roles. Practices that developed practical skills were layered and ordered to ensure the success of each student. Learning how to pray—how to literally form and order the words, what to say and when, the tone to use—can be very intimidating. We tried a variety of exercises to assist students in mastering these skills. Prayer partners encouraged students to pray out loud for someone else, but with an audience of just one, and often in a room where their voice was competing with others. This helped students practice the words, but also grow less intimidated by the idea of being heard. And, the experience of being prayed for by someone else moved them. Those who struggled were driven by the desire to offer that back. We read Psalms out loud, sometimes alone. We prayed as a group, for one person, all at the same time. It was chaos—but it meant that each person in the room practiced praying aloud.

After exercises like this, some leaders who were ready for more advanced work would be asked to pray for the whole group at the start or the end of a meeting. They first might pray for a smaller group of leaders or the core team, increasing their audience from one to three. As this progressed, I could see them get more comfortable—finding their own words, and imitating others less. The final step was to lead prayer in the worship service. Each student chose how they would pray. They could choose and read a prayer written by someone else. They could facilitate the congregation praying in small groups. They could use a prayer cloth, or exchange written prayer requests with each other. The more a particular student led using prayers that were not original, the more likely that student was to move towards offering spontaneous prayer or writing their own prayers.

An undergraduate senior, Eseoghene Obrimah, wrote the following prayer for survivors after successfully gaining confidence in her own voice through the exercises outlined above:

> Lord, we come to you with this cross on our shoulders.
> Backs bleeding, heads banging, tears falling
> From pain not asked for
> Burdens not accepted
> Suffering
> not consented to
> Wanting to be saved.
>
> Lord, we are questioning this suffering
> Not sure if we've failed you
> Or if you've failed us.
>
> Lord, we are searching for hope
> Searching for peace
> Searching for love
> But they all seem out of reach
> Healing
> Salvation
> You
> Seem out of reach.
>
> Lord
> walk with us.
> So that we may find hope
> in our belief that you share this cross with us.
>
> May we find
> "Peace when trouble blows"
> knowing that
> "Jehovah sees, Jehovah knows;
> Because He is our peace, when sorrow nears,
> Jehovah sees, Jehovah hears."[14]
> We know that He goes through all the highs and the lows with us
> and with Him
> we will reach healing.

May we find love in our knowledge that,
Though we live
in a world that tells us that because we are survivors of sexual
violence
we have failed society
failed ourselves and
failed You,
there is nothing that can change your Godliness
and your Godliness is love
and so we know that you have,
you still do and you will always love us.
And that we are never the ones to blame.

In this moment, Lord, we affirm these words:
"It won't always be like this,
The Lord will perfect that concern in me
Sooner or later, turn in my favor,
Sooner or later, turn in my favor
It's turning around for me
It's turning around for me"[15]

It may be hard to believe right now, Lord.

But our faith reminds us
that death, suffering and sorrow
do not have the last word.

We thank you, Lord, because you've shown us
that the story
does not end on this cross on our shoulders
it does not end in depression,
It does not end with a rape kit,
It does not end in a courtroom,
It does not end in a victim-blaming society.
The story ends when love wins.

Maria Harris reminds us that all Christians have a pastoral vocation, an obligation to each other in relationship and community. "We are realizing that the word of God is addressing us, saying something to us, making demands on us, and asking us to live that word in our lives. We are a people called by the gospel called to make a difference in our world."[16] Common Ground's understanding of itself as a Christian community was rooted in an Acts 2 vision of sharing everything in common, coming to the table as full equals who bring their full selves, and delighting in those relationships. Paul's exhortation in the second chapter of Galatians—"carry each other's burdens, and in this way you will fulfill the law of Christ"—defined the public liturgical values of Common Ground. With an Acts 2 foundation, as Harris describes, it was then not the work of the pastor, the staff person, or a professional to do the heavy lifting, but the whole community shouldered the burdens. Each individual student could do that with increasing ability as they built their skills for the mechanics of praying. Growing their prayer life empowered them in other parts of their lives and leadership as well.

I have included two student-authored prayers in this chapter because they illustrate just how powerful the process can be in a student's spiritual recovery after sexual assault. The previous prayer was a part of regular Sunday worship that fell during Sexual Assault Awareness month; the other was written for an interfaith service during that same time of year. These prayers were not spontaneous. Rather, they were thoughtfully crafted by the students after they volunteered or were invited to lead prayer for the community. Thus, they were not typical examples of student prayer authorship. Both students had some leadership experience on campus as peer educators and as vocal advocates for healthy relationships. They also worked with programs to prevent sexual assault as well as caring for survivors. One of these student leaders reflected on her experience with Common Ground:

> I think the greatest training/experience I got from Common Ground was the ability to write prayer that went beyond my faith tradition and instead encompassed the multitude of lived experiences and lives of the people I surrounded myself with . . . Praying from a common space or 'common ground' let me grow in my capacity love.[17]

In order to identify possible community leaders, we might well ask the following questions:

- Who is ready for next steps in their prayer life and public leadership?
- What partners are in their lives or in the community around you, places of development that you can tap into, bringing that development and leadership into worship spaces?
- What experiences do they need to continue to grow?
- What spaces in the common life of your religious community are ripe for training people towards ever more personal, ever more empowered spiritual and prayer lives?
- What places in your public prayer offer the most agency, grace, and love, so that survivors, advocates, caregivers, and more, can bring their messy, deep, and real experiences to the prayers they lead?

Bridging Public and Private Prayer to Move Towards Care

Rabbi Harold Kushner reminds us that "Prayer, when it is offered in the right way, redeems people from isolation. It assures that they need not feel alone and abandoned. It lets them know that they are part of a greater reality, with more depth, more hope, more courage, and more of a future than any individual could have by himself." He adds: "One goes to a religious service, one recites the traditional prayers, not in order to find God . . . but to find a congregation, to find people with whom you can share that which means the most to you. From that point of view, just being able to pray helps, whether your prayer changes the world outside you or not."[18]

Prayer is never static. Even a pre-written prayer—whether repeated every week, said in unison once, or led from the front by an individual—provides us a means to connect us to God that is bound by time and place. Public prayer meets each person and God's Spirit in the ways they are working together. Public prayer impacts private prayer. Our habits in community shape our habits when we are alone. When communities and leaders recognize this and take a developmental approach to designing liturgy, they empower those in their communities to be authors of their own private prayer. This is particularly important for survivors as they take steps to heal and grow spiritually.

The liturgy I was raised with was full of congregational unison prayer. I loved matching my voice to the rhythm of the congregation as I soaked in all of the words. Yet, when I got to college, I was not comfortable praying in public, either spontaneously or with words of my own authoring. Many faith leaders told me that I would not move forward without trying, being uncomfortable, feeling like I was fumbling—but persisting. The more I prayed aloud, both in private and in public, the more the experience mirrored my internal experience of silent prayer or conversation with God. I have used this lesson in my own ministry.

When I transitioned to campus ministry and Common Ground, these experiences helped me to better understand the students in my care. I started to build prayer experiences that led students to take uncomfortable steps towards healing. Individual students were gradually guided towards authoring their own prayers. The whole community's approach to prayer grew so that the individuals in the community could continue to heal and grow. I invited students of a variety of traditions to lead prayer in a row, so that no particular tradition dominated the spiritual rituals. I occasionally led a pastoral prayer where concerns were shared aloud and prayed for at the time. We experimented with contemplative and artistic prayer practices that touched on their other intelligences. It was essential that this mix was organic and grew out of the community's own private practices. Students were encouraged to learn from each other.

As a student grew in their leadership, they were more likely to feel empowered to write their own prayer or even design their own ritual. For instance, a student brought the idea of a prayer board to the community, and then helped me construct it. For years after she left, it was a part of our worship experience every week. To request a prayer, you simply wrote your request on the tag and hung it up on the board. It was public so the requests often felt fairly anonymous to protect privacy. If a student hung up a new tag, they were invited and encouraged to take a tag and pray in the coming week for someone else's request. This whole system was designed by a student, who saw something similar in her hometown. The board was always present at worship and used during gathering and exiting the space. And once a month, another student would choose to lead this practice of prayer during the communal prayer part of the Common Ground liturgy. They would start with directions and end with a short prayer. To be a worship community where prayers for and with survivors could be written by student leaders, Common Ground had to be a community where any student could bring a private practice into the public space and experiment with how it could work. This kind of spiritual development, of both individuals and the whole community, is an act of care, and requires bridging public and private prayer.

As a pastor I seek to understand the internal spiritual lives of the people I serve by listening deeply, empathetically, and compassionately in one-on-one spaces. But observation in the community, when no one knows I am watching, helps to supplement those pastoral care experiences. It is important to state, especially when talking about boundary violations, abuse of power, and violence, that there is an appropriate way to do this. This practice is not intended to foment gossip. It is not to seek information that individuals do not want to tell me. Rather, assessment of learning required in higher education taught me not to discount observation or separate out what I noticed, but to use it to supplement what I might explicitly hear. This is particularly useful when talking about very difficult pastoral concerns that make the private public.

The following are questions that helped me use my observations to minister more effectively:

- Are the people in the room visibly uncomfortable or shaken?
- What kind of discomfort are they feeling? Are there tears? Are they tears of relief or tears of desolation?
- Does the body language in the room show people withdrawing into themselves or opening themselves to both God's Spirit and the community?

Often faith leaders will know when they are dealing with something difficult in community, but every person in the room may not. Prepare for what people will experience, with leaders or counselors available in the space, and additional resources beyond the church in a worship aid or posted in the building. Thoughtfully consider your own steps most appropriate for your community. As a leader who moves from public to private spaces, these steps are key for me, especially as I work to build public practices that influence private prayer and touch on our intimate suffering.

There are limitations to be aware of as well. I cannot share what has been shared with me, but I can share general observations. There will always be appropriate boundaries if we know how the people in our communities are doing internally, and how they are tapping in to God's Spirit. I find being clear about that reality and my role in it freeing as a leader. I cannot share what I am told, I can share what I have learned in broad and inclusive ways. Throughout my time pastoring Common Ground, I learned that our public practices do shape private practices. For example, a student reflected on prayer as an experience of "give and take." She added "Many conversations from a faith perspective will include phrases like, *God has a plan for you*, *everything happens for a reason*, and *God only gives you what you can handle*. These phrases can be ostracizing to individuals who feel let down and harmed by God after a sexual assault or sexual violence. Prayer in both public and private spaces should acknowledge the harm and hurt that has come from those experiences and recognize that the process of healing is unique to the individual."[19] We need to recognize the harm some religious tropes have had on victims of sexual assault.

Often, faith leaders can inflict additional trauma on survivors with their emphasis on purity culture and *God's will*. A Common Ground student wrote: "thinking about religion's emphasis on *purity* particularly *sexual purity* for women, a survivor can feel like they're not worthy of God. Being able to pray publicly and privately in ways that do not seek to hide the experience of sexual violence can affirm that survivors are indeed more than welcome to talk/sit with/be around God."[20] Because it is implicit and invisible, it can be easy to forget that our public practices will influence private prayer and a survivor's relationship with God. If a survivor feels shame for their experience in their faith community's public worship, how will that impact their image of God and how God sees them? If a community ignores the harm present in its own rape culture, abuse culture, or culture of silence and cover-up, how can survivors in that community trust God with their tender experiences of trauma? By being made to feel untrustworthy in worship, they may feel God doesn't trust them. Faith leaders must reflect on all of these questions as they care for victims and promote healing and spiritual growth.

We must understand the power we wield as religious leaders. As a young clergyperson, as a young adult with privileged identities outside of the church, I wanted to distance myself from both my privileges and the authorities I had been granted. If I disagreed with how power was used, I naively assumed that I could just ignore that power and that was enough to resist. These experiences have taught me the real power that our public prayer has in people's private lives. I now work hard to never underestimate the power I hold as a spiritual leader, and how I should use that power with integrity because it impacts people's internal prayer lives, how they understand themselves before God, and how they understand Godself. I always assume that if I am praying about an issue, a current event, even a concern raised by the community, no matter how anonymous it seems, someone in the room is likely to have a personal experience that is related. My public prayer *will* impact their internal relationship with God—knowing this and allowing this truth to shape my public leadership is a form of pastoral care.

Observe your own faith community. What does the prayer life look like for the people in your religious or faith community? How do you know? Ask people you trust to reflect with you on how and why they pray, and what they need to grow in their prayer life. How might you change the ways your community prays in big and small ways together, so that the people in your community are increasingly empowered in their own prayer lives? How can the public spaces of your faith community give people language for bringing their deepest suffering to God in their private prayer life?

Liturgy is never practiced alone. Liberated liturgy can provide a spiritual experience in community that becomes a part of a survivor's journey towards spiritual wholeness. "At the very heart of the ritual experience is the sense of oneness with the source and purpose of creation and so with one's fellow human beings."[21] Sexual and power-based violence violate these connections between humans and God. We cannot assume, however, that ritual will *fix* these violations. But in order to achieve spiritual wholeness in the context of one's faith, ritual must be a part of the healing process. Prayer creates a bridge that allows liturgy to aid in the process of spiritual formation, giving survivors the tools to use as a part of the healing of their whole lives, both public and private.

Conclusion

In a world weary of *thoughts and prayers* after a traumatic event, it can feel awkward to provide meaningful and transformative prayer that contributes to healing. And yet, in many Christian traditions, prayer, worship, and liturgy are tools. Alone, these tools do not solve anything and none of these tools replace God's activity. And yet, we can create spaces that bridge what is going on in our innermost spiritual lives with God's Spirit. These are spaces of healing.

A Common Ground student reflected on her experience with the healing spaces we created. She appreciated how important it was for sexual violence to be openly discussed in our Common Ground liturgies particularly "in a society that strongly encourages hiding and feeling guilty about sexual assault" that often labels victims as "defiled." Often feeling polluted and defiled in the larger society, survivors in the jointly constructed liturgies felt valued and cleansed of the social stigmas placed upon them. These liturgies openly acknowledged the sexual assault as well as the traumatic "pain in a holy space" that was "game changing" for students.[22]

Prayer and liturgy can be active tools for liberation and healing. Faith groups might ask the following questions to provide healing services for sexual assault victims.

- What changes could be initiated in order to create a more loving and healing environment in liturgy or the faith community?
- What opportunities exist in the structures of the current liturgy?
- How might we develop pastoral and prophetic skills among the members of our spiritual community that foster healing spaces for survivors of sexual and power-based violence?
- How can we empower everyone in our faith community to become authors of our liturgy?

Empowering everyone to be co-creators of liturgy is worth the time and energy necessary to encourage and teach members of the community. The process reaps many rewards for members personally on their spiritual recovery but also for the entire community. We can see this powerful healing in a prayer written by a Common Ground student, S. Wilson, for an inclusive and diverse interfaith liturgy.[23]

> Praying for all people
> Today we pray for all people
> who despite suffering from violence,
> continue to care, grow, and fight
> for those around them who have suffered in silence.
>
> We pray for all individuals who have suffered violence
> on account of their partners, families, strangers, and friends.
>
> We pray for all who have experienced sexual violence
> and are not yet able to name their pain
> or look forward to a hope-filled future.
>
> We pray for the strength of all advocates and survivors
> as they work to transform our societies,

which often find it easier to blame victims of violence
then to work toward ending injustice.

Today, we pray that all voices be heard and listened to
no matter race, gender, or sexual orientation.

We pray for a transformation of mind for those
who perpetrate violence, that they may find healing
within themselves and work to end the cycle of violence.

We look forward to an age of peace when violence is banished
and all people are able to love and accept love
in a way that reflects the love of our Creator.

Lord God, grant those who stand against violence peace of mind
and a renewed faith in your protection and care.
Protect us all from the violence of others,
keep us safe from weapons of hate,
and restore to us tranquility and peace.

Everyone benefits spiritually when our communities are places that empower them to author their own prayer, bring their concerns into shared spaces, and connect their internal experiences of God to shared practices of worship and prayer—and these ways of being can particularly benefit survivors of sexual assault and power-based violence in our community. With this in mind, we can find opportunities and invitations in our traditions that help us to create spaces where everyone in our communities can pray and worship as their full selves, inclusive of their experiences of trauma and shame. Creating liturgy is creating culture, and as we celebrate liturgies that offer God's mercy and grace, fully, to survivors, the church can and will be part of a movement towards building a more just society full of healthy, intimate relationships. Towards that end, faith communities can take the following steps:

- Include prayers for and with survivors and against sexual and power-based violence in regular prayer concerns in worship.
- Create a culture of public worship that includes people of faith who are not clergy in the authoring and leading of public prayer.
- Identify leaders ready to deepen their prayer leadership and create next steps tailored to their skills and gifts.
- Bridge public and private prayer, and while doing so, carefully observe how these prayers are received by those present for worship. Be prepared to provide appropriate pastoral care and know how prayer is an appropriate part of providing care.

Liturgy is the bridge between private prayers and public action. When we pray together in public for and with survivors of sexual violence, we create a culture where healthy relationships are valued and encouraged, where violations are named and justice is possible, and where trauma is never a barrier to a relationship with God. Faith communities are not just able to participate in this movement, they are obligated to provide a path forward. Public prayer will come alive with the Spirit of God, and individual prayer lives will be changed as your community liberates liturgy in order to create a more just world. Listen to the community and society around you for people who are marginalized and traumatized. Build authentic relationships and be open to being changed by their presence in your community.

Notes

1 As of 2022, this account exists at @whatiwishpeopleknewaboutmyrapist. Created by @briannaledsome.
2 Annie Selak, "The Power of Memory and Witnessing: A Trauma-Informed Analysis of Anamnesis in the Roman Catholic Mass" in *Liturgy + Power*, ed. Brian P. Flanagan and Johann M. Vento (Maryknoll, NY: Orbis Books, 2016), 30.
3 At the time, Xavier's undergraduate enrollment hovered around 4500–4750 full-time students.
4 Fr. Michael Graham, S.J. "An Open Letter from Fr. Graham" *Xavier Newsire*, September 12, 2018, https://xaviernewswire.com/2018/09/12/an-open-letter-from-fr-graham/.
5 "Facts About Sexual Violence," Center for Disease Control, last modified April 19, 2021, www.cdc.gov/injury/features/sexual-violence/index.html#:~:text=Nearly%201%20in%205%20women,it%20occurred%20before%20age%2010.
6 Eseoghene Obrimah, email to the author, May 6, 2022.
7 Claudio Carvalhaes, *Liturgies from Below: Praying with People at the End of the World* (Nashville, TN: Abingdon Press, 2020), 5.
8 Susan Marie Smith, *Caring Liturgies: The Pastoral Power of Christian Ritual* (Minneapolis, MN: Fortress Press, 2012), 11.
9 Eseoghene Obrimah, email to the author, May 6, 2022.
10 The Constitution of the Presbyterian Church (U.S.A.) Part II, Book of Order, 2019–2023 (Louisville, KY: The Office of the General Assembly, 2019), W1.0102–W1.0102 (hereafter cited as BOO).
11 Ibid.
12 S. Wilson, email to the author, May 16, 2022.
13 Marcus Mescher, "Liturgy as power-sharing: synergy for solidarity" in *Liturgy + Power*, ed. Brian P. Flanagan and Johann M. Vento (Maryknoll, NY: Orbis Books, 2016), 53.
14 Lyrics quoted by the author of the prayer. Lionel Peterson, "Peace," track 6 on *Rejoice Africa*, Hosanna Music, 2010. Compact disc.
15 Lyrics quoted by the author of the prayer. VaShawn Mitchell, "Turning Around for Me," track 8 on *Created4This*, EMI Gospel, 2012. Compact disc.
16 Maria Harris, *Fashion Me a People: Curriculum in the Church* (Louisville, KY: Westminster John Knox Press, 1989), 24.

17 S. Wilson, email to the author, May 16, 2022.
18 Harold S. Kushner, *When Bad Things Happen to Good People* (New York: Anchor Books, 2004), 134.
19 S. Wilson, email to the author, May 16, 2022.
20 Eseoghene Obrimah, email to the author, May 6, 2022.
21 James L. Empereur, S.J. and Christopher G. Kiesling, O.P., *The Liturgy that Does Justice* (Collegeville, MN: The Liturgical Press, 1990), 32.
22 Eseoghene Obrimah, email to the author, May 6, 2022.
23 Though Common Ground is primarily ecumenical and entirely Christian, this was written for a special interfaith service that it hosted.

Bibliography

Carvalhaes, Claudio. *Liturgies from Below: Praying with People at the End of the World* (Nashville, TN: Abingdon Press, 2020).

Cavalletti, Sofia. *Living Liturgy: Elementary Reflections*, trans. Patricia A. Coulter and Julie Coulter-English (Chicago: Liturgy Training Publications, 1998).

Empereur, James L. and Christopher G. Kiesling, O.P. *The Liturgy that Does Justice* (Collegeville, MN: The Liturgical Press, 1990).

Graham, Michael, S.J. "An Open Letter from Fr. Graham" *Xavier Newsire*, September 12, 2018.

Harris, Maria. *Fashion Me a People: Curriculum in the Church* (Louisville, KY: Westminster John Knox Press, 1989).

Kushner, Harold S. *When Bad Things Happen to Good People* (NY, NY: Random House, 2009).

Mescher, Marcus. "Liturgy as power-sharing: synergy for solidarity" in *Liturgy + Power*, ed. Brian P. Flanagan and Johann M. Vento (Maryknoll, NY: Orbis Books, 2016).

Selak, Annie. "The Power of Memory and Witnessing: A Trauma-Informed Analysis of *Anamnesis* in the Roman Catholic Mass," in *Liturgy + Power*, ed. Brian P. Flanagan and Johann M. Vento (Maryknoll, NY: Orbis Books, 2016).

Smith, Susan Marie. *Caring Liturgies: The Pastoral Power of Christian Ritual* (Minneapolis, MN: Fortress Press, 2012).

Chapter 3

Clergy Abuse and Students' Moral Injury

Ashley Theuring and Anne K. Fuller

Introduction

Sexual abuse has historically been understood as an interpersonal trauma, impacting primarily the survivor and perpetrator. But as our understanding of trauma, moral injury, and their effect on both individuals and communities expands, a far-reaching and more complex picture of sexual assault begins to materialize. This is particularly relevant in the context of a religious community, such as with clergy sexual abuse. The moral authority of these religious leaders is not only questioned, but ultimately shattered. In the case of the Catholic clergy sexual abuse crisis, the growing public awareness of the abuse and its internal cover-up has resulted in an expanded community impact. As the church continues to explore the necessary steps to heal the affected individuals of clergy sexual abuse, it must also consider the wider community's need for healing.

One subset of this wider Catholic community to consider is emerging adults (18–25 years old)[1] who have grown up with the public narrative of clergy sexual abuse. As emerging adults begin to explore their own faith lives, many are feeling their moral and ethical beliefs conflict with their faith, especially around issues of gender and sexuality.[2] The reality of the sexual abuse crisis and the church's response has become one more reason why emerging adults may no longer find the faith of their childhood to be a source of community, moral authority, and healing. Even when a Catholic emerging adult is not directly connected to an instance of clergy abuse (i.e., victim or family member), they are still implicated by their religious affiliation, and for some that is difficult or even morally injurious.

Overview of Clergy Sexual Abuse

For all intents and purposes, scholars consider 1984 as the beginning of the modern conversation around clergy abuse in the United States. That year, Fr. Gilbert Gauthe in the Diocese of Lafayette in Louisiana faced civil and criminal charges in widely publicized trials for abusing 37 children. Another watershed moment for the Catholic church and the clergy sexual abuse crisis came in 2002 when the *Boston Globe* published results of their investigation into clergy sexual abuse in the Archdiocese of Boston. The investigation showed not only enough evidence to convict and imprison five abusive priests, but also showed that the church authorities had continued to cover up allegations and defend pedophile priests. This public story marked a shift in laity awareness and concern for clergy sexual abuse, seriously challenging public trust in the church and clergy.[3]

But 2002 was not the last time the United States Roman Catholic church would come into the spotlight following the surfacing of allegations. Public disclosures of decades of clergy abuse repeatedly led to shattered public trust in the church. Equally shocking was the clearly documented system-wide cover-up, which continued after 2002.[4] In 2019, 4,434 sex abuse allegations were filed, triple the number of previous years. This number is expected to continue to rise as more states implement *lookback* laws that removed statutes of limitations from sexual abuse laws. As of December 2020, the United States Catholic church has tallied 17,000 complaints and paid about four billion dollars to victims since the 1980s.[5]

Prevalence

Lack of clear and accurate statistics leads to difficulty in determining the prevalence of sexual abuse. One of the complicating factors is the lack of reporting; and when survivors do report, it is usually years after the abuse. Of the victims surveyed, 6% were under 7 years of age, 16% were 8 to 10 years of age, 50.9% were between 11 and 14 years of age, and 27.3% were 15 to 17 years of age. The John Jay College survey only considered abuse of children under the age of 18 years old.[6] The survey also found that victims who alleged abuse were 81% male and 19% female.[7] A meta-analysis of clergy sexual abuse shows that there is an overrepresentation of male victims in the research being done on this topic.[8]

Causes: Social and Individual

Clergy abuse, like all abuse, stems from both social and individual factors. The most obvious social structure at play is the Catholic church. While the Catholic church is not the only systemic structure, or religious organization, to have problems of sexual abuse, there seems to be a particular culture that has permitted the thriving of abusive clergy and enabled the ongoing cover-up.[9] The Catholic church is not a uniform culture, but much of the authoritative structures of the church include obedience to male authority, deference to the church as a holy structure, privileging of the priesthood, and the denial of the complexities of human sexuality.[10] These cultural aspects reinforce a system of clericalism, that allows for secrecy, unilateral decision-making, and ongoing abuse of laity.[11]

Individual factors which contribute to this problem include the psychological profile and formation of abusive priests. It is unclear if the priesthood unintentionally attracts individuals with abusive tendencies, if some aspects of the formation process and systemic structure of the church encourage abuse, or if there is some interplay of both factors. One logical step is to screen out those who fit the psychological and behavioral profiles of sex offenders. Unfortunately, this is not easily done, as the current clinical measures that attempt to predict abusive behavior are not sufficiently accurate.[12] Also, these psychological and behavioral problems can surface after screening during clergy formation.

Formation is the other potential problem area. Clergy training has failed to name the power imbalance between clergy and laity or set standards for ethical and professional relationships. The boundary between clergy and laity is often mystified and rarely addressed openly. Problematically, clergy do not receive comprehensive training on handling psychological issues such as transference[13] and countertransference.[14] When faced with the reality of those phenomena, countertransference on the counselor's part and transference on the part of the person being counseled, clergy are unable to navigate the situation in a healthy way. One major weakness of clergy formation is the lack of "emotionally integrated, morally coherent, and humane perspectives on human sexuality."[15]

Church Response

Prior to 1985, bishops were advised that individual priests who perpetrated sexual abuse were curable and that spiritual remedies, such as prayer, were legitimate and successful in rehabilitating sexual offenders.[16] It wasn't until 1994 that the United States Council of Catholic Bishops (USCCB) established a committee on the sexual abuse allegations, and in 2002, the National Review Board was formed. At the June 2002 meeting, the USCCB adopted the Charter for the Protection of Children and Young People, which was revised in 2005 and 2006. This included the creation of the National Review Board for the Protection of Children and Young People and authorized and financed studies of clergy abuse against children. The Review Board recommended increased screening, formation, and oversight; better relationships with victims, civil authorities, and laity; and more accountability for bishops and church leaders.[17]

Experts agree the same causes which produced the crisis, lack of sexual abuse education and practices of clericalism, have resulted in the church's failed response. There is a general lack of knowledge in the leadership of the church about clergy sexual abuse. The church's response to the clergy sexual abuse crisis has added to the trauma experienced by victims and the church community. The church has favored the institutional concerns over those of victims and taken an adversarial stance towards those considered to be outside the hierarchy, including victims, laity, the general public, and the media. A major mistake in the church's response to the clergy sexual abuse crisis has been the mistreatment of survivors.[18] The clerical systems of silencing have created a secondary problem: a church-wide cover-up. This "wall of denial and silence"[19] has resulted in a toxic mistrust by the laity, the general public, and the media, closing off the church from possible institutional-saving supports.

Moral Injury

Moral injury is a burgeoning discussion within the fields of psychology and trauma studies. Early writings about moral injury are found in the works of psychiatrist Jonathan Shay. Focusing on the experiences of military veterans, Shay defines moral injury as a "(1) betrayal of what's right (2) by someone who holds legitimate authority (3) in a high stakes situation."[20] This definition reflects the particular context of veterans who exhibit symptoms of moral injury because of their military experiences and witnessing of human suffering and violence. We might expand moral injury beyond the immoral act of a superior to include the actions of the individual as well. In the work of clinical psychologist Brett Litz, moral injury is defined as "the lasting psychological, biological, spiritual, behavioral, and social impact of perpetrating, failing to prevent, or bearing witness to acts that transgress deeply held moral beliefs and expectations."[21] This definition highlights the holistic impact of trauma, in general, and moral injury. In addition, the research, posited by Litz and associates, expands feelings of guilt beyond the direct perpetrator, to include enablers and bystanders of violence.

Moral injury was first observed and studied as a phenomenon in veterans, but researchers have quickly expanded the scope of moral injury beyond the military context. Moral injury can occur in any context where an individual "engages in behavior that is not consistent with and ultimately damages the core concepts of relational and self-schemata that make up her or his morals and values resulting in the affective responses of guilt and shame."[22] Despite these expansive definitions, research remains predominantly military-focused, with a lack of measurement tools designed for civilian experiences.

Symptoms of Moral Injury

While moral injury is not a new experience, it is a new concept in the worlds of psychological and sociological theory, and therefore lacks any agreed-upon strict definition, measurements, or treatments. But the symptoms of moral injury can still be helpful in identifying and differentiating the phenomenon from other traumatic diagnoses such as PTSD (Post Traumatic Stress Disorder). The overlaps between PTSD and moral injury have been well-documented; they share many of the same symptoms and can both be triggered by the same event. But a key difference between PTSD and moral injury is that those who experience moral injury express active feelings of guilt and shame, regardless of their role in the morally injurious event. The defining feature of a traumatic event, which might cause PTSD, is that a survivor feels their life or well-being has been threatened. On the other hand, a morally injurious event threatens a survivor's *goodness* and their sense of *right and wrong*. This explains why psychological treatments for PTSD are less effective with survivors who may also be suffering from moral injury.[23]

Survivors with moral injury experience symptoms of guilt and shame, spiritual/existential conflict (e.g., questioning the meaning of life), psychological problems (e.g., depression, anxiety, anger), and social problems (e.g., loss of trust in others and self-isolation).[24] Many of these symptoms are seen in PTSD, and there is a high rate of comorbidity for moral injury survivors with PTSD. This is especially true because most of the early research on moral injury engaged military veterans, whose morally injurious event is often traumatic. But even in civilian situations of moral injury, overlap occurs.

Moral Injury and Bystanders

As the preceding discussion suggests, various definitions of moral injury exist. In their recent review, Griffin and colleagues frame moral injury as pertaining to experiences of betrayal, perpetration of moral injury, or both in relation to the same incident.[25] While perpetration requires that the morally injured individual be directly involved in the event, experiences that lead to betrayal seem to permit a broader understanding of who may be impacted by such events. Hodgson and Carey cite examples of definitions of moral injury that suggest that one need not be directly involved as either a perpetrator or target in order to be affected.[26] For instance, Hodgson and Carey cite Carey et al.'s 2016 definition, which includes "an [organizational] level, when serious acts of transgression have been caused by or resulted in a betrayal of what is culturally held to be morally right in a 'high-stakes' situation by those who hold legitimate authority."[27] Another example referenced by Hodgson and Carey is Jinkerson's description of morally injurious experiences, which refers to "perceived violations of deep moral beliefs by oneself or trusted individuals."[28] Catholic clergy hold a distinctly privileged and authoritative status within the church. Thus, when considering the clergy sexual abuse crisis, which involves both perpetration of sexual abuse and its cover-up by church authority figures, it is easy to see how individuals who are indirectly or perhaps only peripherally associated with such occurrences (e.g., through identifying as Catholic) may still experience this crisis as a series of morally injurious events.

Effects of Clergy Sexual Abuse Crisis on College Students

As discussed above, there is limited prior research pertaining to measurement of moral injury outside the military context. Yet as noted by Chaplo and colleagues[29] and as is apparent from a review of the literature on this construct, moral injury can occur in a broad range of contexts. In fact, moral injury can extend to those not directly involved in the morally injurious event but who only witness it or are aware of it (i.e., bystanders), as reflected in Litz and colleagues' characterization of potentially morally injurious experiences.[30]

Chaplo and colleagues' development of the *Moral Injury Scales for Youth* offers an example of a quantitative measure of moral injury for a non-military population.[31] The authors note that processes believed to influence moral injury are part of "moral cognitive development across the lifespan."[32] Moreover, they explain that they elected to assess moral injury in emerging adults (a term referring to the developmental period from 18 to 25 years) because this population is closest in developmental status and age to the adults for whom previous measures have been created.[33] Chaplo et al.'s work thus supports the feasibility of measuring moral injury among university students. Moreover, given the salience of both identity and moral development to the emerging adulthood period,[34] there is clear value in examining moral injury related to clergy sexual abuse among students affiliated with the Catholic church via (at minimum) their enrollment in a Jesuit institution.

Students at a midwestern, Jesuit Catholic university participated in this research in exchange for partial course credit. Students completed a questionnaire assessing their religious identification and beliefs, awareness, and impact of clergy sexual abuse in the Catholic church, and experiences of moral injury in relation to the clergy abuse crisis. The items assessing moral injury were intended to examine five domains: moral identity (shame), moral reasoning (disorientation), moral agency (futility), moral relationships (betrayal), and moral institutions (loss of authority/credibility). To facilitate examination of relationships between moral injury and conceptually related mental health constructs, students also completed measures of symptoms of posttraumatic stress,[35] anxiety,[36] and depression (an eight-item version of the Patient Health Questionnaire,[37] which excluded the item that assesses thoughts of death or hurting oneself). Jinkerson includes these measures among his recommendations for "[a]ssessing [s]econdary [s]ymptomatic [f]eatures" of moral injury.[38] Finally, students completed a demographic questionnaire.

The data reported here are from a larger study assessing moral injury among adult survivors of clergy sexual abuse, current employees of Catholic dioceses, and students at a Jesuit university. Of the 224 student participants, six indicated that they were diocesan employees, and five indicated that they were survivors of clergy sexual abuse. As this chapter focuses on moral injury among bystanders, students who identified as diocesan employees or survivors were not included in the analyses described here due to their more direct association with the Catholic church or the clergy abuse crisis. Additionally, only data from students who responded to all the items assessing moral injury were included in the results reported here. These considerations yielded a final sample size of 188 students.

Students reported that they were born between 1987 and 2003, resulting in an average age of approximately 20 years old among those for whom this information was available. Participants endorsed the following gender identities: male (28.7%), female (68.6%), and nonbinary (1.6%). One participant (.5%) indicated that they preferred not to respond to this question, and one participant (.5%) did not provide a response. Regarding sexual orientation, the sample was primarily heterosexual/straight (78.7%). Smaller percentages of students identified as bisexual (12.8%), gay or lesbian (1.6%), or an identification not listed in the survey (4.3%). Four students (2.1%) indicated that they preferred not to respond to this question, and one student (.5%) did not provide a response. Reported racial/ethnic identities included (students could select multiple responses.): White/European American (86.2%), Black/African American (7.4%), Hispanic American or Latinx (4.8%), Asian (3.7%), and American Indian (.5%). Of the two participants (1.1%) who indicated that their race/ethnicity was not listed in the questionnaire, one (.5%) specified a Middle Eastern identity; the other did not indicate their identity. One student (.5%) indicated that they preferred not to respond to the question regarding their race/ethnicity, and one student (.5%) did not respond to the question regarding racial/ethnic identity.

Regarding religious identification and beliefs, 13.8% of students reported that they identified as religious but not spiritual, 31.4% indicated that they identified as spiritual but not religious, 40.4% reported identifying as both religious and spiritual, and 13.3% indicated that they were neither religious nor spiritual. Two students (1.1%) did not respond

Clergy Abuse and Students' Moral Injury   49

to this question. Students were asked to identify their current religious affiliation(s) as well as the religion(s) they were raised with. The survey allowed respondents to select one or more responses in addition to providing an option to indicate that they preferred not to respond. Students indicated the following current religious affiliations: Catholic (50.5%), Protestant (3.7%), non-denominational Christian (12.8%), Jewish (1.1%), Buddhist (.5%), Hindu (.5%), Muslim (.5%), atheist (10.6%), agnostic (14.4%), association not listed (5.9%),[39] and do not currently associate with a religion (13.3%). One participant (.5%) did not indicate their current religious affiliation. Regarding the religions they were raised with, students reported the following affiliations: Catholic (66.5%), Protestant (6.9%), non-denominational Christian (14.4%), Jewish (1.6%), Hindu (.5%), Muslim (.5%), atheist (1.6%), agnostic (1.6%), religion not listed (6.9%),[40] and no religion (3.2%). One participant (.5%) did not respond to this question.

Students indicated the extent of their agreement or disagreement with statements reflecting their belief in and relationship with God or a higher power. The majority of students (78.2%) indicated that they strongly agreed or agreed with the statement, *I believe there is a God or some higher power.* Over half of the students (53.7%) strongly agreed or agreed with the statement, *I have a personal relationship with God.* About two-thirds of students (67.6%) disagreed or strongly disagreed that they are uncomfortable with the concept of "God." Taken together, students' reports of their religious and spiritual identifications and beliefs indicate that most of the participants believed in God and identified with one or more religious affiliations.

In order to assess exposure to potentially morally injurious events (i.e., clergy sexual abuse and its cover-up by Church authorities), students responded to several questions pertaining to their awareness of clergy sexual abuse and its impact on them as well as their community. Most students reported that they were aware of sexual abuse by Catholic clergy (92.6%) and that they were aware that Catholic church authorities had covered up such abuse (87.2%). Over two-thirds of students (69.7%) reported awareness of sexual abuse by a Catholic member of the clergy. Several students reported that a friend, family member, or someone else close to them had experienced clergy sexual abuse (9.0%), that they had advocated for a survivor of clergy abuse (6.9%), or that they had raised a complaint against a member of the Catholic clergy in relation to sexual abuse (1.1%). Most students (58.0%) indicated that they believed that the clergy abuse crisis was a widespread, systemic failure by the church (as opposed to 3.7% of students who believed that only a few individuals were responsible); 38.3% of students indicated that they were not confident they knew enough about the scope of the event. A slight majority of students (52.7%) indicated that they had not been affected by the clergy abuse crisis and authority cover-up; the remaining students indicated that they had been somewhat affected (42.0%) or greatly affected (5.3%). Regarding the effect of the abuse crisis and cover-up on their community, students indicated that their community had not been affected (39.9%), had been somewhat affected (50.0%), or had been greatly affected (10.1%). When asked specifically about the impact on their comfort in their faith community in response to awareness of sexual abuse by priests in the Catholic church, 29.3% of students indicated that it had stayed the same, while 1.1% indicated that their comfort had increased, and 46.3% indicated that it had decreased; 23.4% of students reported that they were not members of a faith community.

The moral injury questionnaire consisted of 74 items rated from 1 (Strongly disagree) to 5 (Strongly agree). When appropriate, items were reverse-scored such that higher scores reflected greater moral injury. Possible total scores on the moral injury measure ranged from 74 to 370. Students' scores ranged from 98 to 290 with a mean of 197.47 and a standard deviation of 39.51. This mean total score yields a mean item score of 2.67, slightly below the midpoint of the scale. Although there is no normative data for this moral injury measure due to its novelty, we can conclude based on this mean score that on average, students were identifying relatively low levels of moral injury. To aid in interpreting the degree of moral injury reflected by students' scores, we compared their moral injury scores to those of 52 adult survivors of clergy sexual abuse (mean = 260.69, standard deviation = 46.42) and 35 diocesan employees (mean = 175.71, standard deviation = 48.21). On average, students' scores were significantly lower than those of survivors, but significantly higher than those of employees.

We examined associations between students' moral injury scores and their scores on measures of symptoms of PTSD, anxiety, and depression. As expected, moral injury was significantly positively correlated with each of these constructs, that are conceptually related to, yet distinct from, moral injury.

To better understand experiences of moral injury among students attending a Jesuit university, total scores for the moral injury items were compared for various groups of students based on demographic characteristics and religious and spiritual identifications. Students who identified as female reported greater moral injury (mean = 201.40, standard deviation = 39.28) than students who identified as male (mean = 187.30, standard deviation = 38.82); students who did not indicate a male or female identity were excluded from this comparison due to the small number of students to whom this applied. Due to the small numbers of students who selected sexual orientations other than heterosexual/straight, students who identified as bisexual, gay, lesbian, or another sexual orientation were combined into a single group and compared to students who identified as heterosexual/straight. Students with a sexual orientation other than heterosexual/straight reported greater moral injury (mean = 222.29, standard deviation = 33.61) than students who identified as heterosexual/straight (mean = 191.57, standard deviation = 38.79).

Moral injury scores were also compared based on whether students identified as religious but not spiritual, spiritual but not religious, both religious and spiritual, or neither religious nor spiritual. Students who identified as spiritual but not religious reported greater moral injury (mean = 210.69, standard deviation = 39.05) than students who reported that they were both religious and spiritual (mean = 187.96, standard deviation = 39.67). There were no other significant differences between the four groups. Results also indicated that the extent of students' agreement that they believed there is a God or some higher power was significantly negatively correlated with moral injury, meaning that students who expressed a stronger belief in a higher power experienced lower moral injury.

Additionally, moral injury scores were compared across groups of students based on their current religious affiliations and the religions they were raised with. To compare moral injury between students based on the religion(s) they were raised with, students were divided into three groups: Catholic (125 students); other affiliation (52 students); and no affiliation, agnostic, or atheist (10 students). The same three categories were also used to divide students into groups based on their current religious affiliations (Catholic: 95 students; other affiliation: 41 students; no affiliation, agnostic, or atheist: 51 students). (Note: For both current religious affiliation and the affiliation they were raised with, any student who selected Catholic was assigned to this group, even if they selected multiple responses to the question regarding religious affiliation. Students who selected any religion other than Catholic were assigned to the "other affiliation" group, even if they also selected agnostic, atheist, and/or no affiliation.) There was no statistical difference in the moral injury scores between the three groups when considering the religions students were raised with. However, when examining moral injury in relation to students' current religious affiliations, there was a statistically significant difference between the three groups. Specifically, the average total moral injury score among students indicating that they had no religious affiliation or were atheist or agnostic (mean = 215.61, standard deviation = 36.82) was significantly greater than that of both Catholic students (mean = 191.77, standard deviation = 38.21) and students reporting a non-Catholic religious affiliation (mean = 186.44, standard deviation = 37.85). Catholic students and those reporting a non-Catholic religious affiliation did not differ from each other with regard to moral injury.

Given the difference in moral injury scores between Catholic students and those with no religious affiliation, as well as the lower number of students who reported currently identifying as Catholic compared to the number who were raised Catholic, we divided students who were raised Catholic into two groups: those who still identified as Catholic (92 students) and those who did not (33 students). A comparison of the total moral injury scores between these two groups indicated that students who no longer identified as Catholic experienced significantly greater moral injury (mean = 217.97, standard deviation = 35.02) than students who continued to identify as Catholic (mean = 191.88, standard deviation = 38.75). This finding suggests that there may be an association between moral injury and students' departure from a Catholic identity that they were raised with, although further research is necessary to better understand this potential relationship. Moreover, it is important to keep in mind that none of the groups of students identified based on current religious affiliation or the religion they were raised with exceeded the midpoint of the moral injury scale, on average. Thus, the extent of moral injury among this group of students appears to be relatively low overall.

Moving Forward: Questions and Insights

As the Catholic church moves forward with addressing the impact of the clergy sexual abuse crisis and public scandal, leaders must consider the wider effects on the broader Catholic community. Examining and repairing the damage done to the trust, moral clarity, and overall comfort in their religious communities of the laity should not be neglected. While, admittedly, this initial study raises more questions than it answers, there are some significant findings to suggest that the moral injury and trauma caused by the clergy sexual abuse crisis and cover-up extend beyond those directly involved. The broader Catholic community has been impacted in ways still not yet clear. What this study suggests is that bystanders to morally injurious events may experience some moral injury. While students' moral injury scores were under the midpoint of the scale and significantly lower than survivors' scores, their scores were significantly higher than diocesan employees, suggesting young people are experiencing some level of moral injury. More significantly, almost half of the college students (46.3%) in this study felt a decrease in their comfort in their faith community because of their awareness of sexual abuse by priests.

More complicated findings show the importance for more research on moral injury in response to the clergy sexual abuse crisis and in the general population. Students who identified as spiritual but not religious experienced higher rates of moral injury in comparison to students who identified as both religious and spiritual. Similarly, belief in God or some higher power was associated with lower moral injury scores. Supporting this, students who reported no religious affiliation or were atheist or agnostic had significantly higher scores than those identifying as Catholic or other religious affiliations. These findings do not reveal causal relationships, however. It could be that identifying as religious and spiritual, belief in God, and religious affiliation are protective factors against moral injury, or perhaps higher moral injury results in identifying with spirituality over religion, a disbelief in God, and a lack of religious affiliation. The finding that students who were raised Catholic, but no longer identified as Catholic experienced moral injury at higher levels than students who were raised and remained Catholic, compounds this relational question. It is unknown whether religion is a protective factor against moral injury, if moral injury causes a loss of religious belief, or if a third factor is at play.

What is also troubling is that students who experienced significantly higher rates of moral injury, female students (compared to male students) and students with a sexual orientation other than heterosexual (compared to heterosexual students), have been historically marginalized in the church. Gender and sexual orientation equity are important for this generation of emerging adults, and they perceive a disconnect between them and the church on these issues.[41] With Catholic church attendance down 18% over the last 20 years,[42] it is important to note that women's attendance is declining at faster rates than men's.[43] Similarly, one-third of religiously affiliated LGBT individuals feel conflict in their faith and disaffiliate at much higher rates than their straight counterparts.[44]

What is clear from this initial study is that clergy sexual abuse has caused damage to the larger church body. This is not an issue that has only impacted victims, perpetrators, and direct friends or family, but rather an event with a fallout zone that extends well beyond those directly involved. The abuse and its cover-up are affecting even the peripheral members of the church body in the laity, including young and already marginalized members as shown in this study. As the church and other religious institutions consider the need for healing in regard to clergy sexual abuse, it is important to understand that such publicized and scandalous traumas implicate and affect far beyond the binaries of victim and perpetrator.

Notes

1 Jeffrey Jensen Arnett. "Emerging Adulthood: A Theory of Development From the Late Teens Through the Twenties," *American Psychologist* 55, no. 5 (May 2000): 469.
2 R. Reinhart. *Placing Faith: Community Commitment Among Millennial Catholics* (ProQuest Dissertations & Theses Global, 2021).

3 Investigative Staff of The Boston Globe. *Betrayal: The Crisis in the Catholic Church* (Boston, MA: Little, Brown and Company, 2002).
4 Crosson-Tower, Cynthia. "Sexual Abuse by Clergy: A Unique Offender," in *Confronting Child and Adolescent Sexual Abuse*, ed. Cynthia Crosson-Tower (Los Angeles, CA: Sage Publications, 2014).
5 Dale, Maryclaire "DOJ Probe of Catholic Church Abuse Goes Quiet 2 Years Later," *AP News*, December 13, 2020.
6 John Jay College Research Team. "The nature and scope of the problem of sexual abuse of minors by Catholic priests and deacons in the United States, 1950–2002: A research study conducted by the John Jay College of Criminal Justice. National Clergy Sex Abuse Report" (New York: City University of New York, 2004).
7 John Jay College Research Team, "The nature and scope," 285.
8 Sauvage, Deborah, and Patrick O'Leary. "Child Sexual Abuse in Faith-based Institutions: Gender, Spiritual Trauma and Treatment Frameworks," in *The Sexual Abuse of Children: Recognition and Redress*, ed. by Yorick Small, Andy Kaladelfos, and Mark Finnane (Clayton, Victoria, Australia: Monash University Publishing, 2016) 146–159.
9 Gonsiorek, John. "Barriers to Responding to the Clergy Sexual Abuse Crisis within the Roman Catholic Church," in *Sin Against the Innocents: Sexual Abuse by Priests and the Role of the Catholic Church*, ed. by Thomas G. Plante (Westport, CT: Praeger Publishers, 2004) 226.
10 Keenan, Marie. *Child Sexual Abuse and the Catholic Church: Gender, Power, and Organizational Culture* (New York, NY: Oxford University Press, 2012) 355.
11 Clericalism can be understood as a deference to the hierarchy of the church, especially to the power of ordained clergy.
12 Sipe, A. Richard, "The Problem of Prevention in Clergy Sexual Abuse," in *Bless Me Father for I Have Sinned: Perspectives on Sexual Abuse Committed by Roman Catholic Priests*, ed. by Thomas G. Plante (Westport, CT: Praeger, 1999) 184. And Terry, Karen, J., Smith, Margaret Leland, Schuth, Katarina, Kelly, James R., Vollman, Brenda, and Massey, Christina. *The Causes and Context of Sexual Abuse of Minors by Catholic Priests in the United States, 1950-2010: A Report Presented to the United States Conference of Catholic Bishops by the John Jay College Research Team* (Washington, D.C.: United States Conference of Catholic Bishops, 2011) 143.
13 Transference refers to unconsciously repeating past behaviors and attributing them to other individuals. [https://dictionary.apa.org/transference]
14 Countertransference describes the ways in which someone providing counseling responds to the recipient of counseling and that individual's transference. [https://dictionary.apa.org/countertransference]
15 Gonsiorek, John. "The Interplay of Psychological and Institutional Factors in Sexual Abuse by Roman Catholic Clergy," in *Clergy Sexual Abuse: Social Science Perspectives*, ed by Claire M., Renzetti, and Sandra Yocum (Boston, MA: Northeastern University Press, 2012).
16 Terry, et al. *The Causes and Context of Sexual Abuse*, 143.
17 National Review Board for the Protection of Children and Young People. *A Report on the Crisis in the Catholic Church in the United States* (Washington, D.C.: United States Conference of Catholic Bishops, 2004) 145.
18 Martin, James. "How Could It Happen? An Analysis of the Catholic Sexual Abuse Scandal," in *Predatory Priests, Silenced Victims: The Sexual Abuse Crisis and the Catholic Church*, ed. by Mary Gail Frawley-O'Dea, and Virginia Goldner (Mahwah, NJ: The Analytic Press, 2007) 35–57. And Rossetti,

Stephen J. "Learning from Our Mistakes: Responding Effectively to Child Sexual Abusers," in *Toward Healing and Renewal: The 2012 Symposium on the Sexual Abuse of Minors Held at the Pontifical Gregorian University*, ed. by Charles J. Scicluna, Hans Zollner, and David John Ayotte (New York, NY: Paulist Press, 2012).
19 Donald B. Cozzens. *Sacred Silence: Denial and the Crisis in the Church* (Collegeville, MN: The Liturgical Press, 2002) 199.
20 J. Shay. "Moral Injury," in *Psychoanalytic Psychology*, 31, no. 2 (2014): 183.
21 B.T. Litz, N. Stein, E. Delaney, L. Lebowitz, W.P. Nash, C. Silva, and S. Maguen. "Moral injury and Moral Repair in War Veterans: A Preliminary Model and Intervention Strategy." *Clinical Psychology Review*, 29, no. 8 (2009): 697.
22 E.A. Dombo, C. Gray and B.P. Early. "The Trauma of Moral Injury: Beyond the Battlefield." *Journal of Religion & Spirituality in Social Work*, 32, no. 3 (2013): 208.
23 H.G. Koenig, G. Harold, D. Ames, N.A, Youssef, J.P. Oliver, F. Volk, E.J. Teng, K. Haynes, Z.D. Erickson, I. Arnold, K.G.N. O'Garo and M.J. Pearee. "The Moral Injury Symptom Scale-Military Version," *Journal of Religion and Health*, 57, no 1 (2018): 249–265.
24 See J.D. Jinkerson. "Defining and assessing moral injury: A syndrome perspective," *Traumatology*, 22, no. 2 (2016): 122–130. Litz, B. T., Stein, N., Delaney, E., Lebowitz, L., Nash, W. P., Silva, C., and Maguen, S. "Moral injury and moral repair in war veterans: A preliminary model and intervention strategy," *Clinical Psychology Review*, 29, no. 8 (2009): 695–706. Drescher, K. D., Foy, D. W., Kelly, C., Leshner, A., Schutz, K., and Litz, B. "An exploration of the viability and usefulness of the construct of moral injury in war veterans," *Traumatology*, 17, no. 1 (2011): 8–13. https://doi.org/10.1177/1534765610395615
25 Brandon J. Griffin et al., "Moral Injury: An Integrative Review," *Journal of Traumatic Stress* 32, no. 3 (June 2019): 355–356. https://doi.org/10.1002/jts.22362
26 Timothy J. Hodgson, and Lindsay B. Carey, "Moral Injury and Definitional Clarity: Betrayal, Spirituality and the Role of Chaplains," *Journal of Religion and Health* 56, no. 4 (August 2017): 1215–1216.
27 Lindsay B. Carey et al., "Moral Injury, Spiritual Care and the Role of Chaplains: An Exploratory Scoping Review of Literature and Resources," *Journal of Religion and Health* 55, no. 4 (August 2016): 1220.
28 Jinkerson, "Defining and Assessing Moral Injury," 126.
29 Shannon D. Chaplo, Patricia K. Kerig, and Cecilia Wainryb, "Development and Validation of the Moral Injury Scales for Youth," *Journal of Traumatic Stress* 32, no. 3 (June 2019): 448. https://doi.org/10.1002/jts.22408.
30 Litz et al., "Moral Injury and Moral Repair in War Veterans," 700.
31 Chaplo et al., "Development and Validation of the Moral Injury Scales for Youth," 448–458.
32 Chaplo et al., "Development and Validation of the Moral Injury Scales for Youth," 448.
33 Chaplo et al., "Development and Validation of the Moral Injury Scales for Youth," 448–449, 456.
34 Daniel Lapsley and Sam A. Hardy, "Identity Formation and Moral Development in Emerging Adulthood," in *Flourishing in Emerging Adulthood: Positive Development During the Third Decade of Life*, eds. Laura M. Padilla-Walker, and Larry J. Nelson (New York: Oxford University Press, 2017), 14–39. https://doi.org/10.1093/acprof:oso/9780190260637.003.0002.

35 Frank W. Weathers et al., *The PTSD Checklist for DSM-5 (PCL-5) – Standard* [Measurement instrument]. (2013). Available from www.ptsd.va.gov/.
36 Robert L. Spitzer et al., "A Brief Measure for Assessing Generalized Anxiety Disorder: The GAD-7," *Archives of Internal Medicine*, 166, no. 10 (May 2006): 1094., https:// 10.1001/archinte.166.10.1092.
37 Kurt Kroenke, Robert L. Spitzer, and Janet B. W. Williams, "The PHQ-9: Validity of a Brief Depression Severity Measure, *Journal of General Internal Medicine*, 16, no. 9 (September 2001): 613, https://doi.org/10.1046/j.1525-1497.2001.016009606.x.
38 Jinkerson, "Defining and Assessing Moral Injury," 127.
39 Responses included Baptist, Episcopalian, Lutheran, non-denominational Christian, Pentecostal, polytheistic, and a response indicating an identity as "[C]atholic in religion but not [associating] with the [C]hurch or many practices."
40 Responses included Apostolic Pentecostal, Baptist, Episcopalian, Lutheran, non-denominational Christian, and Pentecostal.
41 Clare Ansberry. "Young People Say Disconnect Keeps Them From Church," *Wall Street Journal*. October 25, 2021. www.wsj.com/articles/young-people-say-disconnect-keeps-them-from-church-11635163200.
42 Jeffery Jones. "U.S. Church Membership Falls Below Majority for First Time," *Gallup*. March 29, 2021. https://news.gallup.com/poll/341963/church-membership-falls-below-majority-first-time.aspx.
43 Ryan Burg. "Guest Column: Behind the Steep Decline in Church Attendance Among Women," *Barna State of the Church*. March 4, 2020. www.barna.com/changes-behind-the-scenes/.
44 Pew Research Center. "Chapter 6: Religion" *A Survey or LGBT American*, June 12, 2013. www.pewresearch.org/social-trends/2013/06/13/chapter-6-religion/

Bibliography

Ansberry, Clare. "Young People Say Disconnect Keeps Them From Church." *Wall Street Journal*. October 25, 2021. www.wsj.com/articles/young-people-say-disconnect-keeps-them-from-church-11635163200.

Arnett, Jeffrey Jensen. "Emerging Adulthood: A Theory of Development From the Late Teens Through the Twenties." *American Psychologist* 55, no. 5 (May 2000): 469–480. https://doi.org/10.1037//0003-066X.55.5.469.

Burg, Ryan. "Guest Column: Behind the Steep Decline in Church Attendance Among Women." *Barna State of the Church*, March 4, 2020. www.barna.com/changes-behind-the-scenes/

Carey, Lindsay B., Timothy J. Hodgson, Lillian Krikheli, Rachel Y. Soh, Annie-Rose Armour, Taranjeet K. Singh, and Cassandra G. Impiombato. "Moral Injury, Spiritual Care and the Role of Chaplains: An Exploratory Scoping Review of Literature and Resources." *Journal of Religion and Health* 55, no. 4 (August 2016): 1218–1245. https://doi.org/ 10.1007/s10943-016-0231-x.

Chaplo, Shannon D., Patricia K. Kerig, and Cecilia Wainryb. "Development and Validation of the Moral Injury Scales for Youth." *Journal of Traumatic Stress* 32, no. 3 (June 2019): 448–458. https://doi.org/10.1002/jts.22408.

Cozzens, Donald B. *Sacred Silence: Denial and the Crisis in the Church*. Collegeville, MN: The Liturgical Press, 2002.

Crosson-Tower, Cynthia. "Sexual Abuse by Clergy: A Unique Offender," in *Confronting Child and Adolescent Sexual Abuse*, ed. Cynthia Crosson-Tower. Los Angeles, CA: Sage Publications, 2014.
Dale, Maryclaire. "DOJ Probe of Catholic Church Abuse Goes Quiet 2 Years Later." *AP News*, December 13, 2020.
Dombo, E. A., Gray, C., and Early, B. P. "The Trauma of Moral Injury: Beyond the Battlefield." *Journal of Religion & Spirituality in Social Work*, 32, no. 3 (2013).
Drescher, K. D., Foy, D. W., Kelly, C., Leshner, A., Schutz, K., and Litz, B. "An exploration of the viability and usefulness of the construct of moral injury in war veterans." *Traumatology*, 17, no. 1 (2011). https://doi.org/10.1177/1534765610395615.
Gonsiorek, John. "Barriers to Responding to the Clergy Sexual Abuse Crisis within the Roman Catholic Church," in *Sin Against the Innocents: Sexual Abuse by Priests and the Role of the Catholic Church*, ed. by Thomas G Plante. Westport, CT: Praeger Publishers, 2004.
Gonsiorek, John. "The Interplay of Psychological and Institutional Factors in Sexual Abuse by Roman Catholic Clergy," in *Clergy Sexual Abuse: Social Science Perspectives*, ed. by Claire M., Renzetti, and Sandra Yocum. Boston, MA: Northeastern University Press, 2012.
Griffin, Brandon J., Natalie Purcell, Kristine Burkman, Brett T. Litz, Craig J. Bryan, Martha Schmitz, Claudia Villierme, Jessica Walsh, and Shira Maguen. "Moral Injury: An Integrative Review." *Journal of Traumatic Stress* 32, no. 3 (June 2019). https://doi.org/10.1002/jts.22362.
Hodgson, Timothy J., and Lindsay B. Carey. "Moral Injury and Definitional Clarity: Betrayal, Spirituality and the Role of Chaplains." *Journal of Religion and Health* 56, no. 4 (August 2017): 1212–1228. https://doi. 10.1007/s10943-017-0407-z.
Investigative Staff of The Boston Globe. *Betrayal: The Crisis in the Catholic Church*. Boston, MA: Little, Brown and Company, 2002.
Jinkerson, J. D. "Defining and Assessing Moral Injury: A Syndrome Perspective." *Traumatology*, 22, no. 2 (June 2016): 122–130. http://dx.doi.org/10.1037/trm0000069.
John Jay College Research Team. "The nature and scope of the problem of sexual abuse of minors by Catholic priests and deacons in the United States, 1950–2002: A research study conducted by the John Jay College of Criminal Justice. National Clergy Sex Abuse Report." New York: City University of New York, 2004.
Jones, Jeffery. "U.S. Church Membership Falls Below Majority for First Time." *Gallup*. March 29, 2021. https://news.gallup.com/poll/341963/church-membership-falls-below-majority-first-time.aspx.
Keenan, Marie. *Child Sexual Abuse and the Catholic Church: Gender, Power, and Organizational Culture*. New York, NY: Oxford University Press, 2012.
Koenig, H. G., Harold G., Ames, D., Youssef, N. A., Oliver, J. P., Volk, F., Teng, E. J., Haynes, K., Erickson, Z. D., Arnold, I., O'Garo, K.-G. N., and Pearce, M. J. "The Moral Injury Symptom Scale-Military Version." *Journal of Religion and Health*, 57, no. 1 (2018).

Kroenke, Kurt, Robert L. Spitzer, and Janet B. W. Williams. "The PHQ-9: Validity of a Brief Depression Severity Measure." *Journal of General Internal Medicine*, 16, no. 9 (September 2001): 606–613. https://doi.org/10.1046/j.1525-1497.2001.016009606.x.

Lapsley, Daniel, and Sam A. Hardy. "Identity Formation and Moral Development in Emerging Adulthood," in *Flourishing in Emerging Adulthood: Positive Development During the Third Decade of Life*, edited by Laura M. Padilla-Walker and Larry J. Nelson, 14–39. New York: Oxford University Press, 2017. https://doi.org/ 10.1093/acprof:oso/9780190260637.003.0002.

Litz, B. T., Nathan Stein, Eileen Delaney, Leslie Lebowitz, William P. Nash, Caroline Silva, and Shira Maguen. "Moral Injury and Moral Repair in War Veterans: A Preliminary Model and Intervention Strategy." *Clinical Psychology Review*, 29, no. 8 (December 2009): 695–706. https://doi.org/10.1016/j.cpr.2009.07.003.

Martin, James. "How Could It Happen? An Analysis of the Catholic Sexual Abuse Scandal," in *Predatory Priests, Silenced Victims: The Sexual Abuse Crisis and the Catholic Church*, ed. By Mary Gail Frawley-O'Dea, and Virginia Goldner. Mahwah, NJ: The Analytic Press, 2007.

Nash, W. P. "Commentary on the Special Issue on Moral Injury: Unpacking Two Models for Understanding Moral Injury." *Journal of Traumatic Stress*, 32, no. 3 (2019).

National Review Board for the Protection of Children and Young People. *A Report on the Crisis in the Catholic Church in the United States*. Washington, D.C.: United States Conference of Catholic Bishops, 2004.

Pew Research Center. "Chapter 6: Religion." *A Survey or LGBT American*, June 12, 2013. www.pewresearch.org/social-trends/2013/06/13/chapter-6-religion/.

Reinhart, R. *Placing Faith: Community Commitment Among Millennial Catholics*. ProQuest Dissertations & Theses Global. 2021.

Rossetti, Stephen J. "Learning from Our Mistakes: Responding Effectively to Child Sexual Abusers," in *Toward Healing and Renewal: The 2012 Symposium on the Sexual Abuse of Minors Held at the Pontifical Gregorian University*, ed. by Charles J. Scicluna, Hans Zollner, and David John Ayotte. New York, NY: Paulist Press, 2012.

Sauvage, Deborah, and Patrick O'Leary. "Child Sexual Abuse in Faith-based Institutions: Gender, Spiritual Trauma and Treatment Frameworks," in *The Sexual Abuse of Children: Recognition and Redress*, ed. by Yorick Small, Andy Kaladelfos, and Mark Finnane. Clayton, Victoria, Australia: Monash University Publishing, 2016.

Shay, J. "Moral Injury," in *Psychoanalytic Psychology*, 31, no. 2 (2014).

Sipe, A. Richard, "The Problem of Prevention in Clergy Sexual Abuse," in *Bless Me Father for I Have Sinned: Perspectives on Sexual Abuse Committed by Roman Catholic Priests*, ed. by Thomas G. Plante. Westport, CT: Praeger, 1999.

Spitzer, Robert L., Kurt Kroenke, Janet B. W. Williams, and Bernd Löwe. "A Brief Measure for Assessing Generalized Anxiety Disorder: The GAD-7." *Archives of Internal Medicine*, 166, no. 10 (May 2006): 1092–1097. https://10.1001/archinte.166.10.1092.

Terry, Karen, J., Smith, Margaret Leland, Schuth, Katarina, Kelly, James R., Vollman, Brenda, and Massey, Christina. *The Causes and Context of Sexual Abuse of Minors by Catholic Priests in the United States, 1950–2010: A Report Presented to the United States Conference of Catholic Bishops by the John Jay College Research Team.* Washington, D.C.: United States Conference of Catholic Bishops, 2011.

Weathers, Frank W., Brett T. Litz, Terence M. Keane, Palmieri, P. A., Brian P. Marx., and Paula P. Schnurr, *The PTSD Checklist for DSM-5 (PCL-5) – Standard* [Measurement instrument]. 2013. Available from www.ptsd.va.gov/.

Chapter 4

Healing with God's Nonlinear Nonbinary Love

Paul A. Tenkotte

Background

Living in today's homophobic and transphobic environment, it is understandable why some people simply reject organized religion, God, or both. My purpose here is not to convince those who have taken such a path to change their course. Rather, my primary purpose is to offer those trapped in anger towards organized religion, God, or both to let that anger go—even if the only reason to do so is for your own mental, emotional, and physical health. Second, I hope to demonstrate how the queer community can use nonlinear and nonbinary thinking processes that provide alternatives to the linear and binary perspectives that homophobic and transphobic fanatics utilize to make others feel less than human. Third, for those desiring to embrace God anew, I sincerely hope that they come to know God as harmonious with modern science, and further, that God's unconditional love for every human—like the universe itself—is inexhaustible.

Good Luck, Bad Luck, Who Knows?

There is an old fable that has been handed down about a Chinese Daoist farmer who lived centuries ago and raised horses. One day, one of his most beautiful horses ran away. The Daoist farmer's neighbors commiserated with him about what a tragedy had befallen him, asserting that he suffered bad luck. The Daoist farmer looked at his neighbors intently and replied calmly, *Good luck, bad luck, who knows?*[1]

Several months later, the Daoist farmer's horse returned to his farm, with wild horses alongside. The neighbors paid a visit to the farmer, exclaiming their happiness for him and his stroke of good luck. *Good luck, bad luck, who knows?* the farmer retorted. Shortly thereafter, the Daoist farmer's son was attempting to tame one of the wild horses. The horse bucked and threw the farmer's son to the ground, injuring the young man in such a manner that he was no longer able to walk. The neighbors sauntered over to the farmer's house, bemoaning such a terrible accident and bad luck. Patiently, the Daoist farmer asserted, *Good luck, bad luck, who knows?*

A year later, invaders attacked the town, and many of the young men of the village were killed in its defense. However, unable to serve in the army, the Daoist farmer's son survived. The neighbors traversed over to the Daoist farmer's home and declared that he was so fortunate. The Daoist farmer answered, *Good luck, bad luck, who knows?* And the story could go on and on.

The story of the Daoist farmer teaches us to be patient, remembering that nothing in life is as simple as it appears. The universe is infinitely vast and complex, and our human brains—as elaborate as they are—cannot begin to comprehend its size. For 13.8 billion years, the universe has been evolving and expanding. In fact, the statistics are mind-boggling. There are as many as "400-billion stars in our own galaxy" alone, not counting the stars in the other "two-trillion galaxies in our universe."[2]

Likewise, our planet earth is large and diverse. Estimates "for the number of species on Earth" vary "between 5.3 million and 1 trillion."[3] Their diversity is further evidenced by many other astonishing facts. For example, many species of the animal kingdom exhibit homosexual and bisexual behaviors, the subject of countless scientific investigations.[4] Clearly, God must love diversity as the earth and universe abound with it.

Also, the world's human population is vast and diverse. In 2022, our global population was quickly approaching 8 billion people,[5] growing at the rate of more than 80 million people per year."[6] Take a moment to consider the large number of ethnicities and nationalities in that mix, as well as the differences in race, gender, sexual identity, and personality. Further, as any serious study of genetics exhibits, diversity is literally hardwired into our human DNA, a vital component of the continual process of human evolution.

Understanding the vast diversity and complexity of our world, ourselves, and our universe is tantamount to realizing that binary thinking—of good versus evil, rich versus poor, black versus white (with no shades of gray), *us* versus *them*, Republicans versus Democrats, capitalism versus communism, male versus female, gay versus straight, etc.—is severely limiting in its capacity to understand and navigate modern reality. Likewise, linear thinking (also called sequential thinking) is also very confining in attempting to solve the many challenges facing us as humans. Linear thinking proceeds from a general premise through sequences of cause-and-effect events to an ending point/hypothesis. For example, A causes B that leads to C.

In his books, *Understanding Media: The Extension of Man* (1944) and *The Guttenberg Galaxy* (1962), well-known scholar Marshall

McLuhan observed how linear thinking became entrenched in Western civilization. As a matter of fact, his reasoning reflects linear thinking itself. McLuhan asserted that Johannes Guttenberg's introduction of movable-type printing into Europe during the 1400s produced some cause-and-effect results. First, the printing press produced more affordable books. More accessible books, in turn, subsequently led to more people learning to read. And since reading requires linear thinking skills, Europeans began to think in a more homogenous fashion. They started to read the same books that, consequently, popularized similar, linear viewpoints.

The story of the Chinese Daoist farmer is an illustration of the opposite of linear and binary thinking patterns. Rather, it is an example of dialectical (nonbinary, sometimes called cyclical) thinking, which underlies the foundations of many Asian philosophies and religions. This dialectical cognition does not necessarily proceed in a line from beginning to end. Rather, it considers varying perspectives, the influence of time on the determination of an event, and the ability to accept and even embrace contradictions. On the other hand, Western philosophies and religions have largely utilized linear and binary (sometime called Dualism) thinking in their attempts to fashion perspectives of the world.[7]

Ironically, both binary and linear thinking are contrary to some of the greatest discoveries of modern science. For example, in his special (1905) and general/classical (1916) theories of relativity, Albert Einstein theorized that time is relative (not a fixed unit) and that absolute rest and motion do not exist, except only in relation to one another.[8] Likewise, in 1927, Werner Heisenberg posited his Uncertainty Principle, disclosing that both position and momentum (speed) of objects are uncertain. This is connected to quantum mechanics, which explains that all objects behave as both particles and waves. As a result, it is not possible to know both the exact position and the speed (momentum) of a particle at the same time.[9] Also in 1927, Georges Lemaître published a scholarly paper proposing the theory of the expanding universe, followed in 1931 by his formulation of what later was called the Big Bang theory. Meanwhile, in psychology, both Sigmund Freud (1880s) and Carl Jung (1910s) studied what is generally referred to as the subconscious brain.[10] All these scientists confirmed that the universe—and humans—are much more complicated than we originally thought. Indeed, nature does not necessarily abide by unchangeable rules as hypothesized by earlier scientists. Rather, the universe is expanding, evolving, and can prove random and unpredictable.

Discoveries in physics and astronomy were paralleled by technological developments, especially in the information sciences. By the 1990s, the Information Revolution (sometimes called the Third Industrial Revolution) was underway worldwide. Disruptive technological innovations over the next couple of decades literally changed the way people live, work, study, and play. Computers, mobile phones, the internet, and social media require nonlinear thinking skills. Nonlinear cognition is necessary as we are literally beset by multiple messages and tasks arriving electronically, even invasively, into our work and home environments. Multitasking is one very simple example. Another example is critical thinking, that is, the ability to think in a nonlinear fashion. Critical thinking requires us to both analyze (to take apart) and synthesize (to put together) information from various sources/topics and to see where those sources/topics converge, diverge or merge. Further, it does not necessarily dispose of contradictory evidence. Rather, critical thinking often sets aside contradictions for reconsideration or reevaluation later.[11]

With all this modern knowledge of the universe and of ourselves, how is it possible that some people remain rooted in worn-out, disconnected modes of thinking? That tendency is explainable scientifically as well. Psychologists have a term for the anxiety we experience when we learn something new that simply does not fit our commonly accepted worldviews. They call it *cognitive dissonance*. We overcome cognitive dissonance and become mature, engaged adult learners when we discover how to liberate ourselves from false notions implanted within our brains. Indeed, adults learn best when they are willing to face contradictory assumptions, to learn further about the topic under discussion, and to change their opinions as necessary.[12]

"Religion is outraged when an outrage is perpetrated in its name."[13]

An example of cognitive dissonance will furnish us an understandable, yet perhaps painful, mental role-playing exercise. Imagine the cognitive dissonance experienced by a conservative Christian when they learn that someone close to them is LGBTQIA+ (Lesbian, Gay, Bisexual, Transgender, Queer or Questioning, Intersex, Asexual). Perhaps their religion has always taught them that being queer is sinful. Discovering that their loved one is anything other than straight likely results in cognitive dissonance. Our human brains rebel against cognitive dissonance, which causes us tension and anxiety. To resolve the situation, they try to reduce the dissonance. The worst scenario is that they reject us. A better scenario is that they educate themselves about the queer community and learn to accept it for the reality that it is, not the supposed contradiction that they have been taught. The best scenario, of course, is that they educate themselves and others to become loving allies.

Likewise, LGBTQIA+ victims of sexual abuse may also experience cognitive dissonance of their own. The fact that abuse occurred at the hands of trusted clergy elevates the situation to multiple layers of contradictions. The scenario is truly nonlinear and intersectional (intersecting between several layers, for example, between gender, sexual identity, age, as well as structures of power, privilege, and economic status). First, many mainline religions in the United States still regard the LGBTQIA+ community as broken, sinful, and deserving of condemnation.[14] Second, clergy—adults to whom other adults entrusted their children's physical, mental, emotional, and spiritual wellbeing—betrayed that trust in a most egregious and illegal manner. Third, the very act of sexual abuse by a priest, minister or other religious representative is the height of hypocrisy, betraying God and religion itself.[15] Finally, the fact that many abusers tried to manipulate God in their efforts to hide abuse or, worse yet, to make audacious claims that God would punish innocent victims for revealing the abuse to others, is sheer blasphemy. As Gandhi (Siddhartha Gautama) once stated, "Religion is outraged when an outrage is perpetrated in its name."

Over the years, I have struggled with mainline religions' rejection of me and people I care about. Even when other Christians are told to love us, the reality is sometimes more insipid, insidious, and disappointing. Queers are relegated to a lesser status in many organized religions. Religious leaders prevent them from becoming priests, ministers, deacons, elders, or serving on parish councils. They are told in many Christian churches in the United States that they cannot receive communion or be married in a religious ceremony. Some queers have been refused church funerals, as well as burial in church cemeteries. Some social service agencies operated by churches refuse to provide marriage counseling to the queer community, or to consider them as foster or adoptive parents.[16]

The Futility of Anger

The great religious leader, Siddhartha Gautama (Gautama Buddha), once said that "You make things worse when you flare up at someone who's angry. Whoever doesn't flare up at someone who's angry wins a battle hard to win."[17] Scilla Elworthy, a world-renowned peace and civil rights activist, agrees: "Wherever there is injustice, there is anger, and anger is like gasoline—if you spray it around and somebody lights a matchstick, you have an inferno. But anger inside an engine is powerful: it can drive us forward and can get us through dreadful moments and give us power."[18] Responding to anger in a negative manner, such as with vengeance, is a futile exercise. On the other hand, using anger to positively change yourself and others is liberating.

Recently, a colleague confided in me that she was always angry. Her admission was not a startling revelation to me. Her anger showed in nearly everything she tried to do. And I use the word *tried* intentionally here. Despite her best efforts, my colleague's attempts at handling everyday work and life issues were not successful. To make matters worse, she judged herself harshly, pegging each attempt as a failure. This only served to fuel the fire of her anger further. In addition, she often complained about physical health symptoms, for which she was consulting a physician. It was obvious that she was on a downward spiral. I listened patiently, and then did what any compassionate colleague should do. I told her that seeing a counselor was one of the best decisions that I ever made in my life. I suggested that she do so as well, for her own sake. Weeks later, she confided in me that she had taken my advice.

Anger can grow deep roots from a single seed. Any traumatic event can trigger it along with depression. Once rooted, we can feed anger from additional sources. Cynicism can grow in the shadows cast by anger's branches. We may lose our trust in others, and even find it difficult to love again, or least to love as deeply as we humans are fully capable.

Anger caused by sexual abuse and violence can take on additional dimensions with those in the LGBTQIA+ community. Ironically, in a world where binary constructs of both gender and sexuality surround us every day, others sometimes confuse the clear boundaries that do—and should always—exist between the illegality of perpetrators who caused or enabled sexual abuse on the one hand, and the innocence of victims on the other.

Even Poetic Justice is Not Really Satisfying

When I was very young, maybe ten years old or so, I was the victim of a few bullies in elementary school. After school was dismissed each day, I would try to exit the school building as soon as I could and to run as fast as I was able, in order to avoid them. The physics of the matter was simple, however. I carried too many books home each day to be effectively nimble and fleet of foot.

The bullies lived in the same general area, and often caught up with me. When they did, they would proceed to call me names, push or shove me to the ground, take my hat or books and do other things that can make a child's walk home from school filled with fear and trepidation. My ten-year-old heart hated those bullies, and probably entertained notions of seeking revenge if I ever had the ability, which I knew would probably never happen.

One sunny day, I was relieved to discover that the main bully had decided to ride his bicycle home instead. That meant that I was safe, because he would always race by me on his bike, yell something obnoxious, but proceed quickly on to pursue whatever malicious task he had planned for that afternoon. That day he repeated the pattern, racing by me, turning his head and screaming at me. I was almost safely home and breathed a sigh of relief. Unfortunately, he turned his head and yelled just at the point at which the street intersected with the main road. In his distraction, he failed to stop at the stop sign or to note that a car was in the process of turning right onto the main throughfare. The driver could not stop in time, and the laws of basic physics took effect. An object in motion will remain in motion until acted upon by an outside force. The bully was ejected from his bicycle seat, hurled over the handlebar of his bike, and landed on the pavement.

My immediate reaction was that my prayers had somehow been answered by God. For a minute, I felt a sense of spiritual righteousness—even spiritual superiority—over this wretched bully. Then, my humanity snapped back into me quickly. What if he were hurt or, worse yet, dead? I wouldn't want that! I put my books down and ran to the scene. Fortunately, the driver stopped, and the bully was fine, just skinned up a little bit. The next day, and the day after, and from that point forward, that bully never bothered me ever again. We never discussed the incident, and we never had to. He and I both knew the childish 10-year-old, linear/binary thinking that attempted to explain the situation: God had given him a warning sign; next time, it would be punishment central.

Of course, our childish answer was wrong—God was not punishing him. Ironically, that very basic premise, of a punishing God, backfired on me within the year. My grandmother suffered a stroke, and unbeknownst to me, there was no hope of her survival. Each day, my mother went to the nursing home. I begged to go with her, but she knew that I would not be able to process the scene. When I asked if grandma was improving, my mom always replied in the negative. I prayed that my grandmother would be healed. I asked for one big miracle! When one didn't come and grandma died, I was depressed for days. Finally, one evening as my mother was saying my bedtime prayers with me, she asked me why I was so sad. I could contain myself no longer. I replied bravely, but with tears welling from my eyes, *Grandma died, and it's all my fault*! My mother hugged me and exclaimed that grandma's death was part of the natural cycle, that she had lived a full life, grew old and died. I insisted that I had prayed to God, and he didn't hear me, so I must have done something wrong to offend him. Calming me down, my mother reassured me that I had not done anything to displease God, and that—besides—God does not work that way. Quite the opposite, God loves us unconditionally.

"Don't let the perfect become the enemy of the good."[19]

In 2012 I experienced an eye emergency that initially caused my world to tumble. I followed my doctors' orders, however, and slowly achieved—after multiple surgeries—reasonable eyesight in the affected eye. It was not perfect, but that was never the goal. The ophthamologists reminded me of such. In fact, although they were all trained at different medical schools, served fellowships at distinct (and distinctive) hospitals, and were employed by separate medical practices, they shared one thing in common. They had all been taught by professors who told them some variation of the aphorism above—*Don't let the perfect become the enemy of the good*.

In our lives, we spend so much wasted time and effort searching for the perfect. We imagine that others have what we want—the perfect job, spouse, home, or whatever else we inwardly crave. When we recognize that someone has abused or jilted us, or even that life seems to have offered us the short end of the stick, we may become angry or depressed. Further, our anger and depression can make us vulnerable to other unwanted feelings and habits—addiction, self-hatred, vengeance, victimhood, and a general inability to move past the trauma in our lives.

What God is Not

It would take me many years to realize that God is not sitting in heaven waiting to strike us with punishment when we fail to live up to being the best person that we can be. If that were true, God would have heard the prayers of millions of people and killed Hitler, Stalin, Pol Pot and other dictators on the spot. The fact is, though, God does not operate in that fashion. In fact, in gospel accounts of the New Testament, Jesus Christ attempts many times to describe who God is and who God is not.

The Blind Man

The Gospel of John, Chapter 9, relates how Jesus came upon "a man blind from birth." Jesus' disciples asked him, "'Rabbi, who sinned, this man or his parents, that he was born blind?'" "'Neither this man nor his parents sinned,' said Jesus, 'but this happened so that the works of God might be displayed in him,'" The disciples thought that someone—either the blind man's parents or the blind man himself—had to sin to deserve a supposed punishment of blindness. Wow! So, if a person would sin after they were born, it could have convinced God to punish them—in advance—for that later, as-yet-uncommitted sin by creating them blind from birth? How would that be helpful?[20] Clearly, emphatically, and succinctly, Jesus answers that nobody is to blame. Jesus puts mud on the blind man's eyes, then tells him to wash it off. When he does, he sees for the first time in his life. It's an uplifting story, but it doesn't end there.

The Pharisees feel compelled to investigate the healing. Jesus had performed the miracle on the Sabbath, and the Jews required rest, not work, on the Sabbath. Therefore, they concluded that Jesus had broken a religious law in healing the blind man. The Pharisees proceed to interview the healed blind man, his parents, and presumably others. They conclude that Jesus is a sinner for disobeying the Sabbath. And when the healed blind man implies otherwise, "they replied, 'You were steeped in sin at birth; how dare you lecture us!' And they threw him out."[21]

Then, the story gets even better. Hearing that the Pharisees had physically thrown the poor man out of their sight (literally and figuratively),

Jesus sought him out. Jesus reveals himself to the man, and the man proclaims his belief. However, the Pharisees could not let the incident go. Their cognitive dissonance was clearly on full alert. So when Jesus said "'For judgment I have come into this world, so that the blind will see and those who see will become blind,'" they were very unhappy and asked if Jesus was implying that they were blind. Addressing them, Jesus provides an alternative glimpse into God's kingdom, stating, "'If you were blind, you would not be guilty of sin; but now that you claim you can see, your guilt remains.'"[22] In other words, instead of celebrating the miracle at hand, the Pharisees' cognitive dissonance led them to accuse Jesus of sinning. Further, they refused to consider any other options. Clinging to their dogmatism, they persisted in their belief that the blind man and/or his parents were steeped in sin. In turn, Jesus' answer to the Pharisees turns the table on them. He refers to them as spiritually blind since they were not willing to be open to learning about God. They refused to grow in love but persisted in a hard-headed and hard-hearted proclamation that fed their angry and self-righteous accusations. Not learning, not growing, and continuing to point out others' faults, they remained unchanged.

God is Love

The New Testament resounds with the lesson that God is love, yet some of us (as in the story of the blind man) continue to see God as a punishing, anthropomorphic (human-like) authority figure. Perhaps it is because we grew up picturing God as some kind of angry, old, white-bearded man safely ensconced in the heavens, ready to pounce on us if we disobeyed any of the ten commandments. We were taught that God is perfect, and that humans are steeped in sin from the time of Adam and Eve's fall in the Garden of Eden (the so-called *original sin*). Even to those Christians who regard the Adam and Eve account as metaphorical, the results are the same. A binary, linear view common to many Christian religions results. God is perfect and all-loving; humans are not. God is eternal and knows the future; humans do not. God is omnipotent (all-powerful); humans are not.[23]

It is not difficult to see how basic quandaries and doubts evolved from this sort of binary/linear Christian worldview. If God is perfect and all-loving, then why does God allow bad things to happen to good people? If God knows the future, does God essentially predetermine who will go to heaven and who will not? Questions such as these became the heart and soul of Christian philosophy and theology for centuries. In fact, *theodicy* is the official term we use to describe the attempt to study how a good God and human evil can coexist.[24]

Differing theories of theodicy would be one of the reasons why Christianity experienced many schisms in its history. For example, the Orthodox church separated from the Roman Catholic Church in 1054 CE, and the Protestants split from the Catholics 500 years later. Martin Luther, John Calvin, John Wesley and other religious reformers would propose refurbished answers to these perplexing problems of theodicy. The end result was ironic—a further division among Protestants, between the Arminians (named after Jacobus Arminius) and the Calvinists (named after John Calvin).

The Arminian-Calvinist division is actually very complex. However, for purposes here, I provide an understandable, yet simplistic, explanation offered by a colleague of mine. That colleague was the grandson of a Southern Baptist minister and the son of a very conservative evangelical minister. He attended both churches throughout his youth. When I asked him which church he liked better, he explained that he liked his grandpa's church. His grandfather believed that once you proclaimed Jesus Christ as your savior, you were saved. Obviously, you would still sin, but God would never abandon you. God would always pull you back. On the other hand, my colleague did not at all relate to his dad's religion, which believed that you couldn't do anything without risking damnation. For instance, women weren't supposed to wear lipstick or to dress in slacks. No one was allowed to drink alcohol or to dance. Although the lines between Arminianism and Calvinism are very much blurred in modern times, the basic delineation is this. If one proclaims Jesus as their savior, and still sins, God never lets them go, a variant of Calvinism. On the other hand, if one freely chooses evil, does not repent, and risks redemption, then they believe in a form of Arminianism.

In fact, one of the surprising aspects of the Protestant Reformation was its tenacity in clinging to a very Catholic doctrine, that of original sin. Original sin refers to the first sin of humankind, metaphorically explained by the Fall of Adam and Eve in the Garden of Eden by some Christians, while others regard the story as quite literal. The corollaries of the original sin doctrine are that all human beings since the Fall have inherited a sinful nature and are in need of salvation (regeneration). Some scholars argue that this basic tenet of Christian faith was largely absent in the first few centuries of the church but became entrenched in Christian belief through the efforts of Augustine of Hippo (354–430 CE; also known as St. Augustine) and other later philosophers/theologians. The original sin doctrine fit neatly into linear, binary models of thinking, which, in turn, were amplified by studying and incorporating the writings of classical Greek and Roman philosophers.[25]

Among the most resilient of the classical Greek and Roman philosophies was the binary idea of *natural law*. Natural law claimed to be universal, as well as to be consistent with reason. "Christian thinkers especially applied natural law to matters of sexuality. For example, sexual intercourse between married couples in the missionary position, with the intention of producing children, was regarded as natural. On the other hand, sexual outlets not capable of procreation were viewed as unnatural, including cunnilingus, fellatio, masturbation, mutual masturbation, and sodomy."[26] This natural law argument still forms some Christian churches' basic objection to the right of LGBTQIA+ people to establish loving, monogamous relationships.

In some respects, the binary, linear viewpoint of many Western philosophers and theologians created and sustained a kind of *puppet-master* vision of God. According to this viewpoint, God was the great puppet-master, controlling the strings of human puppets. The imagery is theologically insulting to both God and humans, discounting the deep and meaningful relationships that God desires with all of us.[27]

Of course, not all Western philosophers or theologians confined God to such strict parameters. Alfred North Whitehead's (1861–1947) process *philosophy*, which, in turn, influenced the *process theology* of Charles Hartshorne (1897–2000), liberated God and humans from the puppet-master perspective.[28] One of the most interesting of these process theologians was Pierre Teilhard de Chardin (1881–1955; de Chardin was a title, not his surname). His life exemplified the beginning of a new synthesis between scientific and theological ideas into a truly cosmic model of thinking. Teilhard de Chardin was a Catholic priest, trained in botany, geology, and zoology. An adherent of the theory of evolution, he participated in archaeological digs in China, India, and other places worldwide. Although the Catholic church issued a warning against his publications, it never actually placed them on its Index of Forbidden Books. Highly controversial in his lifetime, Teilhard earned recognition decades after his death. In essence, he believed in a God who, with his creation, progressed through a *process* of evolution to one day when all creation would be united into what Teilhard called an *Omega Point* (literally God). Hence, in the words of theologian Ilia Delio, "For Teilhard the creative process which involves a unification of multiplicity is also a redemptive process because unification involves a struggle against the forces of dispersion, the forces of evil. Hence creation and redemption are coextensive with the total space-time continuum."[29]

Teilhard de Chardin's theology rejected the binary, one-sided component of original sin. Rather, he believed that humans and the universe were progressing forward together. His evolutionary views were consonant with emerging scientific theories of his day that increasingly viewed the universe as sometimes random and unpredictable.[30] Indeed, quantum mechanics, our genetic code, and nearly all the significant scientific discoveries of modern times confirm the randomness. So why are religions reluctant to embrace science and a nonlinear/nonbinary mode of thinking? Cognitive dissonance is the answer, of course, strengthened by centuries of tradition.

There are many books and articles available to explore how science and God are compatible. That is not my purpose here. Instead, I cover this topic solely to reject the observation that there is some sort of internal contradiction between an all-loving, all-knowing, all-merciful God and our imperfect world. In a universe where time is the fourth dimension of our brains, and quantum mechanics seems irrational—randomness and contradictions are realities, not problems. Therefore, anything is possible, including some of the basic tenets of Christianity—including free will, miracles, death, and the afterlife. After all, the universe is neither bound by time nor space.[31]

The nonlinear and nonbinary models of thinking also help to explain the central belief of the world's major religions—that God is love. Like the universe, there are no limits to love, to its inexhaustible supply, to its ability to tie all of us and everything together in a web of interconnectedness, to bring hope to the hopeless, and to offer healing to the LGBTQIA+ community.

Unconditional Love

It is not surprising to discover that many of the most loving people we know were victimized and bullied by others. Despite their own sufferings, however, they have managed to overcome the discrimination and hatred dealt them. How do they achieve such an incredible task?

In the Gospel of Matthew, Chapter 22, verses 36–40, the Pharisees asked Jesus a tantalizing question: "'Teacher, which is the greatest commandment in the Law?' Jesus replied: 'Love the Lord your God with all your heart and with all your soul, and with all your mind.' This is the first and greatest commandment. And the second is like it: 'Love your neighbor as yourself.' All the Law and the Prophets hang on these two commandments.'"[32]

Growing up, as I struggled with my sexual identity, I also grappled with these two commandments. Of the first commandment, I worried that perhaps I wasn't deserving of God's love, or maybe God would not hear the prayers of a queer person like me. The second commandment was even more difficult. How could I love my neighbor as myself when I was not actually certain that I even liked me, much less loved me?

Loving God

Looking back to my younger days as a boy, I am embarrassed to admit that I really didn't understand God or how to love God. In Catholic elementary school, we were required to memorize the *Baltimore Catechism*, which outlined the beliefs of the Roman Catholic tradition. I do not recall how many of the answers to the 499 basic questions proposed in the catechism that we memorized. Whatever the case, the memorization did not necessarily lead to practical understanding. In fact, considering what we know about brain development currently, many of the concepts presented were not age-appropriate for young children.

Chapter 6 of the *Baltimore Catechism* then in use in Catholic schools focused on sin. Sadly, as a studious little boy subject to perfectionism, many of the concepts about sin and the afterlife frightened me. I was not alone. My classmates often felt the same. To make matters worse, our pastor was very authoritarian, lacked patience (especially with children), was prone to anger, and raised his voice sternly to both children and adults. My classmates and I were afraid of him. On the other hand, we were supposed to respect and honor him. According to the *Baltimore Catechism*, question 455 quizzed us: "Why should Catholics show reverence and honor to the priest?" The answer was: ". . . because he is the representative of Christ Himself and the dispenser of His mysteries."[33] Although the adults at my parish realized that our pastor was an able administrator and fundraiser, even they questioned his personality and lack of Christian patience. To us children, he did not evidence the love of Jesus Christ.

During the time of this priest's pastorate, a younger, more amiable priest was assigned to our parish. He seemed like a breath of fresh air, at least at first. He was especially close to the altar boys. He took them on adventures after church on Sundays. He offered them snacks and cots to take a nap. Parents trusted him with their children. If the truth about this pedophile priest were known or even suspected at the time, the pastor stated nothing to the parishioners. And the bishop simply moved him from assignment to assignment when congregations identified his predatory behavior. In his wake, this pedophile priest abused dozens of adolescent boys throughout our diocese. The predator was eventually convicted and sentenced to a long prison term. Even from his prison cell, he insisted that he was not a pedophile and that he "really did care and love" the adolescents he sexually abused.[34]

Love Does No Harm

In her book *Love Does No Harm: Sexual Ethics for the Rest of Us*, Marie M. Fortune states that survivors of sexual abuse "are susceptible to the belief that they are consenting because this belief allows them to feel that they are not totally powerless." However, the victims of sexual abuse, she notes, lack moral agency to consent, which requires "that we possess power and resources. . . . Anything which denies or compromises those resources undercuts moral agency."[35] Sexual abusers use manipulative methods to deny us moral agency, and to convince their victims to keep secret their predatory actions. For instance, the pedophile priest described above told his victims that sex was natural and that they were not doing anything wrong. Further, he stated that, if they still believed that they were committing a sin, he would be happy to hear their confessions. On the other hand, another pedophile priest of the same diocese threatened one of his victims not to tell anyone about the sexual abuse or God would send him to hell.

Whatever tactics abusive clergy told children to manipulate them into keeping their sexual assaults secret, the spiritual damage was harmful. Some victims lost their faith in God, others left their church, and some questioned why God did not hear their prayers. As a female victim of another priest of the same diocese expressed, "I didn't trust God for most of my life. I felt like the priest who raped me had a special bond with God, and God had abandoned me."[36] Victims of abuse are individuals. Like every human being, they react to trauma in varying ways. Survivors have already developed some techniques that have worked for them. Perhaps the two most important commandments, according to Jesus, can assist us in refilling our broken and depleted vessels of love.

Refilling the Depleted Vessel of Love with Love

At an initial glance, loving one's neighbor seems reasonable enough. In particular, loving someone who loves us back is rather easy. However, what about loving someone who bullied or abused us? The second commandment of Matthew 22 is easier to approach from a negative perspective—what it is not. It is not stating that we agree with, tolerate or even like our neighbor.

Second, loving our neighbor is a continual process, not a reachable goal or destination. Human beings are capable of tremendous love. In fact, each new step of love that we achieve enables us to love more and more deeply. The journey never ends. Probably our souls continue to learn to love even after our bodies succumb.

Third, note that Matthew 22 does not state that the people whom you love must love you back to complete the circle. Love can, at times, be a one-way street. That may seem like a contradiction, but it is not. It is part of the beautiful spectrum of love.

Fourth, note how Jesus stated to love your neighbor as yourself. This implies that we love ourselves first. If we do not, then we need to go back to step number one, learning to love ourselves. And I believe that loving ourselves begins with liberating ourselves from anger. Doing so will enable us to recharge our emotional and spiritual batteries. Try as we might, and understandably so, to fill ourselves with thoughts of hatred and revenge, those negative feelings will never fill our love void. Only love will fill the emptiness, pain, and sorrow we feel. As hunger is replenished by food, and thirst by water, love restocks our emotional and spiritual wellbeing. Love nourishes love.

Love begins with Empathy

Love begins with empathy. This is perhaps the most difficult part of the equation to understand, especially in terms of someone who has hurt us. However, we are humanly capable of empathizing, and for our own sakes, we might want to at least try.[37]

First, let's review what empathy is not. It is not tolerance, not acceptance, not approval. It is simply the recognition that the person who hurt us is human. Although we might prefer to dismiss them as a rat, snake, or garbage, please be aware that when we dehumanize others, it can become habitual. And let's face it. Dehumanizing others is what racists, homophobes, and transphobes do. We do not want to be like them. In reality, no one but God can judge those who have harmed us.

Nevertheless, we should remain firm in the conviction that we do not admire those who injured us. In no way, do we ever want to be like them. In fact, victims should never feel compelled to see their abusers again, provided that is possible. Further, empathy does not require that we approach abusers face-to-face. For instance, when one of my friends confronted his married, heterosexual adult brother (we'll refer to the abuser as Jack) about how Jack had raped him as a child, Jack proved unrepentant, stating that my friend must have enjoyed it because he became gay.

Healing from sexual abuse is a step-by-step process. By all means, if a person is not ready to empathize with those who hurt them, they are not compelled to do so. Instead, they should surround themselves with people, pets, or hobbies that make them happy. They can try to perform kind deeds for others. We fill our depleted vessels of hurt with more and more love.

Empathy and unconditional love—they are probably the most difficult things we'll ever attempt in our lives. We are survivors and feel the sociobiological need to fight back. Unfortunately, as the victims of great trauma, we can only fill the vacuum of love with more love. Hatred and vengeance will only diminish our reserves. We must learn to love ourselves, heal, and then heal to love.

Learn to Heal and Heal to Love

Each of us is a unique human being. Finding a one-size-fits-all approach to healing from sexual abuse and learning to love is simply not possible. Fortunately, there are many resources available, both on the internet and in print. Seeking the advice of a professional psychologist or counselor is also a good idea. It is worthwhile to experiment to see what works.

Thinking back to my ten-year-old self and the bullies in my life, I was very naive. I thought that if only God moved their parents to another city, or somehow let a big meteor flatten them, then all my problems would be solved. Of course, as those bullies moved on, other bullies and problems replaced them. Decades later, I realized that life is complicated. We learn from even painful circumstances. Not everyone and everything fits into neat, little boxes. The universe is not binary, and neither are humans. Everything does not occur in a linear, cause-and-effect fashion. There is randomness in life. And despite all its uncertainty and pain, life is nonetheless beautiful because there is love. Love is inexhaustible. The more you love, the more it grows. You can love and not be loved back. But love never leaves you. Even when others reject your love, it still remains your gift. Love is also nonbinary. Straight or LGBTQIA+, you can love deeply.

If we study the world's major religions, we'll discover that they all emphasize that God is love. Whatever we ultimately believe, however, we can be assured that love will nearly always win in the end, even if it takes a long time to do so. Therefore, it seems reasonable that our meaning and purpose in life is to learn about love, to grow in love, and to breathe love back to everyone we meet and to everything we encounter.

Notes

1 I have retold this Chinese parable in my own words. Entitled, "Sai Weng Shi Ma" ("The Old Man Who Lost His Horse"), it has many versions and likely had its origins in the 2nd century BCE compilation entitled, *Huainanzi*. "SAIOGAUMA (塞翁が馬) I NRIMO I SAIWENGSHIMA (塞翁失马)," *Intercultural Word Sensei: Understanding Culturally Unique Words through Interdisciplinary Research*, accessed June 2022, https://interculturalwordsensei.org/nrimo-%E5%A1%9E%E7%BF%81%E5%A4%B1%E9%A9%AC/.
2 *NOVA Universe Revealed: Age of Stars*, NOVA, 2021, transcript, www.pbs.org/wgbh/nova/video/nova-universe-revealed-age-of-stars/.
3 "How Many Species on Earth? Why That's a Simple Question but Hard to Answer," *The Conversation*, April 28, 2019, accessed June 2022, https://theconversation.com/how-many-species-on-earth-why-thats-a-simple-question-but-hard-to-answer-114909.
4 Joan Roughgarden, *Evolution's Rainbow: Diversity, Gender, and Sexuality in Nature and People* (Berkeley: University of California Press, 10th anniv. ed., 2013); Simon LeVay, *Gay, Straight, and the Reason Why: The Science of Sexual Orientation* (Oxford, United Kingdom: Oxford University Press, 2nd ed., 2017); James Owen, "Homosexual Activity among Animals Stirs Debate," *National Geographic*, July 23, 2004, accessed June 2022, www.nationalgeographic.com/science/article/homosexual-animals-debate#:~:text=In%20his%20day%20%22the%20birds,unknown%20within%20the%20animal%20kingdom.
5 "Current World Population," worldometer, accessed June 2022, www.worldometers.info/world-population/.
6 "Growth Rate," worldometer, accessed June 2022, www.worldometers.info/world-population/#growthrate.

7 Bart de Langhe, Stefano Puntoni, and Richard Larrick, "Linear Thinking in a Nonlinear World," *Harvard Business Review*, (May–June 2017), accessed June 2022, https://hbr.org/2017/05/linear-thinking-in-a-nonlinear-world; Hiroshi Yama and Norhayati Zakaria, "Explanations for Cultural Differences in Thinking: Easterners' Dialectical Thinking and Westerners' Linear Thinking," *Journal of Cognitive Psychology*, 31, no. 4 (2019): 487–506; Zuo Biao, "Lines and Circles: West and East," The Theosophical Society in America, accessed June 2022, www.theosophical.org/publications/quest-magazine/1286-lines-and-circles-west-and-east.

8 Carlo Rovelli, *Seven Brief Lessons on Physics* (New York, NY: Riverhead Books, 2016); Amir D. Aczel, *God's Equation: Einstein, Relativity, and the Expanding Universe* (New York, NY: MJF Books, 1999); Lawrence W. Fagg, *The Becoming of Time: Integrating Physical and Religious Time* (Durham, NC: Duke University Press, 2003).

9 Carlo Rovelli, *The Order of Time* (New York, NY: Riverhead Books, 2018). See these helpful videos: "Theory of Relativity Explained in 7 Minutes," LondonCityGirl, accessed June 2022, https://www.youtube.com/watch?v=ttZCKAMpcAo; Brian Greene, "String Theory," *TED-Ed*, accessed June 2022, www.youtube.com/watch?v=kF4ju6j6aLE. Chad Orzel, "What is the Heisenberg Uncertainty Principle?" *TED-Ed*, accessed June 2022, https://ed.ted.com/lessons/what-is-the-heisenberg-uncertainty-principle-chad-orzel; "What Does an Atom Really Look Like," *The Science Asylum*, accessed June 2022, https://www.youtube.com/watch?v=EOHYT5q5lhQ; "Quantum Mechanics for Dummies," accessed June 2022, www.youtube.com/watch?v=JP9KP-fwFhk.

10 See this helpful video: "How Does the Subconscious Mind Work?" *MindSet*, accessed June 2022, www.youtube.com/watch?v=Ee2HDmbgZjc.

11 Jeremy Rifkin, *The Third Industrial Revolution: How Lateral Power Is Transforming Energy, the Economy, and the World* (New York, NY: St. Martin's Press, 2011); Carson C. Chow, "Linear and Nonlinear Thinking, *Scientific Clearing House*, October 1, 2014, accessed June 2022, https://sciencehouse.wordpress.com/2014/10/01/linear-and-nonlinear-thinking/. See also the following helpful video: Jimmy Chang, "How to Distinguish Between Linear & Nonlinear: Math Teacher Tips," *eHow*, accessed June 2022, www.youtube.com/watch?v=9To7GhdaCLY.

12 Elliot Aronson, "Cognitive Dissonance," in Alan E. Kazdin, ed., *Encyclopedia of Psychology* (Oxford, Great Britain: Oxford University Press, 2000): Vol. 2, pp. 141–142.

13 "Mahatma Gandhi's essay on Hinduism," *Why I Love Hinduism* (blog), accessed June 2022, https://vedicambassador.wordpress.com/2013/10/01/mahatma-gandhis-essay-on-hinduism/.

14 Frances Fitzgerald, *The Evangelicals: The Struggle to Shape America* (New York, NY: Simon and Schuster, 2017); Mark D. Jordan, *The Invention of Sodomy in Christian Theology* (Chicago: University of Chicago Press, 1997); Ute Ranke-Heinemann, *Eunuchs for the Kingdom of Heaven: Women, Sexuality, and the Catholic Church* (New York, NY: Doubleday, 1990); Frédéric Martel, *In the Closet of the Vatican: Power, Homosexuality, Hypocrisy* (London, United Kingdom: Bloomsbury Continuum, 2019); Thomas C. Fox, *Sexuality and Catholicism* (New York, NY: George Braziller, 1995); John Boswell, *Christianity, Social Tolerance, and Homosexuality* (Chicago: University of Chicago Press, 1980).

15 Michael D'Antonio, *Mortal Sins: Sex, Crime, and the Era of Catholic Scandal* (New York, NY: St. Martin's Press, 2013); Marie Keenan, *Child Sexual*

Abuse and the Catholic Church: Gender, Power, and Organizational Culture (Oxford, United Kingdom: Oxford University Press, 2012); Investigative Staff of the Boston Globe, *Betrayal: The Crisis in the Catholic Church* (New York, NY: Little, Brown and Company, updated ed., 2015).

16 Helpful in understanding the basis of the heteronormative (in which heterosexuality is regarded as the norm, and everything else as aberrant) world in which we live is Linn Marie Tonstad, *Queer Theology: Beyond Apologetics* (Eugene, OR: Cascade Books, 2018).

17 Thanissaro Bhikkhu, trans. of "Akkosa Sutta: Insult." SN (*Samyutta Nikaya*) 7.2, accessed June 2022, www.accesstoinsight.org/tipitaka/sn/sn07/sn07.002.than.html.

18 "Speaker: Scilla Elworthy. Wisdom in Action: Global Peace and a World that Works," Awakin.org, accessed June 2022, www.awakin.org/v2/calls/388/scilla-elworthy/.

19 This expression takes many forms and is not easily attributable to any person in particular. The Enlightenment scholars Montesquieu and Voltaire both used variations of this phrase in the 1700s.

20 While the Jews believed in sin, they did not believe in any conception of original sin: Lawrence A. Hoffman, ed., *We Have Sinned: Sin and Confession in Judaism, Ashamnu and Al Chet* (Nashville, TN: Jewish Lights Publishing, 2012): 4; William L. Coleman, *Those Pharisees* (New York, NY: Hawthorn Books, 1977).

21 Gospel of John, Chapter 9, New International Version, *Bible Gateway*, accessed June 2022, www.biblegateway.com/passage/?search=John%209&version=NIV.

22 Gospel of John, Chapter 9, New International Version, *Bible Gateway*, accessed June 2022, www.biblegateway.com/passage/?search=John%209&version=NIV.

23 John Sanders, *The God Who Risks: A Theology of Providence* (Downers Grove, IL: InterVarsity Press, 1998).

24 Michael Tooley, "The Problem of Evil," *Stanford Encyclopedia of Philosophy*, accessed June 2022, https://plato.stanford.edu/entries/evil/; Harold S. Kushner, *When Bad Things Happen to Good People* (New York, NY: Avon Books, 1981).

25 Patricia A. Williams, *Doing without Adam and Eve: Sociobiology and Original Sin* (Minneapolis, MN: Fortress Press, 2001).

26 Paul A. Tenkotte, "Cleaning the Church Attic: Discarding 'Uniformity and Division' for 'Unity in Diversity," in Debra Meyers and Mary Sue Barnett, eds. *Crisis and Challenge in the Roman Catholic Church* (Lanham, MD: Lexington Books of Rowman & Littlefield, 2020): 24.

27 Thomas H. Green, *Weeds among the Wheat, Discernment: Where Prayer and Action Meet* (Notre Dame, IN: Ave Maria Press, 1985): 23–29.

28 John B. Cobb Jr., *Religions in the Making: Whitehead and the Wisdom Traditions of the World* (Eugene, OR: Cascade Books, 2012); Marc A. Pugliese and John Becker, eds., *Process Thought and Roman Catholicism* (Lanham, MD: Lexington Books of Rowman and Littlefield, 2022); Robert L. Kinast, *Process Catholicism: An Exercise in Ecclesial Imagination* (Lanham, MD: University Press of America, 1999); Norman Pittenger, *Catholic Faith in a Process Perspective* (Maryknoll, NY: Orbis Books, 1981); John C. Moskop, *Divine Omniscience and Human Freedom: Thomas Aquinas and Charles Hartshorne* (Macon, GA: Mercer University Press, 1984); Nicholas Rescher, *Process Philosophy: A Survey of Basic Issues* (Pittsburgh, PA: University of Pittsburgh Press, 2000).

29 Ilia Delio, "Teilhard de Chardin and the Future of God," *New Creation*, Center for Christogenesis, accessed June 2022, https://christogenesis.org/teilhard-de-chardin-and-the-future-of-god/.
30 David Grumett, "Pierre Teilhard de Chardin's Theological Trouble," *The Christian Century*, July 11, 2018, accessed June 2022, www.christiancentury.org/article/critical-essay/pierre-teilhard-de-chardins-theological-trouble; Pierre Teilhard de Chardin, *The Phenomenon of Man* (New York, NY: Harper, 2008 ed.).
31 John F. Haught, *God after Darwin: A Theology of Evolution* (Boulder, CO: Westview Press, 2008); John Polkinghorne, *Quarks, Chaos and Christianity* (New York, NY: Crossroad Publishing, 2005); Rocco Boni, *Quantum Christian Realism: How Quantum Mechanics Underwrites and Realizes Classical Christian Theism* (Eugene, OR: Wipf and Stock, 2016); Richard Rohr, *The Divine Dance: The Trinity and Your Transformation* (London, United Kingdom: Promoting Christian Knowledge, 2016).
32 Gospel of Matthew, Chapter 22, verses 34–40, New International Version, *Bible Gateway*, accessed June 2022, www.biblegateway.com/passage/?search=Matthew%2022&version=NIV; Amy-Jill Levine, *The Misunderstood Jew: The Church and the Scandal of the Jewish Jesus* (New York, NY: Harper Collins, 2006).
33 Rev. Bennet Kelley, ed., *Saint Joseph Baltimore Catechism: The Truths of Our Catholic Faith Clearly Explained and Illustrated.* Official revised ed. No. 2 (New York, NY: Catholic Book Publishing Co., 1969): 214.
34 Cindy Schroeder, "Bierman in Denial until the End," *Cincinnati Enquirer*, June 19, 2005, accessed June 2022, www.bishop-accountability.org/news3/2005_06_19_Schroeder_BiermanIn.htm.
35 Marie M. Fortune, *Love Does No Harm: Sexual Ethics for the Rest of Us* (New York, NY: Continuum Publishing, 1995): 28.
36 Cindy Schroeder, "Bierman in Denial until the End," *Cincinnati Enquirer*, June 19, 2005, accessed June 2022, www.bishop-accountability.org/news3/2005_06_19_Schroeder_BiermanIn.htm.
37 David Stoop, *Forgiving What You'll Never Forget* (Grand Rapids, MI: Revell, 2nd ed., 2016); Fred Luskin, *Forgive for Good: A Proven Prescription for Health and Happiness* (New York, NY: HarperCollins, 2002).

Bibliography

Adams, Carol J. and Marie M. Fortune, eds. *Violence against Women and Children: A Christian Theological Sourcebook*. New York, NY: Continuum, 1995.

Boni, Rocco. *Quantum Christian Realism: How Quantum Mechanics Underwrites and Realizes Classical Christian Theism*. Eugene, OR: Wipf and Stock, 2016.

Brown, Gregory Scott. *The Self-Healing Mind: An Essential Five-Step Practice for Overcoming Anxiety and Depression, and Revitalizing Your Life*. New York, NY: HarperCollins, 2022.

Cobb Jr., John B. *Religions in the Making: Whitehead and the Wisdom Traditions of the World*. Eugene, OR: Cascade Books, 2012.

Fagg, Lawrence W. *The Becoming of Time: Integrating Physical and Religious Time*. Durham, NC: Duke University Press, 2003.

Fortune, Marie M. *Love Does No Harm: Sexual Ethics for the Rest of Us*. New York, NY: Continuum Publishing, 1995.

Haught, John F. *God after Darwin: A Theology of Evolution.* Boulder, CO: Westview Press, 2008.

LeVay, Simon. *Gay, Straight, and the Reason Why: The Science of Sexual Orientation.* Oxford, United Kingdom: Oxford University Press, 2nd ed., 2017.

Luskin, Fred. *Forgive for Good: A Proven Prescription for Health and Happiness.* New York, NY: HarperCollins, 2002.

Martin, James. *Building a Bridge: How the Catholic Church and the LGBT Community Can Enter into a Relationship of Respect, Compassion, and Sensitivity.* New York, NY: HarperCollins, revised ed., 2018.

Polkinghorne, John. *Quarks, Chaos and Christianity.* New York, NY: Crossroad Publishing, 2005.

Pugliese, Marc A. and John Becker, eds. *Process Thought and Roman Catholicism.* Lanham, MD: Lexington Books of Rowman and Littlefield, 2022.

Rohlheiser, Ronald. *Forgotten among the Lilies: Learning to Love Beyond Our Fears.* New York, NY: Doubleday, 2005.

Rohr, Richard. *The Divine Dance: The Trinity and Your Transformation.* London, United Kingdom: Promoting Christian Knowledge, 2016.

Roughgarden, Joan. *Evolution's Rainbow: Diversity, Gender, and Sexuality in Nature and People.* Berkeley: University of California Press, 10th anniv. ed., 2013.

Rovelli, Carlo. *Seven Brief Lessons on Physics.* New York, NY: Riverhead Books, 2016.

Rovelli, Carlo. *The Order of Time.* New York, NY: Riverhead Books, 2018.

Spring, Janis Abrahms. *How Can I Forgive You? The Courage to Forgive, the Freedom Not To.* New York, NY: HarperCollins, 2004.

Stoop, David. *Forgiving What You'll Never Forget.* Grand Rapids, MI: Revell, 2nd ed., 2016.

Tonstad, Linn Marie. *Queer Theology: Beyond Apologetics.* Eugene, OR: Cascade Books, 2018.

Chapter 5

Somatic Spirituality for the Traumatized

Hye Hyun Han

Introduction

Sexual abuse is experienced by many leaving behind physical, psychological, and spiritual scars. Yet, reporting rates do not exceed 10 percent in the United States.[1] Even if a report is made, victims hide their abuse from those around them and live without adequate treatment for Post-Traumatic Stress Disorder (PTSD) and any associated symptoms resulting from these unbearable events. According to the U.S. Department of Health and Human Services, at least 20 percent of the U.S. population are victims of sexual abuse, accounting for 60 million people.[2]

What is the background behind this phenomenon, and what happens in the victim's inner world as a consequence of such an overwhelming experience? Many victims report that after experiencing a traumatic event in their lives, the way they think and react changes. Additionally, victims often suffer ongoing eating disturbances, sleep difficulties, relationship problems, feelings of isolation, depression, anxiety, shame, guilt, increased risk for suicidal ideation, low self-esteem, social phobia, and unusual sexual behavior.[3] These symptoms reflect the variety of physical, mental, and spiritual problems that sexual trauma causes in a person's life.

Sexual Objectification

The underlying factor in sexual violence is the sexual objectification of the victim's body. The victim's suffering is often caused by the process of sexual objectification of their existence, which treats the female body as an object designed to satisfy men's sexual desire without recognition of the victim's human rights, self-determination, and dignity. Neil J. Kressel identifies three motivations of rapists: "(1) to hurt or humiliate the victim, (2) to demonstrate power over the victim, and (3) to satisfy the desire for sex."[4] These evil intentions leave serious wounds, not only on the victim's body but also on their spirit.

The concept of sexual objectification has been examined in gender studies chiefly in relation to pornography issues. Scholars also suggest the recognition of the female body as a sexual object is related to capitalism.[5] They mainly deal with the various ways that female bodies are consumed to satisfy men's sexual needs. However, sexual objectification is the most fundamental cause of multiple types of sexual offenses, which go beyond women's bodies simply being consumed as sexual objects. Objectification is also the primary reason for the trauma of those who have been sexually assaulted. The victim experiences an ontological and spiritual violation that is more serious than any other violation because of the damage to their basic human dignity.

Sexual objectification is applied to the female body more than the male body in androcentric societies. This phenomenon is more pronounced in a patriarchal society where the leverage of men creates a social culture centered on the male gaze. The process through which the powerful class becomes the social subject, and the lower class is objectified by the subject's gaze, is repeated historically. This process also applies to the sexual objectification of transgender bodies, people of color, and African American women within the United States.[6] The fact that the sexual objectification of women's bodies has taken root in culture points to a society in which men are the subjects, and in which the centrality of men's gaze has been long maintained. The problem entails perpetrators experiencing no guilt associated with sexually objectifying victims' bodies because they grew up and were educated in an androcentric society. As a result, victims have not been appropriately compensated anywhere for their damage and do not have access to holistic healthcare. This situation affects the lives of all women in male-dominated societies, not just the victims of sexual violence. Women, who have lived in an androcentric society that perceives them as sexual instruments, become sensitive when the male gaze comes into contact with their bodies. The fear that every man could turn them into a sexual device often incapacitates them. The further problem is self-objectification, where women too begin to perceive their bodies as sexual instruments. They cannot exist or express themselves as they are and choose instead to cultivate and express themselves prescribed by a rape culture. The male gaze becomes the standard for this situation, and it becomes normative that the value of being a woman is to be the object of a man's sexual desire.[7] When a woman realizes that she is the object of a man's sexual desire, her life becomes an experience of awareness that her body is being sexually evaluated by the male gaze.[8] Women take the prevailing culture for granted, accept and internalize it without recognizing the reasons and background behind it. Self-objectification also takes place at this point. The moment external injustice is internalized, oppression becomes the natural environment, and humans who must survive in that environment are doomed to accept injustice.

Trauma Caused by Sexual Objectification

Trauma results from situations that can cause physical damage or threaten life, such as war, sexual assault, physical or mental abuse, disaster, accident, loss, etc. The word trauma originated from the Greek word, τραυμα, which means wound or injury on the body caused by violence.[9] Trauma today not only applies to physical wounds, but also to psychological and spiritual wounds that affect one's whole life. Traumatic memory does not disappear and is trapped within the body, making the amygdala—the part of the brain that senses danger—overactive when a trigger appears without going through the brain-conscious-body command system. As a result, people who have experienced traumatic events have stronger and more intense responses to specific stresses than those who have not. This is because trauma stimulates instinctive fears related to survival beyond the level of consciousness.[10] People suffering from this syndrome experience various physical symptoms, including physical pain, shortness of breath, and insomnia accompanied by nightmares. They also have excessive anxiety, fear, and impulsive tendencies, which change their personality and perspective on life.[11] The victims of trauma experience the same physical pain they felt when experiencing traumatic events through flashbacks during the day and nightmares at night. If the pain persists unbearably, they fall into a state of dissociation where they feel as if they are not themselves.

Traumatic experiences are largely classified into two types; namely, incident traumas caused by natural disasters or unexpected accidents and threats to personal dignity, i.e., traumas caused by human evil. The latter case leaves a deeper wound because the one who caused the victim's pain still exists, and the evil of the perpetrator who left a deep inner injury on the victim persists. Traumatic events are caused by the perpetrator's evil intention to agitate the victim's whole existence, and the awareness of their powerlessness and vulnerability impoverishes their lives. Sexual violence occurs at the intersection of two causes: the offender's evil intentions and the victim's vulnerable body. The wickedness of the perpetrators is also linked to selfishness. They infringe on the bodies and existence of victims to achieve what they want through sexual violence. The first thing that happens is the objectification of the victim from the perspective of the perpetrator. The perpetrator perceives the victim as an object that can be used as desired, not as a human being, an independent subject with the right to self-determination. Serious problems arise in this process. The wounds experienced by victims who have been deprived of their rights over their bodies are deeper and more painful than any other wounds that occur in the process of violence or human objectification. In the process, the helplessness experienced by the victims and the embarrassment at the suddenness of a situation immobilizes them. The problem is even worse if they grew up in a patriarchal culture and were not educated to express their opinions strongly to men. They also tend to suffer from a sense of shame because they have lost the sexual innocence that the patriarchal system demands. Memories of the event/s make them feel shameful and dirty, extending even to their very existence. Many people manifest symptoms of social avoidance, depression, loss of self, or self-harm due to sexual trauma. These effects are linked to the defensive responses of victims. The phenomenon of separation from oneself is a particularly defensive reaction for coping with the evil they have suffered and a means of survival for living in a social culture that makes them feel polluted. When they encounter a stimulus that evokes their past wounds, victims manifest the shock and painful emotions of that time even if they do not directly recall it. Unfortunately, victims must live with their abused bodies every day leading to continuous triggers that transport them back to the traumatic event. The process of making a victim of sexual trauma feel secure must be carried out more delicately than with other traumas, otherwise victims may experience secondary trauma and victimization during the counseling process.[12]

According to Elaine Storkey, population-based research published by the Archives of General Psychiatry and the *American Journal of Psychiatry* finds that those who experience sexual violence have a higher risk of PTSD than those who have endured other forms of extreme trauma, such as sudden bereavement, war, or disaster.[13] More than people realize, and more than the victims themselves are aware, the effects of sexual violence remain deep scars within their beings, constantly remembered in their bodies. The various symptoms that victims confess are, after all, a sign of their wounded existence.

Many trauma researchers have found that physical therapy, such as yoga, dance therapy, sensorimotor psychotherapy, and bodily relaxation meditation techniques, can assist victims of sexual violence.[14] In particular, Bessel van der Kolk found that traditional yoga relieves the effects of trauma on the body and helps a person reach a state of complete relaxation and a safe mindset essential for recovery from trauma as a practice to unite mind and body.[15] However, he also recognized that the various yoga movements could suddenly have the effect of unsealing previously suppressed intense sensations of the body. In particular, traditional movements related to the pelvis lead to flashbacks of sexual violence. In a follow-up study, van der Kolk argued that people with trauma need a slightly different and more cautious approach. They need to feel safe and become familiar with the sensations generated in the body in order to escape from the trauma.[16]

Various art therapy techniques—painting, music, theater—can help victims traumatized by sexual objectification recognize and familiarize their inner self with the sensations generated in the body. Little is known about the exact aspects of traumatic stress that expressive therapy impacts, and it is difficult to prove the value of such therapy scientifically. However, in many cultures around the world, music and dance are used in various therapeutic ways.[17] This is possible because there are people who have experienced the positive effects of artistic expression on those with trauma in the field.

Sexual Objectification and Damaged *Imago Dei*

The reason sexual objectification is more spiritually dangerous than other forms of human objectification is that the layers of oppression are much more complex and potentially fatal. A male-centered social structure that makes sexual objectification possible, and perpetrators who do not feel guilty about sexually objectifying women's bodies, lead to the silence of female victims who cannot easily talk about their terrible experiences after being harmed. This is also deeply connected to why victims cannot easily reveal sexual violence in their societies. If the victim is a woman, she is particularly exposed to the risk of being criticized in a patriarchal society. The male gaze commonly found in patriarchy, which perceives the female body as seductive, applies in this situation.

Nussbaum identifies seven concepts of objectification: "Instrumentality, denial of autonomy, inertness, fungibility, violability, ownership, and denial of subjectivity."[18] Rae Langton adds three more features to Nussbaum's list: "1) Reduction to the body: Treating the other person as identified with their body, or body parts. 2) Reduction to appearance: Treating the other person primarily in terms of how they look or appear to the senses. 3) Silencing: Treating the other person as if they are silent, lacking the capacity to speak."[19] The characteristics of objectification suggested by these two scholars demonstrate the reason why women cannot reveal their experiences, the depth of their oppression, and why they often experience self-objectification based on loss of subjectivity. The self-objectification of their bodies commonly experienced by such victims is particularly problematic spiritually because it presupposes division within the self. Various deforming forces that attack our souls exist outside of us but also within us. When the sexual objectification experienced by victims is internalized, they experience spiritual problems related to self-isolation. Victims of multiple and repeated sexual violence often use the psychological response mechanism of dissociation to protect themselves from the experience of the abuser invading their body. Dissociation is the separation of consciousness from the feelings the body experiences. If the survival mechanism of dissociation is repeated, the perception of reality is dulled, making the victim less sensitive to other violence and exploitation. This is a common phenomenon in sexually exploited women also. Victims of sexual exploitation often abuse alcohol and drugs to forget the pain, and their suicide attempt rate is 48 percent, which is twenty-three times higher than the general population.[20]

In the understanding of theological anthropology, all human beings possess dignity as the *imago Dei*, the image of God. According to the first creation story in Genesis 1, God wanted to extend the divine presence on the earth through God's image in human beings. Similarly, J. Richard Middleton suggests humans were the cosmic temple or earthly house where God dwelt and he emphasizes that humans became living beings and not objects due to the breath of God.[21] He states, "The image was thus 'transubstantiated'—that is, transformed from an inert object into a living, breathing, a manifestation of the deity on earth."[22] As a demonstration of the divine being, humans are breathed into with the living breath of God and are no longer objects, but a living and breathing presence of God on the earth.

In sexual objectification, however, the victim's integrity and value as God's image are diminished due to the objectifier's view. Victims are treated as fungible objects, and their individuality and uniqueness are not considered.[23] Such a view dilutes the meaning of a person's existence and does not acknowledge the presence of the divine in that person. Human objectification occurs because people think there is a hierarchy in the worth of human beings, and the malicious intentions of the perpetrator tread on the dignity of the victim. From the viewpoint of theological anthropology, human beings are equal and inherently dignified because God made them in the divine image with a unique destiny to be with God's spirit.[24] We often focus on the damaged humanity and dignity of the victim, but in situations where human objectification occurs, the humanity and dignity of the perpetrator who degrades the victim's humanity are also compromised. The two faces of human evil—sin and suffering—degrade the humanity of both perpetrators and victims.[25]

Theology of the Body for Victims of Sexual Violence

The most important assistance that religious organizations can provide for victims of sexual violence is pay attention to their suffering and offer them a safe space to heal. However, religious organizations often cover up the issue of sexual violence and engage in secondary victimization that understands the victims as those who seduce men into sin like Eve in the second creation story in Genesis. These responses are related to the theology of glory, which encourages the church to see suffering as something that needs to be quickly overcome. The church has long been immersed in the theology of glory, which is attributed to scholastic philosophy. This theology focuses on the resurrection rather than on Jesus' crucifixion and incarnation as one who came to this earth to sympathize with and participate in human suffering. A church that focuses on the resurrection event and a theology of glory is a problem for those who suffer because it is difficult to find a safe place to heal in such a church. Much like Job, those who suffer are often characterized by other church members as under punishment from God for their sins and are hurt by a theocratic understanding that perceives their suffering as God-given. The theocratic view that God determines everything that happens also leads to the understanding that God is the one who causes unbearable suffering, thereby creating the image of a violent and merciless God. This is in direct opposition to the image of a God who did not turn away from human suffering, sympathized with it, and died on the cross as a human being. This theology of the cross has emerged as a criticism of the theology of glory and theodicy that dominated Christianity until the middle of the twentieth century.

In the second half of the twentieth century, theologies of suffering and the theology of the cross led to a significant turning point in this trend. As part of this turn, Dorothee Sölle focused on a suffering God alongside humans;[26] Johann Baptist Metz emphasized solidarity with others' memories of suffering;[27] Jürgen Moltmann created the image of the crucified God from the suffering of Jesus;[28] and more recently, other theologians have been actively putting trauma in conversation with theology. Shelly Rambo transforms traditional theology that interprets the crucifixion as redemptive suffering based on trauma theory and the analysis of Holy Saturday as a time of God's silence. She focuses on the remaining act and love of the Spirit for traumatized people who live between death and life.[29] Along the same lines, Serene Jones focuses on the Gospel of Mark's unending story, which means God's never-ending actions and grace for human sin.[30] These methods of understanding God, Jesus, and Spirit in human suffering demonstrate the change in the theologian's role in the postmodern world. Rita Nakashima Brock and Rebecca Ann Parker declare, "We wanted theology to redefine salvation—not only as forgiveness for sinners but also as healing for those who had been the victims of sin, for the brokenhearted."[31] Their language reminds us of the need to make a safe space and healing for the suffering ones that we have neglected.

The first task of any theological discussion concerning the victims of sexual crime is to consider their suffering thoughtfully. When religion loses its ability to sympathize with human suffering, it is easy to create violent gods. However, God is more complex than humans can comprehend especially when it comes to understanding evil and suffering. We must also bear in mind that our understanding of God is never perfect or complete due to human limitations and the prevalence of perceptible blind spots in our logic. When we fail to recognize this limitation, it is easy for us to universalize fragmentary theologies that only provide glimpses of the incomprehensible God and hurt people by traumatizing or oppressing them. It is necessary to escape any theology based on over-realized concepts of God's victory and glory over evil and instead appreciate theology from the perspective of the suffering, oppressed, and marginalized.

Female victims of sexual violence have already suffered enough, and they need a religion that shares their pain and provides healing for their broken hearts. It is difficult to find a safe place to express the pain of trauma, especially in the case of sexual violence. If victims meet a group that offers a safe space to reveal the truth and that listens to their painful stories, recovery becomes possible.[32] I see the hope of Christianity as a healing religion for victims of sexual violence through the life and death of Jesus. In the suffering moment, people need those who have experienced similar suffering to understand their painful memories and have empathy because when they share similar experiences, their suffering turns into mutual healing. The body of Jesus hanging on the cross was not his own. That body was naked, dominated, objectified, tortured, and killed.[33] Jesus' passion and the silence of God in his suffering on the cross can be a comfort to the victims of sexual violence. Their bodies were also dominated and objectified, and they continue to suffer from traumatic memories of sexual abuse and the objectification of their bodies.

Jesus' life was spent with the oppressed, suffering, and marginalized. Jesus demonstrated what #WithYou truly means in the world. (#WithYou supports the victims of sexual violence who reveal their traumatic memories through the #MeToo movement.)[34] Love is walking into another's suffering without fear. Understanding means coming down from where we stand and taking a position below that of the other person. The faith community should remember the life of Jesus, who walked into the suffering of the human world and came down from heaven to be with us. Christianity can provide a safe space and healing for victims' broken hearts and bodies based on a considerate theology and understanding of their suffering within Jesus' #WithYou spirit.

Reconsidering Dualism: Spiritual Body

It is easy to overlook the fact that sexual violence is not simply a matter of bodily violation. When we look at the catastrophic effects that the victim experiences, this event is not only a violation of the body, but is also linked to human dignity and to spiritual issues that disturb a person's very existence. Victims, especially those exposed to persistent sexual violence, frequently experience dissociation while enduring these traumatic situations and then choose to separate from themselves in order to live within their victimized bodies. This separation leads to the self-objectification in which victims see themselves through the eyes of their perpetrator. It is also evident that sexual violence is a form of abuse distinct from other types of violence, creating deeper internal trauma and greater PTSD.[35]

The origins of the limited thinking that recognizes this problem as an infringement of the body are found in ontological dualism. This dichotomous thinking, based on Greco-Roman constructions of the body, has long dominated the ontological understanding of the human being in the Western world. One of the problems with the body-soul dichotomy lies in the setting of obvious boundaries. It is the essence of a dichotomy to draw a boundary between two areas that were previously connected without separation. This is why dichotomous thinking is dangerous when it is applied to human beings. As the word *individual* suggests, our body, mind, and soul exist as an indivisible *one being*. Assuming that the body, mind, and soul are interconnected, it is evident that the violations and negative effects of sexual violence do not simply end as bodily damage.

However, dichotomous thinking, stemming from Greco-Roman philosophies, Gnosticism, and René Descartes' dualism, which has dominated Western notions for a long time, plays a central role in conceptualizing the sexual violence as mere physical abuse.[36] The impact of the spiritual invasion experienced by the victim begins to emerge when we move beyond this ontological dichotomy and consider the body and the human spirit as connected. The mental and spiritual symptoms of sexual violence demonstrate that our bodily senses are connected to our psychological and spiritual senses. In this matter, Resmaa Menakem explains the concept of the soul nerve in light of psychiatrist Stephen Porges' understanding of the Vagus nerve.[37] She describes the soul nerve as the largest regulatory organ of the body's fundamental functions in the human autonomic nervous system. She writes, "The largest part of your soul nerve goes through your gut, which has about 100 million neurons, more than your spinal cord. This is why we sense so many things in our belly—and why some biologists call the gut our 'second brain.'"[38] This idea is related to concepts of conscious body and somatic psychology, which raises the question about dualistic devaluations of the body.[39] Also, the recent achievements of various physical integration techniques used in the treatment process of trauma lead us to reconsider distorted perceptions of the body, and the importance of the body for human well-being. This transition has led many scholars, including van der Kolk, Peter A. Levine, Pat Ogden, and Cathy A. Malchiodi, to concentrate on bodily therapy for the traumatized, with somatic therapy emerging as an effective means of helping people recover from PTSD.[40]

This trend demands an integrated somatic model of spirituality for those traumatized by sexual violence based on trauma theory and the idea of the body connected with the soul, rather than the use of a contemplative spiritual practice, which can often cause trauma victims to experience re-traumatizing flashbacks. Jesus' incarnation, resurrected body, and Paul's term, "spiritual body (σῶμα πνευματικόν)" in 1 Corinthians 15:44, provide an essential clue to the spiritual body and somatic spirituality. The incarnated and resurrected body of Jesus challenges the tendency to separate body and soul and to see death as the liberation of the soul from the material world, which the Gnostics claimed at the time of Jesus.[41] However, negative perceptions of the body and ontological dualism still prevail in Western and Western-influenced Christianity.

Furthermore, Christian spirituality mainly involves spiritual practices based on such a separation and hierarchy of body and soul. Also, the meaning of the words influenced by dualism—such as body/soul (mind), physical/spiritual, and material/immaterial, which were already formed in English-speaking culture—has become dominant in the Western world.[42] Cyprian Consiglio points out that despite the denials of many theologians, Christianity has never escaped the ancient dualism related to Platonism and Gnosticism, which assume that the body is less dignified than the human soul.[43]

The fact that Jesus appeared bodily before his disciples in his resurrected state refutes the discourse about the finitude of the body, and Jesus' incarnation demonstrates God's embodiment in the human being among creation. The body of the resurrected Jesus directly challenges the Greco-Roman and Gnostic understanding that only the soul is resurrected and will last forever. Nevertheless, negative perceptions of the body and the discourse on its finitude are still valid in Christian circles. Christians thus need to recover the meaning of the spiritual body (σῶμα πνευματικόν) as a space of divine incarnation.

Somatic Spirituality for Those Traumatized by Sexual Violence

The concept of somatic spirituality has not been discussed in depth in Christian spirituality until now, primarily due to the negative perception of the body based on the body-spirit dualism found throughout Christianity. Christianity mainly focuses on the spirit and mind, rather than the body, in approaching God. However, many spiritual practices in Christian spirituality, such as pilgrimage, prayer posture, and bodily praise, are based on the spirituality of the body.

This recognition creates a spiritual experience within the framework of somatic spirituality that allows victims of trauma to change their understanding of the value of their bodies, stemming from the memory of sexual objectification. Recognition of the positive meaning of the victims' bodies, which have been invaded by someone's gaze or abuse, is an essential part of their healing process. A shift in awareness is a crucial element in positive acceptance of their bodies and in overturning any negative images.

Those traumatized by sexual objectification are deprived of their humanity, self-determination, ownership, autonomy, and subjectivity. In such a situation, perpetrators have gone beyond a simple ontological violation and have blasphemed the deity in the victims. It is not so easy to disparage people as sexual objects if there is recognition that the Spirit of God dwells in them and if their existential value as *imago Dei* is taken into consideration. However, perpetrators do not recognize the rights and dignity of their victims' existence and consider themselves as subjects and others as objects. The most fundamental value of a human being is the vitality that resides in that existence. In Christianity, this vital force, understood as the living Spirit of God, is what makes a human being live and breathe and is what reveals their dignity. As long as life continues, all human beings have the right to exist in this world as an image resembling God with the subjectivity God has given them. Violation of the body is recognized as a superficial problem of sexual objectification, but what causes more severe pain is the spiritual violation. Victims need to discover the resilience behind the vulnerability caused by trauma, and they can do this through somatic spirituality. Levine states, "While studying the effects of accumulated stress on the nervous system, I began to suspect that most organisms have an innate capacity to rebound from threatening and stressful events."[44] As he puts it, everyone has the power to recover from their wounds within themselves, from the divine beauty that was already created within us. As the image of God, everyone is the most mystical and valuable existence in the world. People have the resilience to heal themselves within their beings, especially in their bodies.

Various practices of somatic spirituality based on the body and bodily sensations can assist victims in overcoming the disconnection from their bodies and reconcile with their being. These somatic practices include:

- Contemplative drawing with the breath
- Experiencing the Word through the body via *bibliodrama* or holistic play
- The embodiment of the Word in *lectio divina* and meditative drawing
- Bodily prayer.[45]

These practices also introduce ways victims can communicate with themselves and move toward God, who has created resilience within us. The body acts as a storehouse that contains our whole life and connects our inner and outer worlds, and it is a spiritual space in which God dwells. We should reconsider the discourse on the body in the field of Christian spirituality for those traumatized by sexual objectification.

In the New Testament, the body is expressed in two ways as the physical body (σάρξ, sarx) and the spiritual body (σῶμα, soma). The difference between these two bodies is whether or not they contain the Spirit of God, the Holy Spirit. However, in the process of describing the body of the resurrected Jesus, the word spiritual body (σῶμα πνευματικόν) that appears in 1 Corinthians 1:44, gives us a concept beyond this dimension. The body that contains the Spirit of God is not a spiritual body; the body itself is spiritual. This concept still echoes in the flow of Western spirituality, which has not completely erased the influence of Gnosticism. Western spirituality thinks separately about the body and spirit and does not pursue spirituality through the body. Jesus was not only resurrected as a spirit, however, and the event of his resurrection was itself a challenge to the Gnostic understanding of the body at the time. The body's reaction to trauma may offer a similar challenge to modern-day people who think in isolation of their being and who devalue the meaning and influence of their bodies.

Conclusion

The reason why sexual violence, one of the most common traumas, is particularly problematic is that victims cannot experience proper healing since they are not easily able to expose their victimization. Furthermore, victims live with their violated bodies, which constantly remind them of the trauma for the rest of their lives. Unless the victims have a positive perception of their bodies, these traumas remain dark shadows for a lifetime.

The survivor's invaded body is not an object. The body is a spiritual space, and each organ and sense of the body is connected to the spiritual senses. The two-dimensional spiritual issues experienced by the victim are also something we need to consider, along with the healing of the body and mind. First, the damaged dignity stemming from the violation of the perpetrator means that the source of power that a person possesses has been damaged. The frequent use of the word *overwhelmed* to describe traumatic situations indicates a shift in our perceptions of the world: the perception of the vulnerability of our existence resulting from suffering beyond endurance. In addition, during the victim's painful experience, the distorted perception of a merciless God, which seems to be consistent with the silence that accompanies the theocratic understanding of God, inflicts further pain on victims, drawing them away from God or the absolute.

For these victims, God who participates in human suffering through the existence of Jesus and his cross, God who demonstrates embodiment in the human body through the incarnation, and Jesus' spiritual body, which is resurrected in a form that retains the wounds of life, provides a clue to their holy bodies and somatic spirituality. The somatic spirituality that recognizes victims' bodies, which have been objectified and violated by the perpetrator's desires, are a sacred space in which God dwells and restores the inner resilience that makes it possible to regain their source of power. The victims of sexual objectification need the self-awareness to realize their subjectivity and the inner strength to overcome the objectification that has undermined their dignity. As a starting point for such awareness, recognizing one's body can be a practical first step. Communication with their bodies helps victims overcome the disconnection between their objectified physical being and their true self, to the point where they can become reconciled with their wounded inner being.

Notes

1 George B. Palermo and Mary Ann Farkas, *The Dilemma of the Sexual Offender* (Springfield: Charles C. Thomas, 2013), 178.
2 Andrea Vilela Araujo, "An Integral Solution to Healing Sexual Abuse Trauma," *Journal of Integral Theory and Practice* 3, no. 4 (2008), 125–126.
3 Margaret M. Feerick and Kyle L. Snow, "The Relationships between Childhood Sexual Abuse, Social Anxiety, and Symptoms of Posttraumatic Stress Disorder in Women," *Journal of Family Violence* 20, no. 6 (2005), 409.
4 Neil J. Kressel, *Mass Hate: The Global Rise of Genocide and Terror* (Cambridge: Worldview Press, 2002), 37; John M. Rector, *The Objectification Spectrum: Understanding and Transcending our Diminishment and Dehumanization of Others* (New York: Oxford University Press, 2014), 40.
5 See Rae Langton, *Sexual Solipsism: Philosophical Essays on Pornography and Objectification* (Oxford: Oxford University Press, 2009).
6 See Mirella J. Flores, Laurel B. Watson, Luke R. Allen, Mudiwa Ford, Christine R. Serpe, Ping Ying Choo, and Michelle Farrell, "Transgender People of Color's Experiences of Sexual Objectification: Locating Sexual Objectification within a Matrix of Domination," *Journal of Counseling Psychology* 65, no. 3 (2018); Laurel B. Watson, Dawn Robinson, Franco Dispenza, and Negar Nazari, "African American Women's Sexual Objectification Experiences: A Qualitative Study," *Psychology of Women Quarterly* 36, no. 4 (2012).
7 See Chizuko Ueno, *Hate Misogyny*, translated by Il-deung Na (Seoul: Eunhaengna, 2012), 263.
8 Ibid., 271.
9 John P. McTighe, *Narrative Theory in Clinical Social Work Practice* (Cham: Springer, 2018), 43.
10 See Jinhee Lee, *Practice to be Free from Bad Memories* (Seoul: Pampas, 2018), 34.
11 Ibid., 80.
12 Secondary victimization is the action of victim-blaming, which holds that the victim contributed to the cause of sexual violence. See Rebecca Campbell and Sheela Raja, "The Sexual Assault and Secondary Victimization of Female Veterans: Help-Seeking Experiences with Military and Civilian Social Systems," *Psychology of Women Quarterly* 29, no. 1 (2005), 99–100.
13 Elaine Storkey, *Scars Across Humanity: Understanding and Overcoming Violence Against Women* (London: SPCK, 2015), 124.

14 See Pat Ogden, Kekuni Minton, and Clare Pain, *Trauma and the Body: A Sensorimotor Approach to Psychotherapy* (New York: W. W. Norton, 2006); Pat Ogden, "The Different Impact of Trauma and Relational Stress on Physiology, Posture, and Movement: Implications for Treatment," *European Journal of Trauma & Dissociation* 5, no. 4 (2021); Peter A. Levine, *In an Unspoken Voice: How the Body Releases Trauma and Restores Goodness* (Berkeley: North Atlantic Books, 2010); Cathy A. Malchiodi, *Trauma and Expressive Arts Therapy: Brain, Body, and Imagination in the Healing Process* (New York: Guilford, 2020).
15 Bessel A. van der Kolk, *The Body Keeps the Score: Brain, Mind, and Body in the Healing of Trauma* (New York: Viking, 2014), 268–273.
16 Ibid., 275–277.
17 Ibid., 244–245.
18 Martha C. Nussbaum, "Objectification," *Philosophy & Public Affairs* 24, no. 4 (1995), 257.
19 Langton, *Sexual Solipsism*, 228–229.
20 Hyejeong Park, *Sex work, Not Prostitution, But Sexual Exploitation* (Incheon: Yeoldabooks, 2020), 59.
21 J. Richard Middleton, *A New Heaven and a New Earth: Reclaiming Biblical Eschatology* (Grand Rapids: Baker Academic, 2014), 48.
22 Ibid., 49.
23 See Rector, *The Objectification Spectrum*, 16.
24 See Storkey, *Scars Across Humanity*, 204.
25 Wendy Farley, *Tragic Vision and Divine Compassion: A Contemporary Theodicy* (Louisville: Westminster John Knox Press, 1990), 52.
26 Dorothee Sölle, *Suffering* (Philadelphia: Fortress Press, 1975).
27 Johann Baptist Metz, *Faith in History and Society: Toward a Practical Fundamental Theology*, trans. David Smith (New York: The Seabury Press, 1980).
28 Jürgen Moltmann, *The Crucified God: The Cross of Christ as the Foundation and Criticism of Christian Theology* (New York: Harper & Row, 1974).
29 Shelly Rambo, *Spirit and Trauma: A Theology of Remaining* (Louisville: Westminster John Knox Press, 2010).
30 Serene Jones, *Trauma and Grace: Theology in a Ruptured World* (Louisville: Westminster John Knox Press, 2009).
31 Rita Nakashima Brock and Rebecca Ann Parker, *Proverbs of Ashes: Violence, Redemptive Suffering, and the Search for What Saves Us* (Boston: Beacon Press, 2001), 6.
32 See van der Kolk, *The Body Keeps the Score*, 244.
33 See Michael Trainor, *The Body of Jesus and Sexual Abuse: How the Gospel Passion Narratives Inform a Pastoral Response* (Eugene: Wipf & Stock, 2015), 254.
34 Hye Hyun Han, "Objectification of Comfort Women and the Theology of #WithYou," *Political Theology*, September 3, 2020. https://politicaltheology.com/objectification-of-comfort-women-and-the-theology-of-withyou/.
35 See Patricia A. Frazier and Margit I. Berman, "Posttraumatic Growth Following Sexual Assault," in *Trauma, Recovery, and Growth: Positive Psychological Perspectives on Posttraumatic Stress*, ed. Stephen Joseph and P. Alex Linley (Hoboken: Wiley, 2008), 161.
36 Dale B. Martin, *The Corinthian Body* (New Haven: Yale University Press, 1995), 3–15, 105–108.
37 Stephen W. Porges, "The Polyvagal Perspective," *Biological Psychology* 74, no. 2 (2007), 116.

38 Resmaa Menakem, *My Grandmother's Hands: Racialized Trauma and the Pathway to Mending Our Hearts and Bodies* (Las Vegas: Central Recovery Press, 2017), 79.
39 See Bruce Burger, *The Body As Consciousness* (Berkeley: North Atlantic Books, 1998).
40 See van der Kolk, *The Body Keeps the Score*; Levine, *In an Unspoken Voice*; Ogden, Minton, and Pain, *Trauma and the Body*; Malchiodi, *Trauma and Expressive Arts Therapy*.
41 Chapter 15 of 1 Corinthians demonstrates the problematic awareness of the body and spirit held by the members of the Corinthian church. See Martin, *The Corinthian Body*, 104–136.
42 Martin, *The Corinthian Body*, 3–4.
43 Cyprian Consiglio, *Spirit, Soul, Body: Toward an Integral Christian Spirituality* (Collegeville, MN: Liturgical Press, 2014), 10.
44 Peter A. Levine, *Healing Trauma: A Pioneering Program for Restoring the Wisdom of Your Body* (Boulder: Sounds True, 2008), 1.
45 See Hye Hyun Han, "Art-Based Spiritual Practice for the Victims of Human Objectification," *Korea Presbyterian Journal of Theology* 53, no. 4 (2021), 180–185.

Bibliography

Araujo, Andrea Vilela. "An Integral Solution to Healing Sexual Abuse Trauma." *Journal of Integral Theory and Practice* 3, no. 4 (2008): 125–53.

Brock, Rita Nakashima, and Rebecca Ann Parker. *Proverbs of Ashes: Violence, Redemptive Suffering, and the Search for What Saves Us.* Boston: Beacon Press, 2001.

Burger, Bruce. *The Body As Consciousness.* Berkeley: North Atlantic Books, 1998.

Campbell, Rebecca, and Sheela Raja. "The Sexual Assault and Secondary Victimization of Female Veterans: Help-Seeking Experiences with Military and Civilian Social Systems." *Psychology of Women Quarterly* 29. no. 1 (2005): 97–106.

Consiglio, Cyprian. *Spirit, Soul, Body: Toward an Integral Christian Spirituality.* Collegeville: Liturgical Press, 2014.

Farley, Wendy. *Tragic Vision and Divine Compassion: A Contemporary Theodicy.* Louisville: Westminster John Knox Press, 1990.

Flores, Mirella J., Laurel B. Watson, Luke R. Allen, Mudiwa Ford, Christine R. Serpe, Ping Ying Choo, and Michelle Farrell, "Transgender People of Color's Experiences of Sexual Objectification: Locating Sexual Objectification within a Matrix of Domination." *Journal of Counseling Psychology* 65, no. 3 (2018): 308–23.

Feerick, Margaret M., and Kyle L. Snow, "The Relationships between Childhood Sexual Abuse, Social Anxiety, and Symptoms of Posttraumatic Stress Disorder in Women." *Journal of Family Violence* 20, no. 6 (2005): 409–19.

Han, Hye Hyun. "Objectification of Comfort Women and the Theology of #With You." *Political Theology*, September 3, 2020. https://politicaltheology.com/objectification-of-comfort-women-and-the-theology-of-withyou/.

Han, Hye Hyun. "Art-Based Spiritual Practice for the Victims of Human Objectification." *Korea Presbyterian Journal of Theology* 53, no. 4 (2021): 159–89.

Jones, Serene. *Trauma and Grace: Theology in a Ruptured World.* Louisville: Westminster John Knox Press, 2009.
Joseph, Stephen, and P. Alex Linley, ed. *Trauma, Recovery, and Growth: Positive Psychological Perspectives on Posttraumatic Stress.* Hoboken: Wiley, 2008.
Kressel, Neil J. *Mass Hate: The Global Rise of Genocide and Terror.* Cambridge: Worldview Press, 2002.
Langton, Rae. *Sexual Solipsism: Philosophical Essays on Pornography and Objectification.* Oxford: Oxford University Press, 2009.
Lee, Jinhee. *Practice to Be Free from Bad Memories.* Seoul: Pampas, 2018.
Levine, Peter A. *Healing Trauma: A Pioneering Program for Restoring the Wisdom of Your Body.* Boulder: Sounds True, 2008.
Levine, Peter A. *In an Unspoken Voice: How the Body Releases Trauma and Restores Goodness.* Berkeley: North Atlantic Books, 2010.
Malchiodi, Cathy A. *Trauma and Expressive Arts Therapy: Brain, Body, and Imagination in the Healing Process.* New York: Guilford, 2020.
Martin, Dale B. *The Corinthian Body.* New Haven: Yale University Press, 1995.
McTighe, John P. *Narrative Theory in Clinical Social Work Practice.* Cham: Springer, 2018.
Menakem, Resmaa. *My Grandmother's Hands: Racialized Trauma and the Pathway to Mending Our Hearts and Bodies.* Las Vegas: Central Recovery Press, 2017.
Metz, Johann Baptist. *Faith in History and Society: Toward a Practical Fundamental Theology.* Translated by David Smith. New York: The Seabury Press, 1980.
Middleton, J. Richard. *A New Heaven and a New Earth: Reclaiming Biblical Eschatology.* Grand Rapid: Baker Academic, 2014.
Moltmann, Jürgen. *The Crucified God: The Cross of Christ as the Foundation and Criticism of Christian Theology.* New York: Harper & Row, 1974.
Nussbaum, Martha C. "Objectification." *Philosophy & Public Affairs* 24, no. 4 (1995): 249–91.
Ogden, Pat, Kekuni Minton, and Clare Pain. *Trauma and the Body: A Sensorimotor Approach to Psychotherapy.* New York: W. W. Norton, 2006.
Ogden, Pat. "The Different Impact of Trauma and Relational Stress on Physiology, Posture, and Movement: Implications for Treatment." *European Journal of Trauma & Dissociation* 5, no. 4 (2021): 97–106.
Palermo, George B., and Mary Ann Farkas, *The Dilemma of the Sexual Offender.* Springfield: Charles C. Thomas, 2013.
Park, Hyejeong. *Sex Work, Not Prostitution, but Sexual Exploitation.* Incheon: Yeoldabooks, 2020.
Porges, Stephen W. "The Polyvagal Perspective." *Biological Psychology* 74, no. 2 (2007): 116–43.
Rambo, Shelly. *Spirit and Trauma: A Theology of Remaining.* Louisville: Westminster John Knox Press, 2010.
Rector, John M. *The Objectification Spectrum: Understanding and Transcending our Diminishment and Dehumanization of Others.* New York: Oxford University Press, 2014.
Sölle, Dorothee. *Suffering.* Philadelphia: Fortress Press, 1975.

Storkey, Elaine. *Scars Across Humanity: Understanding and Overcoming Violence Against Women*. London: SPCK, 2015.
Trainor, Michael. *The Body of Jesus and Sexual Abuse: How the Gospel Passion Narratives Inform a Pastoral Response*. Eugene, OR: Wipf & Stock, 2015.
Ueno, Chizuko. *Hate Misogyny*. Translated by Il-deung Na. Seoul: Eunhaengna, 2012.
Van der Kolk, Bessel A. *The Body Keeps the Score: Brain, Mind, and Body in the Healing of Trauma*. New York: Viking, 2014.
Watson, Laurel B., Dawn Robinson, Franco Dispenza, and Negar Nazari, "African American Women's Sexual Objectification Experiences: A Qualitative Study." *Psychology of Women Quarterly* 36, no. 4 (2012): 458–75.

Chapter 6

Deconstruction and Reclamation
A Healing

Annette Williams

Introduction: The Constructed Self

Early experiences are foundational in shaping our psyches and the way we interact with and walk in the world.[1] This exploration will address childhood sexual abuse from the macro perspective of socio-historical and cultural factors contributing to its existence and from the micro perspective of its impact on women's lives.[2]

"William James offered an alternative to the notion that self-identify is based in a mental or self substance. Personal identity is, he said, an idea that a person constructs."[3] The personal self is constructed from the accumulation of experiences, responses, and feedback one receives throughout life. Donald Polkinghorne adds:

> The human disciplines attribute the development of the notion of personal identity and the self to symbolic and bodily interaction within the social environment
> ... The concept of self ... is a construction built on other people's responses and attitudes toward a person ... In order to come to a unified and concordant self concept and personal identity, then, the person needs to synthesize and integrate the diverse social responses he or she experiences.[4]

Because this is also my story, I wondered if perceptions of Black women's sexuality are projected onto the Black female child, and how these perceptions have been fostered. With this in mind, I look at a common stereotype of Black female sexuality that resonates in my own experience. Employing a structured research format has facilitated the telling of painful personal history.

Childhood sexual abuse leaves scars that are deep, and it invariably impacts adult functioning.[5] Accounts by women who have experienced childhood sexual abuse vary as to its impact in their lives.[6] The trajectory of their self-development was altered by the experience and trauma

DOI: 10.4324/9781003323631-7

of childhood sexual abuse. "Violence sends deep roots into the heart."[7] Childhood sexual abuse is described as "a bodily violation of extreme humiliation and devastation . . . It silences our voices, numbs our bodies, warps our thinking, and closes our hearts."[8]

As a Black woman who was subjected to childhood sexual abuse, I echo the thoughts of a Black woman who survived rape at the hands of Black males: "how could they do that to one of their 'own.'"[9] As I acknowledge the extent to which incidents of childhood sexual abuse impacted my sense of self and personal identity, Charlotte Pierce-Baker's question echoes in anguished tones because I suffered abuse at the hands of male family members.

Indeed, how could they do that to one of their own? What in their cosmology, in their sense of relationship to self and the universe, enabled them to feel entitled to use my body for their gratification? And what was my cosmology that I seemingly acquiesced or would perceive victimization as acquiescence?

The process of deconstruction might take a lifetime, although a full deconstruction is highly improbable given the complexity of interwoven factors that constitute the individual. "Because sexual abuse is just one of many factors that influence your development, it isn't always possible to isolate its effects from the other influences on your life."[10]

However, in an effort to unlock the mystery, I turn to Elaine Pagels[11] to develop my understanding of the theological ground from which modern dysfunctional views of sexuality sprouted. Severe attitudes towards women and children held by the early Christian church fathers shaped philosophical thought and the reality of human lives for centuries and continue to do so. Yet, it must be recognized that sexual abuse of children predates the early church by centuries.[12] For the earlier Bronze Age warrior, women and children were often the spoils of war to be disposed of as the warrior chose.[13]

In concert with the above, as a Black woman I try to understand the socio-historical and cultural determinants of the way Black women's sexuality is commonly perceived. Views of the Black woman's body and sexuality are rooted in the insidious institution of slavery. In this part of the investigation I turn to Dorothy Roberts, bell hooks, and Carolyn West for their insight and theoretical understanding.

The current exploration of childhood sexual abuse is also an excavation. I want to dig deep and extract the last vestiges of memory, the memory that clings to my cells and causes flesh, bone, and psyche to recoil from intimacy and trusting. This is memory that is only partially available to conscious awareness. Most of the memory is hidden from consciousness, emerging intermittently in dreams and in the form of somatic[14] resonance to people, environments, or situations. I know of a memory's truth by way of somatic confirmation that gives rise to emotional response.

"Memory (and history) is an embodied phenomenon."[15] I have learned that my aloof and detached mind does not always speak truth, rather it often obscures truth for the sake of effective daily functioning.

Investigational Approach

The advantage of remembering is that "the previously ostracized experiences can return to the fold, and the increased wholeness resulting from these new integrations favors greater well-being."[16] Allowing unassimilated aspects of self stemming from childhood sexual abuse an opportunity to emerge and be heard is a microcosmic take on the tradition of feminist scholarship that provides opportunities for "other persons and other experiences that have not been valued or privileged within the dominant culture to speak their own stories with their own voices and opportunities for these voices to be listened to and honored."[17] In the case of one's own psyche, it is the intrapersonal politics of dominant ego and suppressed realities.

Subjective knowledge grounded in experience is valued within feminist epistemologies.[18] A woman's personal experience has the power to speak to more than her individual encounter for it reflects the larger sociohistorical, cultural, and political context of its occurrence. In this way, the personal is political. I believe the subjugation of women and children, and the exploitation of Black women's sexuality are formed in the same socio-historical and cultural aberrations spawned by patriarchy and supported by patriarchal theology, philosophy, and politics. This view resonates with the thinking of Patricia Hill Collins who states:

> Viewing relations of domination for Black women for any given sociohistorical context as being structured via a system of interlocking race, class, and gender oppression expands the focus of analysis from merely describing the similarities and differences distinguishing these systems of oppression and focuses greater attention on how they interconnect.[19]

It is the interconnection of these systems of oppression that makes the task of self-deconstruction—the finding of the essential self—daunting.

Clark Moustakas, in *Heuristic Research: Design, Methodology and Applications*, lays the ground rules and provides the methodological framework for this current research. Heuristic research is research into the self, buttressed by traditional approaches to inquiry. "The self of the researcher is present throughout the process and, while understanding the phenomenon with increasing depth, the researcher also experiences growing self-awareness and self-knowledge."[20]

At minimum, placing the self at the center of scholarship has seemed narcissistic in my estimation. However, a good friend reminded me of the dialectic that exists between personal and social transformation—you try and change the world you change yourself, you change yourself you change the world. It is not an either/or relationship. Moustakas echoes this when he writes, "The question is one that has been a personal challenge and puzzlement in the search to understand oneself and the world in which one lives. The heuristic process is autobiographic, yet with virtually every question that matters personally there is also a social—and perhaps universal—significance."[21]

Using the heuristic paradigm, the journey of recovering wholeness is discussed. The central place of spirituality within this process is also revealed. This spirituality is based on the West African Yoruba Ifá tradition that was brought to the Western Atlantic region with the slave trade. African-based spirituality is earth-based; as such it is embodied and comes alive in one's life through practice and application. Central to my reclamation process is an altar that I constructed honoring my child-self and asking for the guidance, love, and support of Yemaya.

Yemaya is the Ifá orisha (deity) associated with the nurturing of children and the general affairs of women. She is aligned with our dreams. She is the mother of the oceans, teeming with life. "There is no mountain of trouble that Yemaya cannot wear down; no sickness of heart that She cannot wash clean; no desert of despair that She cannot flood with hope."[22]

Relevance

The effects of sexual abuse suffered in childhood are far-reaching. Women who were sexually abused as children frequently engage in self-destructive behaviors, including self-mutilation and suicide. "In clinical outpatient samples, an estimated 50% to 60% of women with sexual abuse histories have attempted suicide, compared to 23% to 34% of women without sexual abuse histories."[23] The same study points out that when the abuse is kept secret, when the child does not tell, this contributes to self-blame. Self-blame has been shown concomitant with shame, low self-esteem, substance abuse, feelings of alienation, as well as self-destructive behaviors.[24]

As I have awakened to the ability to face, the courage to verbalize, and the capacity to heal the personal dysfunctions attendant to childhood sexual abuse, hopefully my process can be of service to other women who want to embark on a similar journey.

Contributing Factors to Abuse and Oppression Internalization

Elaine Pagels assists in understanding modern repressive attitudes towards sexuality and the feminine. Grounded in biblical scholarship, her work is an exploration of the Genesis creation myth as interpreted in the first four centuries of the Christian church's existence. The Gnostics' interpretation of the creation story as an allegory that concerns the process of spiritual self-discovery and depicts "Eve—or the feminine spiritual power she represented—as the source of spiritual awakening"[25] was very different from the literal orthodox interpretation. One telling example is what Tertullian, a second century church leader, had to say of women: "You are the devil's gateway ... you are she who persuaded him whom the devil did not dare attack." Tertullian underscores his misogyny stating *"Do you not know that every one of you is an Eve? The sentence of God on your sex lives on in this age: the guilt, of necessity, lives on too."*[26]

Believed to be inaccurately attributed to Paul, but nonetheless reflecting his apparent misogyny, 1 Timothy expresses a view of women held today by fundamentalists in many areas of the world. Women are to "learn in silence and submissiveness. I permit no woman to teach or to have authority over men; she is to keep silent ... Yet woman will be saved through bearing children, if she continues in faith and love and holiness, with modesty."[27]

The author of 1 Timothy directs men to "manage his own household well, keeping his children submissive and respectful."[28] A man is "(o)ne that ruleth well his own house, having his children in subjection with all gravity."[29] Women and children thus fall under the sanctioned dominion of men. This gospel has been translated into the vernacular with sayings such as: *a man's home is his castle*; or, *man is the king of his castle*, with all rights and privileges of his gender.

My father was a Jehovah's Witness adhering to a conservative Christian literal interpretation of the bible. Two teachings from childhood reverberate in my consciousness: *spare the rod, spoil the child*; *children are seen and not heard*. Corporal discipline is often used to help ensure that children walk a path pleasing to Jehovah. The place of the wife and children in the family structure is clearly delineated within the religion. The husband/father is the undisputed head of his household. Christian orthodoxy, unable to see the divine as immanent within the individual and seeing woman as a chalice of evil responsible for the downfall of man and all attendant misery, believes that control and repression of woman is both deserved and righteous.

If women and the feminine are generally disparaged and male superiority intoned by religious patriarchy, Black women are subject to "a complex set of stereotypes that deny Black humanity in order to rationalize white supremacy."[30] Within its pages, *Killing the Black Body* by Dorothy Roberts looks at stereotypes of Black female sexuality. In particular she describes how these stereotypes were used and are continually used to justify sexual exploitation of Black women from slavery to the present day. Harkening back to Eve, the "construct of the licentious temptress served to justify white men's sexual abuse of Black women."[31]

During slavery, Black women were sexually exploited as broodmares. Miscegenation did not spare the child the toils of slavery. Children were sent to work in the fields by age eleven and many before age seven. Women who did not reproduce were "exposed to every form of privation and affliction."[32] However, sexual exploitation was not exclusively reserved for women of childbearing age. Black females were vulnerable to sexual exploitation early in life. In 1881, Black Episcopalian minister Alexander Crummel wrote, "In her girlhood all the delicate tenderness of her sex has been rudely outraged . . . No chance was given her for delicate reserve or tender modesty. From her childhood she was the doomed victim of the grossest passion. All the virtues of her sex were utterly ignored."[33]

In her essays, bell hooks explores contemporary manifestations of the stereotypes and exploitation of Black female sexuality. One very interesting manifestation is the phenomenon of white college males' desire to have sex with others, i.e., non-white females. This act of having sex with others is envisioned by the young men as self-altering and thus as a rite of passage or "ritual of transcendence." In her analysis hooks asserts, "the presence of the Other, the body of the Other, was seen as existing to serve the ends of white male desires."[34]

Three prevalent Black female archetypes are examined in the literature. These are Sapphire—dominant and angry; Mammy—nurturing and self-sacrificing; and Jezebel—lascivious, wanton temptress.[35] This latter archetype encapsulates the stereotype of Black women's sexuality promulgated since slavery that feeds the imaginations of many individuals. What are the early influences that might determine its internalization?

I would posit that inappropriate childhood sexual encounters led to conflating love, acceptance, and security with sexuality—more exactly, being sexually pleasing to men was internalized as a precondition to receiving love and nurturance. "A child is naturally dependent on adults for nurturance, guidance and support. This fundamental right of the child is broken when the child is sexually victimized."[36]

There is a myth of power tied to sexuality that is a distortion of the truth of victim and victimizer. According to Carolyn West the rationalization of the rape and forced breeding of enslaved Black women was justified through the Jezebel archetype. "Instead of acknowledging this sexual victimization, slave owners portrayed Black women as promiscuous, immoral Jezebels who seduced their masters. This image gave the impression that Black women could not be rape victims because they always desired sex."[37] This image also created the fallacy that Black females hold power over their victimizers.

Victim-blaming has survived with the negative archetype. In a study of undergraduates presented with a date rape scenario, researchers "found that a forced sexual encounter would be perceived as less serious if the victim were a Black woman than if the victim were a White woman."[38]

In terms of the implications of this archetype for childhood sexual abuse, telling is the response of a law enforcement official to a 12-year-old Black female who was raped by her mother's boyfriend: "(A) man cop asked me all these questions and I felt really, really dirty. He asked me, Do I 'switch'[39] around the house?"[40] The child suffers secondary victimization at the hands of the authority who is supposed to be her ally and protector against the perpetrator. Here the child is the perceived Jezebel, seducing her adult abuser.

Abusers often project attributes or qualities onto the children they abuse. These attributes are false and are just in the mind of the abuser. A perpetrator may create false beliefs about a child's wishes, desires, and likes, or try to bring the child up to their peer level (imagining a sexual attraction or relationship with them). They may believe the child wants them to do the sexual acts. We often hear ridiculous statements from abusers such as, "he/she was a seductive child"; which is complete nonsense.[41]

I have no memory of being told not to disclose my early abuse, but I knew not to tell. Although upwards of 80,000 incidents of child sexual abuse are reported annually,[42] it is believed that "the number of unreported instances is far greater, because the children are afraid to tell anyone what has happened, and the legal process of reporting can be difficult" and may compound the trauma.[43] Even though an incident of abuse occurred in a car full of my allies and protectors, I was silent. I already internalized the message that I would be blamed for my uncle's behavior. The family is instrumental in socializing children. John Hodge writes, "It is in this form of family where most children first learn the meaning and practice of hierarchical, authoritarian rule. Here is where they learn to accept group oppression against themselves as non-adults, and where they learn to accept male supremacy and the group oppression of women." He adds, "Here is where the relationship of superordination-subordination, of superior-inferior, of master-slave is first learned and accepted as 'natural.'"[44] Even if no male is present in the household, this behavior is modeled from the mother's interaction with other males and from society in general.

I cannot remember the role of men in my early household. Life in Jamaica revolved around my grandmother and aunts. I do remember thinking my aunts beautiful and remember their gift-giving male friends. I remember watching the dance of relationship and even remember once a group of us mischievous cousins or *bad pikni* spying on my aunt and her male friend engaged in courtship.

Beauty–sex–power became a confused trinity that made subsequent victimization acceptable. Indeed, the sexual predatory behavior of another male relative when I was 14 carried this false veneer of power. Why else would this man come after me? It must be something I am doing or exuding? I acquiesced to a disembodied sexual experience, with myself the numb observer. The fallacy of power in connection with the Jezebel archetype is seen in the description of a young woman appearing on a television talk show:

> Connie, a slender, 17-year-old wearing a small tight vinyl dress... She says to both an audience member and her sister, who redress her about her promiscuity, "If I want to have yo' man, I'll take yo' man."[45]

I wonder at Connie's understanding of personal power. I wonder how she would answer a question Bass and Davis use to help individuals take stock of the effect of childhood sexual abuse in their lives: "Do you feel your worth is primarily sexual?"[46] Unfortunately, through gathering stories of women who were abused as children, the Women's Research Center has a ready answer to the question: "A child—particularly a child who is deprived of affection except as it is disguised as sexual abuse—learns that her primary value is sexual."[47]

The message of love, acceptance, and security that is linked to sexuality is a message generally reinforced within our culture and which some young women have learned to turn to advantage. bell hooks states:

> Popular culture provides countless examples of black female appropriation and exploitation of 'negative stereotypes' to either assert control over the representation or at least reap the benefit of it... Many black women singers, irrespective of the quality of their voices, have cultivated an image which suggests they are sexually available and licentious.[48]

In my own reality, while I had learned to turn male desire to my advantage, primarily in the form of evoking adulation and praise as surrogates for love, at a young age I had become dissociated from my body and ultimately from intimate sexuality. A deadening of my body had resulted, where sexuality was enacted rather than deeply felt. Sexuality was often in the service of another, not necessarily felt as a coerced duty, but rather rationalized as a service or act of kindness mainly because physical and psychological boundaries and the ability to say *no* were impaired. Imbibed notions of Black femaleness along with religious tenets to which I was exposed, and which permeate society and collective consciousness disadvantageously informed my young mind.

A Heuristic Journey

One's heuristic journey wends its way from a place of inner awareness—"only the experiencing person... can validly provide portrayals of the experience"[49]—unfurling at its own pace, leading to self-transformation.

Thoughts, feelings, senses, dreams (the numinous), and immersion in experience are all welcome epistemologies. "The focus in a heuristic quest is on recreation of the lived experience; full and complete depictions of the experience from the frame of reference of the experiencing person."[50]

Unlike a formal heuristic study where the experiences of several individuals would be considered in order to find a pattern joining the experiences, mine is a solitary heuristic process to find the pattern that links the experience of childhood sexual abuse to my current lived reality. As nothing occurs outside of context, part of the heuristic process into childhood sexual abuse involves ascertaining how social constructions inform childhood sexual abuse, especially that of the Black female child.

The heuristic research process entails six phases: initial engagement, immersion, incubation, illumination, explication, and creative synthesis.[51] Each will be looked at in turn with regard to this project.

Initial Engagement

"The task of initial engagement is to discover an intense interest, a passionate concern . . . During this process one encounters the self, one's autobiography, and significant relationships within a social context."[52] I confront my significant relationship with an uncle (and other Black male relatives) within the social context of patriarchal psychosis manifesting in childhood sexual abuse.

The earliest full memory I have of my childhood sexual abuse is of an incident that left me feeling utterly helpless and without voice—too ashamed to speak, to say *stop* out loud, to ask for help. I was in a car full of loving women—my grandmother and aunts. As a four- or five-year-old, I was told to sit on my uncle's lap in a back window seat. With my legs turned toward that window, my uncle proceeded to put his hand under my dress, then under the elastic edge of my cotton panties. He was maneuvering his finger between the lips of my immature vulva, and no matter how I squirmed or tried to twist my legs forward, he did not stop.

When he removed his hand, it was to smell his finger and sink more deeply into the thick leather seat of the old car as he sighed with contentment and rapture. I looked at him relieved because he had stopped and in disbelief at what I saw. I so clearly remember his response and my being simultaneously shocked, repulsed, and fascinated. I do not think I had the conceptual language to identify the source of my fascination as being the thought that the little area between my legs could cause such an evidently strong response. But that is the message my psyche absorbed.

Similarly, memories of incidents that occurred much later with other male relatives were never forgotten. It was not until after my mother's death when I was 30, while I was living through the grief of her loss, that

I remembered this incident with my uncle. My mother's death catalyzed a long, ongoing journey to reclaim and heal splintered aspects of self.

There is another early childhood memory of abuse that over a period of years has lived with me in somatic recall, images, and dreams. All the particulars of this incident are not in focus. I know it happened before the incident with my uncle described above. I see a few non-threatening images but hear no sound. "Survivors . . . may remember the context in which the abuse took place but not the specific physical events."[53] Also, "most memories from early childhood, especially before ages 5 and 6, will usually be just a 'snapshot' process."[54]

This submerged incident is intrinsic to certain aspects of my self-definition, particularly to the internalization of the image of Black female sexuality as contained in the Jezebel archetype. I started this heuristic process hoping for more clarity regarding what I feel is my foundational sexual abuse experience. What follows is a sharing of the personal component of my heuristic process.

Immersion

During the immersion phase, "the researcher lives the question in waking, sleeping, and even dream states."[55] I have been immersed in the process of coming to terms with the reality and impact of my childhood sexual abuse for many years. It started with my long investigation of rape—what is rape, why men rape, women's rape responses, and rape recovery—that culminated in my master's thesis. Writing, for many survivors, is an important step in the healing process.

I immersed myself in the process of trying to understand the damage caused by rape to self and soul, and of finding ways of healing. During the process of researching rape, I came to understand the power dynamics that constitute rape and came to understand why statutory rape is indeed rape—the initial engagement that launched my investigation. A 40-something male copulating with a 14-year-old girl is rape.

The bottom line is that sexual abuse is about power and control.[56] Outright coercion or violence are extreme manifestations of this reality. More subtle, or even unspoken, forms of power and control are often exerted. For instance, the abuser, to serve the abuser's end, often manipulates a child's genuine affection. A 40-year-old man holds power over a 14-year-old girl. Besides the privilege that comes with gender, he also holds the authority that comes with age. A conventionally reared 14-year-old, generally, feels compelled to obey her elder out of instilled respect or fear.

Through extensive research I learned of the social context within which rape and sexual abuse are situated. Dreams have been my guide in coming to terms with my personal history of abuse and in assisting me in the journey out of victimization. My own dreams have been instructive, and the dreams received for me by a close friend and gifted dreamer have been particularly helpful. "In heuristic investigations, I may be entranced by visions, images, and dreams that connect me to my quest."[57]

As part of my immersion into heuristic process, I incorporated elements contained in *The Healing Wisdom of Africa*. I created a shrine for the spirit of my child-self and her healing/transformational process. Author Malidoma Somé states, "A shrine is where one goes to enter into communication with the Other World. It is a place of beauty and mystery, and also the place of memory."[58] On the shrine are images of myself as a child of three, four, and seven years of age. A candle to the mothering orisha or deity, Yemaya,[59] also graces the shrine.

In part, I made the shrine to encourage my child-self to communicate with me and in this regard employed Moustakas' self-dialogue technique that is similar to the Jungian technique of active imagination. Active imagination is used as a means to bring unconscious material into consciousness. It is an invitation to the unconscious to speak, knowing that the conscious mind is paying attention. Active imagination is a counterpoint to dreams, developed by Jung for working with dreams.[60]

While dreams simply occur, through active imagination one directly engages the dream and dream elements—asking questions, confronting images, and generally dialoging with the unconscious as it becomes manifest. Moustakas' self-dialogue is not employed exclusively with dreams, however. The process of attunement, of establishing deep inner connection, is key to self-dialogue.[61]

The self-dialogue or active imagination process is not as mysterious as it might seem. Most of us have some form of dialogue happening in our minds on a daily basis—we imagine how an important interaction will play out, for example. The difference is that here we are directly engaging with elements of our unconscious or elements of our dreams. The process does involve temporarily displacing left-brain primacy and diving into the uncharted waters of the non-rational or numinous. I invited my child-self to visit with me; I spoke to her with affection and listened to her with openness and respect.

The night I built the shrine and did the self-dialogue, I had two series of significant dreams. Each series contained three dreams. The number three is a gateway number. "Three is the numerical vibration that opens the gateways to the higher planes . . . Dreams themselves are the gatekeepers and thus vibrate to the number 3 . . . Thus when three shows up in a dream, it is a signal that requires attention."[62] For Jung, the number three symbolized in dreams signals the descent process into the soul from which one emerges with gifts of insight and the ability to be in alignment with the soul's individuation process.[63] Clearly, I needed to pay attention to these dreams.

Incubation, Illumination, Explication

Incubation is described as "a process of spontaneous mental reorganization uncontrolled by conscious effort."[64] Because of time limitations, the heuristic process was not allowed to unfold organically. I feel that it is ongoing and that although I am at the explication stage, it is explication of an early phase in a multi-tiered incubation process.

Through immersion in the *tangible* (traditional scholarship) and *nontangible* (dreams and tacit knowing), I have gained insight into and illumination on the area of childhood sexual abuse and my personal experiences. Traditional research has helped me see that my responses are normal and shared by many women who have been similarly traumatized.[65] Contact with the numinous has shed light on my personal journey in relation to childhood sexual abuse and presented me with the promise of healing and transformation. "The purpose of the explication phase is to fully examine what has awakened in consciousness in order to understand its various layers of meaning."[66] As such I have been able to write about the personal impact of larger socio-historical and cultural forces that operate in childhood sexual abuse and in the internalization of this form of oppression for myself as a Black female.

Ascertaining how the larger socio-historical and cultural forces impact my personal experience of childhood sexual abuse is the task of deconstructing this self. It is an undertaking not yet completed. This exploration is an overview and introduction more than an explication of complete understandings.

Creative Synthesis

An incredibly healing aspect of this heuristic exploration has been reconnecting with the playful, creative spirit of my seven-year-old self. This reconnection was made manifest through a spontaneous impulse to color and play jump-rope. The reconnection itself feels like a creative synthesis, although this is not how Moustakas employs the term. Generally, the creative synthesis is a tangible creative work arising from the distillation of the insights and results of the heuristic process.[67] Artwork and poetry were features of my creative synthesis.

I believe that the contact made with this seven-year-old aspect of myself and feeling her energy as distinct from energy I am accustomed to experiencing are a distillation and result of the heuristic process. They have produced an embodied creative synthesis of highly transformational value.

My hypothesis regarding the reason for my seven-year-old's manifestation is that she feels safe because she knows I will protect her with Yemaya's blessing, and she feels honored to be given the opportunity to be heard. I must be patient and allow her to tell her story in her time.

The process of reclamation will unfold organically, as will the process of integrating our energies.

Coda and Discussion

One very early morning while in the hypnopompic space between sleep and waking, I faced the thought or worry that Black men will feel threatened, hurt, or angry at my disclosure. In this liminal space of predawn consciousness, a Black male student of my acquaintance either demonstrated this thought or simply represented Black men. In either case, I erupted in a seismic outburst of anger and was able to vociferously use masterful Billingsgate[68] to fully express my rage. It was bodily felt, and a very cathartic experience. The experience was a purging, a releasing of the burdensome internalized obligation to protect my abuser.

This phenomenon of group allegiance in relation to childhood sexual abuse is addressed by Bass and Davis who state that "when a group of people has been discriminated against, there is a need to maintain a united front. This can make it more difficult to acknowledge abuse within the group."[69] Black men have been victims of the hegemonic dominant culture but have also internalized its tenet of male privilege. As in the dominant culture, this patriarchal domain of influence is power over the family, the home, women, and children.

Pierce-Baker eloquently addresses the dilemma of Black women who are victims of sexual abuse by Black men stating:

> For black women, where rape is concerned, race has preceded issues of gender. We are taught that we are first black, then women. Our families have taught us this, and society in its harsh racial lessons reinforces it. Black women have survived by keeping quiet, not solely out of shame, but out of a need to preserve the race and its image. In our attempts to preserve racial pride, we black women have often sacrificed our own souls.[70]

At the end of this heuristic process, I do not have any clearer a picture of what happened to me in the greenish walled room, on the prickly, thin straw mattress of my earliest, fragmented, and vague memory. But as a fellow survivor of childhood sexual abuse put it: "Really, I think you have to be strong enough to know. I think that our minds are wonderful in the way they protect us, and I think that when I'm strong enough to know, I'll know."[71]

Although I have not grasped the elusive brass ring of whole memory, this heuristic process has brought me many gifts and blessings. Seeing childhood sexual abuse in its larger context is one such gift. I am closer to a synthesis of the socio-historical and cultural factors involved in childhood sexual abuse and the interrelationship of these factors with the dynamics of internalization of that abuse. This synthesis will enable me to deconstruct the self of this particular Black woman and perhaps provide a pathway for other individuals. The synthesis will enable me to relinquish shame, guilt, and self-blame. Relinquishing self-blame means discarding the personal sense of responsibility for my own abuse.

What the socio-historical and cultural factors involved in childhood sexual abuse and the dynamics of the internalization of oppression have in common is the element of domination. Collins speaks of "the social relations of domination" and the "matrix of domination" as fundamental to the issue of oppression.[72] It was informative to look at the theological ground of these beliefs through the work of Elaine Pagels. The early fathers of the Christian church clearly articulated their belief in female inferiority and sanctioned the dominance of man over woman and child.

A second gift is that I have once again had confirmed the value of the loving, clear guidance of dreams. And most significantly, I have been blessed to experience a transformative reconnection with the spirit of my seven-year-old self—the little girl who holds so much pain along with her capacity for play and creativity. Feminist scholarship embedded in a transpersonal research paradigm provided the fertile soil from which this experience could arise.

Further Thoughts

From a personal perspective, excavating repressed memories of sexual abuse and placing sexual abuse within a larger socio-cultural context is liberating. In this chapter, I spoke to the release of self-blame, shame, and guilt that can accompany contextualization of sexual abuse as an expression of patriarchal derangement. On an individual level, excavation—even partial—can lead to greater self-understanding and self-acceptance.

As my memories emerged, I could affix reasons to the difficult dynamics I had with certain men. I could look back at my 14-year-old self and understand my acquiescence, releasing my sense of responsibility and shame. At the level of intimate relationships, there was a sense of renewal. I came to see why I disliked certain expressions of affection—why intimate touch could send me out of my body, leaving me disconnected from my partner. Being able to share my realizations with a loving, patient partner has resulted in greater intimacy and continued healing.

Dreamscape

Dreams are a window into the unconscious. The most important aspect of actively working with your dreams is recording your dreams. This can be done using a journal dedicated to your dreams or using a voice recorder. Regularly recording your dreams seems to act as a signal to the subconscious to send you pertinent information. Over time, dreams become clearer and more coherent.

Dreams are ephemeral; they tend to dissipate quickly once one awakens. So, record them right away. Keep paper and pen or phone recorder next to your bed. If you awaken in the middle of the night with a dream on the edge of consciousness, write what you remember. No need to get every detail at this point. What elements stand out most? What is the message? Making these notes will help your recall when you can more fully record the dream. There are books and classes dedicated to the art of dreaming and dream analysis. Two books of interest by Rosemary Guiley, are *Dreamwork for the Soul: A Spiritual Guide to Dream Interpretation*, and *The Dreamer's Way: Using Proactive Dreaming to Heal and Transform Your Life*.

As tools of spiritual technology, such as dreams, are used to assist and guide you in your healing journey, be cognizant of the larger socio-cultural matrix within which damage to the self and soul are often situated. The personal is political.

Notes

1 John W. Santrock, *Life-Span Development* (Madison, WI: WCB Brown & Benchmark Publishers, 1995).
2 Statistics vary but indicate that approximately 1 in 4 girls and 1 in 13 boys suffer childhood sexual abuse. (Centers for Disease Control, "Fast Facts: Preventing Childhood Sexual Abuse," www.cdc.gov/violenceprevention/childsexualabuse/fastfact.html.)
3 Donald Polkinghorne, *Narrative Knowing and the Human Sciences* (Albany, NY: SUNY Press 1988), 149.
4 Ibid., 150.
5 Stephen Fleming and Sheri Bélanger, "Trauma, Grief, and Surviving Childhood Sexual Abuse," in *Meaning Reconstruction and the Experience of Loss*, ed. Robert Neimeyer, 311–325 (Washington, DC: American Psychological Association, 2001).
6 Ellen Bass and Laura Davis, *The Courage to Heal: A Guide for Women Survivors of Child Sexual Abuse* (New York: Harper Collins, 1994).
7 Pat Conroy, *The Prince of Tides*, (NY: Houghton Mifflin, 1986), quoted in Charlotte Pierce-Baker, *Surviving the Silence: Black Women's Stories of Rape* (NY: W. W. Norton, 1998), 63.
8 Ruth King, *Healing Rage: Women Making Inner Peace Possible* (Berkeley, CA: Sacred Spaces Press, 2004), 10.
9 Charlotte Pierce-Baker, *Surviving the Silence: Black Women's Stories of Rape* (NY: W. W. Norton, 1998), 63. (Although her research concerns rape, I nonetheless cite Charlotte Pierce-Baker. Her book contains the stories of Black women who have been victims of rape, herself included. Some of these women also endured childhood sexual abuse.)
10 Bass and Davis, *Courage to Heal*, 38.
11 Elaine Pagels, *Adam, Eve, and the Serpent* (New York: Random House, 1988).

12 Florence Rush, *The Best Kept Secret: Sexual Abuse of Children* (New York: McGraw-Hill Book Company, 1980).
13 Monica Sjoo and Barbara Mor, *The Great Cosmic Mother: Rediscovering the Religion of Earth* (San Francisco: Harper & Row, 1987).
14 Somatic: "of the body, as distinguished from the soul, mind, or psyche; corporeal; physical." Definition taken from Collins dictionary (www.collinsdictionary.com/us/dictionary/english/somatic).
15 Paul Stoller, *Sensuous Scholarship* (Philadelphia: University of Pennsylvania Press, 1997), xvii.
16 William Braud and Rosemarie Anderson, *Transpersonal Research Methods for the Social Sciences* (Thousand Oaks, CA: Sage Publications, 1998), 44.
17 Ibid., 45.
18 Linda Alcoff and Elizabeth Potter, *Feminist Epistemologies*. Thinking Gender (New York: Routledge, 1993).
19 Patricia Hill Collins, "Black Feminist Thought in the Matrix of Domination" in *Black Feminist Thought: Knowledge, Consciousness, and the Politics of Empowerment* (Boston: Unwin Hyman, 1990), pp. 221–238. www.hartford-hwp.com/archives/45a/252.html.
20 Moustakas, *Heuristic Research*, 9.
21 Ibid., 15.
22 Luisah Teish, *Jambalaya: The Natural Woman's Book of Personal Charms and Practical Rituals* (New York: HarperCollins, 1985), 119.
23 Debra K. Peters and Lillian M. Range, "Self-blame and Self-destruction in Women Sexually Abused as Children," *Journal of Child Sexual Abuse* 5, no. 4, (1996): 20.
24 Ibid.
25 Pagels, *Adam, Eve, and the Serpent*, 68.
26 Tertullian, *De Cultu Feminarum* 1, 12. Emphasis added, quoted in Pagels, *Adam, Eve, and the Serpent*, 63.
27 1 Timothy 2.11–13 and 15. Revised Standard Version.
28 1 Timothy 3.4. RSV.
29 1 Timothy 3.4. King James Version.
30 Dorothy Roberts, *Killing the Black Body: Race, Reproduction, and the Meaning of Liberty* (New York: Random House, 1999), 8.
31 Ibid., 11.
32 Ibid., 26.
33 Alexander Crummel, "The Black Woman of the South: Her Neglects and Her Needs," in *Africa and America: Addresses and Discourses* (Miami, 1969), 64 quoted in Beverly Guy-Sheftall, *Daughters of Sorrow: Attitudes Toward Black Women, 1880–1920* (Brooklyn, NY: Carlson Publishing, 1990), 60.
34 bell hooks, *Black Looks: Race and Representation* (Boston: South End Press, 1992), 24.
35 Carolyn M. West, "Mammy, Jezebel, and Sapphire: Developing an 'Oppositional Gaze' Toward the Images of Black Women," in *Lectures on the Psychology of Women*, eds. Joan Chrisler, Carla Golden, and Patricia Rozee (New York: McGraw-Hill, 2004), 236–251.
36 Fleming and Bélanger, *Trauma, Grief, and Surviving*, 318.
37 West, *Mammy, Jezebel, and Sapphire*, 246.
38 Ibid.
39 Black slang from the 1960s meaning to sway one's hips provocatively while walking.

40 Pierce-Baker, *Surviving the Silence*, 156.
41 "Sexual Abuse/Trauma," www.allaboutcounseling.com/sexual_abuse.htm#sa7.
42 American Academy of Child & Adolescent Psychiatry, "Facts for Families: Sexual Abuse" no. 9 Updated November 2014, https://dev.aacap.org/AACAP/Families_and_Youth/Facts_for_Families/FFF-Guide/Child-Sexual-Abuse-009.
43 Ibid.
44 John L. Hodge, "Dualist Culture and Beyond," in *The Cultural Basis of Racism and Group Oppression*, ed. John L. Hodge, Donald K. Struckmann, and Lynn Dorvand Trost (Berkeley, CA: Two Readers Press, 1975), 233, quoted in bell hooks, *Feminist Theory: From Margin to Center*, (Boston South End Press, 1984), 36.
45 Shawna V. Hudson. "Re-creational Television: The Paradox of Change and Continuity Within Stereotypical Iconography," *Sociological Inquiry* 68, (1998): 246 quoted in West, *Mammy, Jezebel, and Sapphire*, 246.
46 Bass and Davis, *Courage to Heal*, 42.
47 Women's Research Center, *Recollecting Our Lives: Women's Experience of Childhood Sexual Abuse* (Vancouver, Canada: Press Gang Publishers, 1989), 105.
48 bell hooks, *Black Looks: Race and Representation*, 65.
49 Moustakas, *Heuristic Research*, 26.
50 Ibid., 39.
51 Ibid., 27–32.
52 Ibid., 27.
53 Bass and Davis, *Courage to Heal*, 78.
54 "Sexual Abuse/Trauma," www.allaboutcounseling.com/sexual_abuse.htm#sa7.
55 Moustakas, *Heuristic Research*, 28.
56 Brian N. Sweeney, "Gender-Based Violence and Rape Culture," in *Companion to Women's and Gender Studies*, ed. Nancy Naples (Oxford, UK: Wiley-Blackwell, 2020): 285–302.
57 Ibid., 11.
58 Malidoma Patrice Somé, *The Healing Wisdom of Africa: Finding Life Purpose Through Nature, Ritual, and Community* (New York: Putnam, 1999), 134.
59 Introduced earlier, she is a member of the West African Yoruba spiritual pantheon.
60 Carl G. Jung (1875–1961) and Joan Chodorow, *Jung on Active Imagination* (Princeton, NJ: Princeton University Press, 1997).
61 Moustakas, *Heuristic Research*.
62 Rosemary Ellen Guiley, *Dreamwork for the Soul* (New York: Berkeley Books, 1998) 157–158.
63 Charles Bebeau, "Praxis II" (seminar, Avalon Institute, Boulder, Colorado, Spring 1997).
64 Polanyi, Michael, *Science, Faith, and Society* (Chicago: University of Chicago Press, 1964), 34, quoted in Moustakas, *Heuristic Research*, 29.
65 Bass and Davis, *Courage to Heal*; Fleming and Bélanger, *Trauma, Grief, and Surviving*; King, *Healing Rage*.
66 Moustakas, *Heuristic Research*, 31.
67 Moustakas, *Heuristic Research*, 32.
68 Used for "Billingsgate, a London fish-market dating from the 16th c., known for the invective traditionally ascribed to the fish-porters" (Oxford English Dictionary, 142).
69 Bass and Davis, *Courage to Heal*, 70.

70 Pierce-Baker, *Surviving the Silence*, 84.
71 Bass and Davis, *Courage to Heal*, 92.
72 Collins, *Black Feminist Thought*, 1990.

Bibliography

Alcoff, Linda and Elizabeth Potter. *Feminist Epistemologies*. Thinking Gender. New York: Routledge, 1993.
American Academy of Child & Adolescent Psychiatry, "Facts for Families: Sexual Abuse" no. 9. Updated November 2014. https://dev.aacap.org/AACAP/Families_and_Youth/Facts_for_Families/FFF-Guide/Child-Sexual-Abuse-009.
Bass, Ellen and Laura Davis. *The Courage to Heal: A Guide for Women Survivors of Child Sexual Abuse*. New York: Harper Collins, 1994.
Bebeau, Charles. Praxis II Seminar – Avalon Institute. Boulder, Colorado. Spring 1997.
Braud, William and Rosemarie Anderson. *Transpersonal Research Methods for the Social Sciences*. Thousand Oaks, CA: Sage Publications, 1998.
Centers for Disease Control, "Fast Facts: Preventing Childhood Sexual Abuse," www.cdc.gov/violenceprevention/childsexualabuse/fastfact.html
Collins, Patricia Hill. "Black Feminist Thought in the Matrix of Domination." In *Black Feminist Thought: Knowledge, Consciousness, and the Politics of Empowerment*, 221–238. Boston: Unwin Hyman, 1990. www.hartford-hwp.com/archives/45a/252.html.
Fleming, Stephen and Sheri Bélanger. "Trauma, Grief, and Surviving Childhood Sexual Abuse." In *Meaning Reconstruction & the Experience of Loss*, edited by Robe Neimeyer, 311–325. Washington, DC: American Psychological Association, 2001.
Guiley, Rosemary Ellen. *Dreamwork for the Soul*. NY: Berkeley Books, 1998.
Guy-Sheftall, Beverly. *Daughters of Sorrow: Attitudes Toward Black Women, 1880–1920*. Brooklyn, NY: Carlson Publishing, 1990.
hooks, bell. *Feminist Theory from Margin to Center*. Boston: South End Press, 1984.
hooks, bell. *Black Looks: Race and Representation*. Boston: South End Press, 1992.
Jung, Carl G. (1875–1961) and Joan Chodorow. *Jung on Active Imagination*. Princeton, NJ: Princeton University Press, 1997.
King, Ruth. *Healing Rage: Women Making Inner Peace Possible*. Berkeley: Sacred Spaces Press, 2004.
Moustakas, Clark. *Heuristic Research: Design, Methodology, and Applications*. Newbury Park, CA: Sage Publications, 1990.
Pagels, Elaine. *Adam, Eve, and the Serpent*. New York: Random House, 1988.
Peters, Debra K., and Lillian M. Range. "Self-blame and Self-destruction in Women Sexually Abused as Children." *Journal of Child Sexual Abuse* 5, no. 4 (1996): 19–33.
Pierce-Baker, Charlotte. *Surviving the Silence: Black Women's Stories of Rape*. NY: W. W. Norton & Company, 1998.
Polkinghorne, Donald. *Narrative Knowing and the Human Sciences*. Albany, NY: SUNY Press, 1988.
Roberts, Dorothy. *Killing the Black Body: Race, Reproduction, and the Meaning of Liberty*. New York: Random House, 1999.

Rush, Florence. *The Best Kept Secret: Sexual Abuse of Children.* New York: McGraw-Hill Book Company, 1980.
Santrock, John W. *Life-span Development.* Madison, WI: WCB Brown & Benchmark Publishers, 1995.
"Sexual Abuse/Trauma," www.allaboutcounseling.com/sexual_abuse.htm#sa7.
Sjoo, Monica and Barbara Mor. *The Great Cosmic Mother: Rediscovering the Religion of Earth.* San Francisco: Harper & Row, 1987.
Somé, Malidoma Patrice. The Healing Wisdom of Africa: Finding Life Purpose Through Nature, Ritual, and Community. New York: Putnam, 1999.
Stoller, Paul. *Sensuous Scholarship.* Philadelphia: University of Pennsylvania Press, 1997.
Sweeney, Brian N. "Gender-Based Violence and Rape Culture." In *Companion to Women's and Gender Studies*, edited by Nancy Naples, 285–302. Oxford, UK: Wiley-Blackwell, 2020.
Teish, Luisah. *Jambalaya: The Natural Woman's Book of Personal Charms and Practical Rituals.* NY: HarperCollins Publishers, 1985.
West, Carolyn M. "Mammy, Jezebel, and Sapphire: Developing an 'Oppositional Gaze' toward the Images of Black Women." In *Lectures on the Psychology of Women*, edited by Joan Chrisler, Carla Golden, Patricia Rozee, 236–251. NY: McGraw-Hill, 2004.
Women's Research Centre. *Recollecting Our Lives: Women's Experience of Childhood Sexual Abuse.* Vancouver, British Columbia (Canada): Press Gang Publishers, 1989.

Chapter 7

A Spiritual Being Having a Human Experience

Quanita Roberson

My Black mother and my white stepfather had begun studying with Jehovah's Witnesses when I was a teenager. The first step was to learn what the Bible teaches in Bible study groups. Next, they needed to practice what they learned in Bible study. In other words, they needed to make significant changes to both their thinking and behavior before being baptized into the church. This baptism was a concrete symbol of their rebirth—their new dedication to God with a clean conscience. Part of this preparation for joining the church included 'truth telling.'

I was 15 when my stepfather confessed to my mother that he had been sexually abusing me.

He picked me up from school, as he often did, but he was unusually quiet. I didn't know that my life was about to change. When I stepped into the kitchen, my mother said three words that shattered my life forever. With a tear-stained face, she quietly said that he told her. My mother never cried. I felt like the world was suddenly moving in slow motion. Nothing would ever be the same. Then she asked what I wanted her to do? I was stunned. I was 15. I didn't know what I wanted her to do. I could barely even think in that moment as my brain whirled making me dizzy and unstable. I just stood there unable to move for fear of falling. And then she said the word that would change me and my relationship with her forever. *I know what we need to do, we need to forgive.*

Forgive? We needed to forgive?

From that moment forward I began carrying her and my stepfather's pain and anxiety in a way that I wouldn't understand for years to come. This burden was immense, and it would take decades for me to unpack, dismantle, and heal from this affliction.

The three of us moved to the living room to talk. Well, I mostly listened. My mother explained that early in their marriage she had cheated on my stepfather. Applying her newly acquired Bible study knowledge, she insisted that no sin was greater than another. Thus, the three of us needed to forgive each other.

That's it? My mind exploded. There's no accountability? No punishment? No restitution? No justice? Just forgive, forget, and move on? How can this be happening?

Then she asked me if I wanted my stepfather to leave. I said yes—at least that would be some justice. He packed a small bag and left to stay at his parent's house. I finally felt like I had a voice in this cataclysmic event. My world seemed more stable. But this wasn't going to be a solution.

My stepfather returned after only a few days of peace. I was so angry! It felt like yet another violation. Not only did he sexually abuse me, but now he had the power to force me to deal with it on his schedule and under his terms. His truth telling purge to save his soul set off a chain of events that threw me into my healing journey early, not in the natural order of things. Not in my own timing and readiness.

Up until that fateful day, I really believed in my heart that if my mother only knew that her husband was sexually abusing me, she would move mountains to punish my perpetrator and heal my deep wounds. But my mother's insistence on forgiveness rather than justice and her aversion to protecting and healing me, led to only one conclusion. I was worthless and unlovable. After all, if my own mother didn't think I was valuable, then maybe I really had no value.

I started to have nightmares. I was being attacked by people I knew every time I would go to sleep. Everyone seemed to be a rapist. I tried not to sleep, which you can't do for too long without it adding to the craziness. So, I searched for a therapist that would see me for free. I told her what had happened, and by law she had to report it to the department of human services. This chain of events put me on another roller coaster. Authorities scheduled my human services interview at the same time as my stepfather's appointment, which meant that I had to ride in the car with him to the appointment. At best this was awkward, at worst it furthered my trauma. After the interview I asked if they could place me somewhere else. Someplace safe from my abuser. My mother hadn't done anything illegal, and she was my legal guardian, so no. They could not even take me out of the house that had become a living nightmare for me. No one seemed to be interested in protecting me, much less helping me to heal. I felt that I could not escape my nightmare. I was trapped.

One thing about trauma is that it makes you believe that God left you and that now you are responsible for your own survival. It took me years to learn that that wasn't true My job is to keep my focus on how I'm living. My job is to tap into my own unique gifts in the world and then give them away.

The department of human services gathered our versions of what had happened and forwarded the information to the prosecutor's office. I was then contacted by a prosecutor who basically told me that it was up to me if they moved forward with this case or not because they didn't have a case without me. I remember asking if I could take some time to decide what I wanted to do. I didn't share with my mom or my stepfather that I was in this discernment process. As I think back on it now, it must have been a surprise to them when there was a grand jury scheduled to see if there was enough evidence to move forward with an indictment. This step gave me some much-needed confidence in my own ability to control my life.

"God protects us from nothing but sustains us in all things."[1]

When I was fifteen, I went to court and filed charges against my stepfather for sexual abuse. Technically the state filed charges and I agreed to be a witness. They didn't have a case unless I was willing to testify in front of the grand jury. I remember taking the whole summer to decide what I wanted to do. I decided to take back my life.

Unfortunately, my extended family did not see things from my perspective. My grandmother told me that I needed to think about my mother and her marriage. Of course, I should put other's needs ahead of my own. My aunt accused me of trying to get back at my mother for some alleged grievance. And my father, as always, never protected me or came to my aid. I felt abandoned by everyone that I loved. When I decided to testify and charges were filed, I was living with my mother and stepfather, so things got worse. I started having anxiety attacks. It got so bad that I had trouble riding the bus and I began missing a lot of school.

It's important to note that I didn't make the decision to testify because I felt like my perpetrator deserved to be held accountable. I agreed to testify because I needed to know that even if the people I trusted were not able or willing to stand up for me, I could stand up for myself. There was a part of me that knew that I would die if I didn't do it. I needed to be worth fighting for. I did it for me. I needed to not abandon myself in this moment. This isn't the right choice for everyone, but it was for me.

I first testified in front of the grand jury, which after deliberation, indicted my stepfather who then pled guilty to the lesser charge of contributing to the delinquency of a minor. This process took months. And all that time we were all living in the same house. Right before we entered the courtroom for my stepfather's sentencing, the attorney who had been representing me all these months informed me that he wouldn't be joining me. He had to be somewhere else, so another attorney, a person I did not know would be in the courtroom with me. I was standing, alone, on one side of the courtroom with the prosecutor. My mother and stepfather were standing together on the other side of the courtroom as he was sentenced to serve ninety days on weekends so he could go to work during the week. The judge decided that he would stay in the house with my mom and me during the week and go to jail on the weekends. I didn't realize until years later how traumatizing this day and the following couple of years were for me. I was just trying to survive it. As a matter of fact, I didn't feel much of anything. I was numb. I left the courtroom and walked to school, a place that had become refuge for me, and then later that evening I went home as if nothing had happened. What else could I do?

The school I attended was a magnet school for the performing arts. It was created because of a lawsuit that found that the schools in my area were unintentionally segregated based on the racially segregated neighborhoods. In a concerted effort to avoid mandatory busing, the district decided to create four magnet schools to facilitate voluntary busing and desegregation. My school's goals included integration through the arts. I earned my place in this selective school as a music major with a creative writing minor. This art-focused school forced us to respect ourselves and reflect deeply on our gifts that might be shared with the world. Some indigenous people don't even have a word for art because it is thought of as spirit brought to the ground. Art for me was a refuge. I would go to school early in the morning so that I could close myself into the fine arts library and sing classic Italian music, show tunes, and whatever else we were working on in choir at the time. I would walk the perimeter of the room singing and it would feel like I was flying. This was one of the ways that I could escape what was happening in my life. This is one of the effective vehicles of sanity and healing that I use to this day. It's important to note that my schoolteachers instilled sustainable confidence in us. I believed in myself. I believed I could do anything. This belief formed the foundation for my decision to take my stepfather to court.

Clearly, the systems that we have in place for sexual violence victims—the department of human services and the legal system—failed me. But these systems only relate to my human journey. The *undocumented systems did not fail me*. These *undocumented systems*, such as relationships with my gift-giving teachers, are essential to the healing and spiritual growth process since we are spiritual beings having a human experience and not human beings that sometimes have spiritual experiences. This core belief changes how I view the world and my place in it.

Our spiritual journey through *undocumented systems* provides support for our human experiences. Since the spiritual systems move quicker than those of the earthly world, we can heal first on a spiritual level, then on an emotional level, and finally on a physical level. Our spiritual selves and human selves overlap each other, so as we make leaps in our spiritual journey it is mirrored in our human journey.

> *When you risk sharing what hurts you in the presence of someone who won't invade or abandon yourself you learn to not invade or abandon yourself.*
>
> James Findley[2]

I call these *undocumented systems* because they are not the professional and institutionalized systems that we have created to deal with sexual violence. Instead, these are systems that operate in the spiritual realm. We often call these undocumented system events or encounters coincidences. But I argue that there is a divine order at play.

A friend once asked me what questions might I ask myself that would help me to change my life? After careful reflection, I formulated two questions that would guide my healing.

- If I embraced a belief that everything was in divine order, how would I walk through the world differently?
- How might I treat other people differently?

Undocumented systems related to my life-changing questions have often been revealed to me in the form of what I would call my earthly angels, people who show up at the precise moment that I need them. Earthly angels provide me with information or support that I didn't even know that I needed.

One such angel was a prosecutor. I don't remember how we met. He wasn't the prosecutor assigned to me, but he treated me like a valuable human being. At some point he gave me his contact information and I started visiting him in his office every now and then. My school was walking distance to his office, so it was easy for me to drop by on my way to my bus stop. The best way I can explain those visits was that he witnessed me in my healing journey. He never asked for anything in return and there was such healing in this simple act for me. Especially significant that it was from this White man in this patriarchal system that represents the law that did little to protect me when it sent me back to live with my perpetrator. Those visits were reconciling something within me. Something personal and something ancestral. There was a healing happening between this wound that I personally carry as a Black female incest survivor with a White man as my perpetrator. And at the same time there was an ancestral healing between the relationships of my Black female ancestors and the White men in their lives.

A part of the ancestral legacy of slavery was being healed in my family lineage through me. Through this Black girl and this White man. The violent roots of enslavement continue to reverberate through our communities because the pain that has not been transformed is always transferred. Sexual violence is not about sex. It is all about power, control, and pain. It is one of the ways that we transfer our pain on to another in an attempt to find some temporary relief from anguish. I don't say this to excuse anyone for their actions. Just the opposite is true. Healing our pain, regardless of its origin, is always our responsibility.

I now know that my stepfather transferred his own unhealed pain to me. And my mother had her own unhealed pain that prevented her from addressing my pain. I used to think that she chose her husband over me, but I now realize that she chose to deal with his pain over her own. I really was not even part of her decision-making process. She couldn't see my pain because she could not even examine her own.

Another earthly angel who assisted me in my spiritual recovery was a substitute teacher at my school. I didn't know her very well. I think I had only been in her class a handful of times. When I was 16 and suicidal, I was hospitalized and put into the psych ward. At this time, adolescent patients and adult patients were housed together and treated much the same. The only real difference was that a teacher visited with the teenagers for a few hours during the school week.

My earthly angel heard that I was in the hospital and came to visit me. I'm not completely sure what compelled her to come, but I feel like we had a spiritual connection with each other. Our bond grew and I stayed with her and her family when I was released from the hospital until the end of that school year. I was devastated when she abandoned me after she saw my less-than-stellar final grades.

It would be many years before I was ready to interact with my substitute teacher and her family again. Many years went by before my earthly angel and her husband invited me and my family to come to see their quartet performance. I agreed. On the way there I started crying uncontrollably. I wasn't quite sure why I was crying, but I pulled myself together using prayer as I often did. I asked the divine and all my ancestors to help me process the grief that was flowing through me without blocking it. When we arrived at the church where they would be singing, we greeted each other briefly and then parted so that we could find our seats. My family and I sat about three rows back in the center. The moment they started singing tears began flowing again. I cried through the whole performance.

I was flooded with the positive experiences I had as part of my teacher's household. Singing in the church choir that she led. Packing school lunches together. Sharing our daily events over dinner. Laughing. I grieved for the life that had been taken from me. The Spirit reminded me that the events that led to our alienation really weren't about me. My teacher was not ready to confront all the issues that precipitated my rejection from this family. The Spirit comforted me with the knowledge that I had reaped all that I could from that relationship—both positive and negative. I drew from that portion of my life all the knowledge, survival skills, and compassion that I needed to create my own loving family. The knowledge, survival skills, and compassion I gleaned from living with my earthly angel has impacted more than just my nuclear family relationships. They have contributed to my career choices and all my professional and social relationships.

I often refer to some of the younger earthly angels as my *community children*. I met one of my community children while working at the American Red Cross, a twelve-year old volunteer. Years later, he contacted me and asked if I would go with him and his sister to petition the court. They were petitioning the court for early release for their oldest sister, who had served more than seven years of a ten-year sentence for killing their mother. Her plan had been to take her own life after her mother's. When I told my community child that I would accompany him to court, it hadn't occurred to me that the last time I was in a courtroom was more than twenty-five years earlier when my stepfather was sentenced. Being in that courtroom with them that day didn't just touch my spirit; it transformed me. It changed me forever.

The court date occurred on the Monday after the Sandy Hook School massacre in Newtown, Connecticut. This family only had one opportunity to petition the court. If the judge denied the petition, the sister would have to serve her full sentence. It was bad luck to be sure that their court date happened to fall when the entire nation was mourning the murder of so many small children in their school.

I took my seat in a courtroom in the same building where I had stood alone for my stepfather's sentencing. My mother was by his side, supporting him, instead of me. I could still hear the lies that his attorney told the judge—that I agreed that my family should stay together and work things out for ourselves. This building was the place where I told the judge that my stepfather's lawyer was lying. I had never talked to his attorney. This place where I, all alone, took a stand for myself.

I didn't know that I was going to experience a spiritual death and rebirth that day with my former volunteer and his family. I didn't know that I would go into the courtroom as one person and come out completely changed, completely transformed. If we open ourselves up, the Spirit will bring us back around full circle to experience how much we have grown or to push us the rest of the way through a block that sometimes we don't even know that we face. By being there with his family, I was able to relive my trauma story differently—experience a sort of forgiveness and reconciliation of my own. Only this time the community showed up. The courtroom was packed with people. There were so many people that people had to stand up in the back. It wasn't until then that I understood my sacred contract with this young man that used to volunteer for me and the American Red Cross.

When he was younger, I was able to give him a place to go, a place that he could be witnessed. And, in return, he would come back one day, this day, and save me. His sister's lawyer explained that the family could have petitioned the court earlier, but they wanted to wait until they felt it was the right time. The siblings all had a hereditary eye disease and were slowly losing their vision. They wanted to get their oldest sister settled into a place to live before she completely lost her vision. The family recognized that many of the women who were released from prison would end up re-incarcerated, mainly because they didn't have job skills and found it hard to support themselves and their families. So, his family took proactive measures to ensure her successful transition. They found grant funding to start a green training program in the prison, which not only helped to improve the conditions that the prisoners lived in, but it gave the women who were in prison job skills to assist in a smoother transition into society.

In addition, a former neighbor who grew up next door to this family stood up and explained that she knew if this woman was released the family planned to petition the courts to allow her to move out of town to where her sister was currently living. In the meantime, the neighbor and her husband were offering to open their home to her. Then the siblings' Auntie walked to the front of the courtroom to speak and said, *I am here from India representing the grandparents and aunts and uncles on both sides of the family. We believe what she has done is morally wrong and she has started and will continue to make amends to her family and to the community. I pledge to serve as Godmother to her for the rest of my life.*

When she was done a gentleman walked to the front of the room to address the court. He shared that he owned a business that built single family green homes in the city where the petitioner wanted to relocate. He was prepared to offer her a job. He knew it might take some time before she would be given permission to move, and he was willing to allow her to work remotely until a move could happen.

Tears were streaming down my face as my former volunteer stood up to speak. His first words were, *this has been a journey of learning about unconditional love.* In that moment, these words threw me into my own journey in a way I have never felt before. That's the moment, those are the words that changed me forever. I didn't know how yet. I just knew I was different. He went on to say that for the past seven and a half years he and his sister have flown into town and driven 40 minutes each way for a three-hour visit every month. He told the judge that he had hoped for the day that he and his sisters could go shopping together and could eat a meal together. He then said something to the judge that I thought was remarkable. *Whether or not you release my sister today, that day would still come, either now or in two-and-a-half years, but I'm asking you to please release my sister.*

At this point I am sitting on the bench sobbing. The unfolding of this case in front of me cracked something open deep inside that I think was slammed shut the last time I sat in this courthouse. I was not the only one crying. There were tears flowing throughout the courtroom. His words about hope and forgiveness for his sister and the surrender I felt from him for whatever was to come in that next moment changed me.

His sister spoke and expressed remorse for taking her mother's life—she said that she learned early on in prison that talk was cheap. All she could do is use her life to make amends for what she had done. Then she thanked the judge for his willingness to hear her. The prosecutor stood up and said, *It was nice that all of these people showed up but where were they when she killed her mother—that our system isn't just about rehabilitation but about punishment as well and that Anne could have gotten twenty to life, but she entered into a plea bargain for five to ten years and she should have to complete the whole ten-year sentence.* She reminded the judge that he has never let anyone off early on a plea bargain and that he needed to be consistent in his ruling. It just so happens that the judge was retiring that Friday and decided to sign her release for the next day.

I didn't know I was going to die again that day, but I went into that courtroom as one person and walked out as someone different. I didn't quite understand just how much my life had and would change. It would take another couple of weeks for things to fully unfold, for things to fully crack open.

About a month after the courtroom experience, I was driving home from my morning workout at the gym. It was 6 a.m. as I drove up to the house. I sat in the van in my driveway for a couple of minutes and then I started feeling what it felt like to be in that courtroom years ago with my mother and my stepfather. Feelings rushed through me—feelings that until then, I had never really felt. I wasn't strong enough when it happened, so I just stored the pain in my body and now I needed to flush it out. As I sat in my van, this grief started pouring out of me. The dam that had held it for all these years just broke. The final blow to its foundation had happened just a month before in that courtroom with my former youth volunteer and his family. That was the beginning of the end. Up until then there was a part of me that didn't realize I had survived it. I had been carrying this trauma around with me, in me, for all this time. I thought it was normal. It had become a part of the lens through which I viewed the world. But now I was finally strong enough to let it flow out of me. I was finally strong enough to feel it and let it go. I have said since then—that was the day I grew up.

Someone once described *disassociation*—a detachment from reality—as a use of spirituality to hide within ourselves. And healing was the ability to bring the spirituality that we found inside ourselves out into the daylight. We need to find in our spirituality the strength and courage to face our lives as they are and to heal from disassociation.

I believe we are spiritual beings having a human experience and are co-creators of everything in our lives. We call up these experiences to grow our souls. Often when I say this people will think I am blaming victims for the things that happen to them. But that is not what I am doing. We often confuse shame, blame, and guilt with responsibility. We think that shame, blame, and guilt are emotions, but they are where we go to hide from emotions. When I hear these emotions expressed in healing circles, I'll ask, *What are you trying not to feel?* Often, it's just deep grief and sadness. We embrace shame, blame, and guilt so that we don't have to take responsibility. Responsibility simply means the ability to respond.

Trauma can make us feel like the divine has left us. It can push us to believe that now we are solely responsible for our own survival. But it's not true. The trauma lies to us. We think in those traumatic moments we were alone. It may be true that in those moments we were by ourselves, but we are never ever truly alone. We live with this myth of independence, but we are all always dependent because we breathe the same air, drink the same water, and walk on the same earth as the Spirit of our ancestors. We are dependent on each other and those who came before. I believe that the myth of independence is a trauma response. It comes from the belief that the Divine abandoned us. When we understand that we are dependent on each other, then we can ask what kind of dependence do we share? Is it co-dependence or is it interdependence? If it is rooted in scarcity and fear, it is co-dependence. If it is rooted in love and abundance, it is interdependence. But it's always dependence. Acknowledging this interdependence can provide us with guidance to secure our own healing as well as pave the way for the healing of others.

Most of the systems that we encounter as victims of sexual violence compound the violence. If system service providers are emotionally intelligent enough to offer emotional healing, it usually does not include spiritual healing. Emotional healing deals with the ego, while spiritual healing deals with the soul. Undoubtedly, the healing journey is very difficult and filled with many obstacles. The journey requires us to face ourselves and those who have harmed us in many ways that are painful. It requires us to be open to learning how to forgive, not for the perpetrator, but for ourselves, for our ancestors, and for our children. We are not often told that every wound has a gift to offer us. We are not told that we only get access to that gift by being willing to sit with our pain, feel our grief, and release all the emotions that are connected to that wound. We do not know that the universe is assisting us and will send earthly angels to help us move forward on our road to recovery. If we are open to receiving this help, we will see it. This step takes courage. Unfortunately, we often wait to feel courageous before we take steps toward healing in our journey. But the problem with that is that courage is not a feeling. Courage is a choice and an action. The feeling that accompanies courage is fear. We must embrace the fear, choose to act courageously, and begin the deep healing that is necessary.

The beginning of the word courage, *cou*, comes from the French word *coeur* meaning heart. The second part of the word is rage. Courage = Heart + Rage. Anger is personal while rage is communal. When we choose to act courageously, we move from our personal fear into a collective truth. And in this process, we honor the divine and find our true freedom.

Notes

1 James Finley, "Finding Refuge in the Interior Space with James Finley." Podcast, https://open.spotify.com/episode/4QGLC56flmiGnnqsL4w5Uw?si=iQ0cYdllSLO5a1x54bMmbQ&nd=1.
2 Ibid.

Chapter 8

Ancestral Releasing of Trauma Through Ritual

Sandra Saucedo

Historically, women have been at the center of power in Indigenous cultures like the Aymara.[1] The Aymara healers reunify (via soul-retrieval) the *ajayu* (soul) with the biological body through ceremonial practices, plant medicine, dream walking, astral work, as well as through death and rebirth rituals. The Aymara embrace a concept called *susto* (fright) where through a traumatic experience part of the soul leaves the body.[2] Aymara healers do not have names for diseases; instead, they describe their means of healing the soul to restore balance, because all sicknesses start in the spiritual body, which are then manifested in the other four bodies: mental, emotional, and sexual bodies that exist within in our biological bodies. Their practices have been developed through millennia to help people cope with the many traumas we must deal with in our life journeys, starting with birth.

When traumatic experiences happen to us, part of that energy, the traumatized part, leaves our body. However, the detached part of the soul—although missing from our selves—is not lost forever, but is stored by our loving Pacha Mama (Mother Earth)[3] to be reunited with the soul when our being is ready to face and heal from the traumatic event/s. Pacha Mama is the giver of life and the main source of healing for all earthlings, and Latina women have been instrumental in the healing of their families and communities by relying on both their nature-based inner spiritual connection and ancestral medicine. I believe the driving force for their courage and determination to leave their previous lives and venture to an alien land is their spirit. It is their spiritual essence, which in part is sexual, that helps sustain and nourish their being to transform fear into opportunity. The Aymara culture values the spiritual connection women have to the divine through all their senses, including their sexuality. After all, it is through our sexuality that women can bring spiritual beings into this world. To the Aymara, sexuality was sacred until colonizers used rape as a weapon that caused women's connection to their spirituality to be severed. That is one of the many ways that colonization created *soul loss* among people of Indigenous origins that has resulted in a cultural amnesia of shamanic and Indigenous relationships to self. But not all was lost. Women continue to be spiritually connected to Pacha Mama as the mothers of humanity and the keepers of ancestral knowledge to ensure the continuation of our cultures.

Natural disasters and socio-political problems have destabilized most Latin American countries, which has forced many women to migrate. Women have been central in the movement of populations across borders all over the world, but women often find themselves heading to the United States to start a new life. María Pilar Aquino observed that at the end of the twentieth century, the four most prominent characteristics of the global reality, particularly for women, were an increasing growth of poverty, inequality, social exclusion, and social insecurity.[4] These realities are not properly dealt with by the U.S. healthcare system that treats displaced populations on a charity-based program that neglects the soul loss, among other losses, that most immigrants experience.

The distrust Latinas have for the health services of the United States is well-founded with experiments that affect the continuation of our species as a culture. Experiments on female sterilization methods have been used on Puerto Ricans and other women of color as a practice that was legitimized not only in the United States, but throughout Latin America.[5]

Consequently, Latinas may not seek help for medical or mental conditions due in part to fear of becoming human test subjects for U.S. doctors. Immigrant women often look for alternative modes of assistance that include shamanic Indigenous practices. They seek assistance within the various religious groups that also deliver services like childcare, English as a second language classes, lawyer referrals, and a place where they might feel safe.

To understand the Latina experience, it is critical to look at the split that occurred between their spiritual and sexual selves due to colonization and Western patriarchy that was forced upon them. The spiritual history of Latinas includes the gender norms of colonizers and their legacy of patriarchy that informs the frame of mind with which Latinas grow up and by which they are influenced. Because they held their culture superior to Indigenous cultures, colonizers did not care to learn from the Indigenous people whom they invaded, and a clash of cultures was the result.

Differing gender ideologies is an example of the colonizers' clash with Indigenous peoples. It was shocking to the colonizers to see that Indigenous peoples revered women and gender-fluid men as sacred healers, priestesses, and oracles, as central to their spiritual and everyday life.[6] Today, Indigenous practices are central in the empowerment of gender-fluid people who, with proper training, can be the keepers of the spiritual life of their community. Colonizers forced patriarchal values upon those colonized, and that gave rise to different forms of male chauvinism, and thus male entitlement ensured the power to rule women and gender-fluid people as if ordained by god, for the colonizers believed they were on a mission from their god to spread their Christianity and ideologies, and eradicate *herejes* (heretics).

In addition, the colonizers idealized men who showed lack of emotions, increased aggressiveness, jealousy, and fearlessness, and those who consumed large amounts of alcohol without getting drunk; they are known as *machos* (Spanish for male, in the animal kingdom).[7] Maria G. Murguia says machismo is believed to be a common view of male behavior that started at the time of the conquest.[8] It is assumed that all machos are heterosexual, have a stronger sexual drive than females, are arrogant, and believe in their superiority over women in interpersonal relationships.[9] Another characterization of machos is that these males have unquestioned authority in the family to uphold family pride and honor; the macho man works outside the home to provide for his family, and by doing all these duties he deserves the respect and obedience of his family.[10]

Marianismo is a term coined by Evelyn P. Stevens in 1973. With roots in Italy, this term attempts to describe and summarize the perceived positive attributes of the Virgin Mary. Under the constraints of Catholic patriarchal colonization, Latin cultures developed alternate ways to view women relegated to a lower status. This philosophy refers to women as semi-divine, morally superior, and spiritually stronger than men. The marianismo female known as *mariana* is patient towards the imperfect nature of men, displays abnegation and submissiveness to men's demands, and is perpetually patient and sad as a result of man's sinful behavior.[11] The semi divine attribute is only used so women will see men as childlike creatures who need forgiveness and rearing to help them advance into heaven, since women are taught to believe the road to heaven is more difficult for men than for women, and even impossible to traverse successfully without the intercession of women on men's behalf.[12] *Hembrismo* is a term coined by Maria Elvira Bermudez in 1995 to describe the artificial amplification of the characteristics ordinarily considered as feminine: weakness, passive attitude towards men, inertia at the infidelity of their partners, and the subsequent abnegation that is expressed through loud crying and talking about her sacrificing behavior to uphold the family.[13] Hembrismo also connotes an animal strength to defend her home (as a lioness defending her cubs); the hembrismo woman also shows perseverance, flexibility, and survival ability in order to help her family, even at the expense of her own well-being.[14]

The machismo, marianismo, and hembrismo stereotypes continue in new forms and provide the foundation for all patriarchal cultures, not just Latina cultures. Latina scholars, theologians, and activists agree that along with patriarchal values, new forms of colonization of minorities continue in the United States. Jeanette Rodriguez, a scholar of Mexican American women, describes the struggle she faced being raised within a cultural and religious context that never taught Mexican American literature, history, customs, native traditions, or foods, but instead she was forced to study worldviews of European culture as the norm and as superior to her own heritage. She said, "sometimes the Latina in me doesn't understand or is in contradiction to the Anglo-educated side of me. Sometimes I feel like one cancels the other. And I feel like nothing."[15] This sentiment is shared by many Latina women raised in the United States and is at the "root of their psycho-social religious worldview, their role in the family, and [is a result of] the impact of acculturation."[16] Acculturation, which Rodriguez explains is the forced teachings of the dominant culture onto minorities,[17] is one way colonization continues in the United States.

Roberto Segundo Goizueta notes that the most devastating consequence of Western rationalism is the declaration of symbolic ritual, narrative, metaphor, poetry, music, and the arts of minorities as "unacademic and unscholarly."[18] Therefore, as Nancy Pineda-Madrid states, in the late nineteenth and early twentieth centuries, New Mexican writers like Nina Otero-Warren chronicled the staggering loss of culture, language, land, livelihood, and a painful awareness of the physical and institutionalized violence against the Spanish, the Mexican, and the Indio.[19] As a result, the dominant culture's forcing native peoples' histories and achievements to be invisible has caused a sense of inferiority among minorities and a false sense of pride among the dominant culture. That ancestral invisibility of the achievements of Latina cultures, as well as the rape of Indigenous women and the traumas of the many perilous journeys to migrate has caused a generational soul loss in the Latina culture of the United States that is rarely taken into consideration when dealing with the mental, spiritual, sexual, and biological health of Latinas.

In response to the spiritual loss of Indigenous and immigrant populations, Latina scholars like Ada Maria Isasi-Diaz developed Mujerista Theology (womanist theology) as "a liberative praxis of reflective action that has as its goal liberation for all Latina women around the world."[20] Isasi-Diaz's studies on Hispanic theology include the Bible, oral traditions, and the Indigenous teachings from a Christian perspective that reflect the many cultures of which the Americas are comprised. However, Latina culture is syncretic with shamanic practices often in conflict with Catholic teachings that are daily practiced along their religious beliefs without causing dissent.

Isasi-Diaz realized it was through *lo cotidiano* (everyday living) that Latinas experience the divine in their lives. Isasi-Diaz notes lo cotidiano "has been belittled and scorned, often related to the private sphere, to that sphere of life assigned to women precisely because it is considered unimportant."[21] However, it is through everyday living that immigrants heal the various traumas women face before migrating, during migration, and after migration while living at the margins of the dominant society. It is by the "coming together of peoples, with no one being excluded and at the expense of no one"[22] that displaced populations help each other reconcile their past with their present to create a new life for themselves and their families. This reconciliation must begin from deep inside to reconcile the colonizer and shaman within.[23]

We must "affirm a plurality and embrace ambiguity, something those of us who live at the margins know much about."[24] These margins force Latinas to strive to remember their spiritual wholeness, while keeping their families safe from harm and reminding them of their glorious past because their offspring will not hear about it in the schools of the dominant class. Authors like Sandra Cisneros, in her book *The House on Mango Street*[25] (which has been banned in some U.S. schools[26]), tells the story of Esperanza Cordero who is the daughter of an immigrant father and a Latina woman. Esperanza moves to a Latino neighborhood where many young girls her age deal with death, rape, work, and taking care of their families long before they are old enough to reasonably take on these harsh realities. Cisneros, through Esperanza, depicts the thousands of young immigrant girls or daughters of immigrants who are burdened with the responsibility of helping raise younger siblings while their parents work. Cisneros provides a pathway forward for Esperanza by connecting her with her ancestral spiritual beings who remind her she is not alone and to trust her to change her life.

Latino culture has an important Indigenous foundation and a connection to Pacha Mama through ancestral teachings—like animism, herbal, elemental, and ancestral spirit guides—that are oral in nature. In our native lands we have our elders to pass on this wisdom, but immigrants living in the United States may not have those elders to teach children their shamanic past, and books could help fill that void. In 2009, the superintendent of Orestimba High School (Newman, California) banned the book *Bless Me, Ultima* from the school's English classes after parents complained of profane and anti-Catholic themes.[27] In *Bless Me, Ultima*, Rudolfo Anaya narrates the story of a boy, Antonio, and the teachings he receives from an old healer-teacher, Ultima. The story talks about the conflicts Indigenous peoples have with Catholic teachings, and the importance of understanding the nature of Indigenous peoples' connection to the land and self-healing. She was the Ultima (last one) who could teach him about the ways of the *curandera* of herbs, divination, animism (totems or *nahuals*), and to live in harmony with the spirit world by learning to trust his own ancestral wisdom to lead his people on a pathway to healing.[28]

Anaya and Cisneros remind us that Catholic teachings negate shamanic teachings like animism, herbal, elemental, and ancestor spirit guides by deeming them a sin. Yet those teachings are deeply rooted in the people who look for herbal remedies and spiritual helpers to heal the five basic bodies that we are all comprised of: our mental, emotional, spiritual, and sexual bodies each manifest in our biological body that strives to live in harmonic balance. The mental body needs to grow constantly by reading, writing, and creating. The emotional body needs to mature without fear, shame, or self-sabotage. The spiritual body is eternal and knows more than our conscious mind is aware of; therefore, meditating and being in nature are the best ways to remember what spirit knows innately—that we are divine. The sexual body of most women must be healed from ancestral and other traumas to be free to express itself through various ways without hurting self or others. The biological body is where all the other bodies and senses manifest; therefore, getting to know how our body reveals pain, pleasure, or joy is important to living a healthy integral life. A constant evaluation of each of the bodies is needed to keep growing and to allow our evolution to continue without repression, guilt, shame, or self-sabotage.

In this tradition, our five basic bodies strive to live in harmony because we are innate healers. We can heal from a scrape, surgery, a broken heart, or self-abandonment because we can regenerate cells, thoughts, and habits *with the proper training*. A healer must spark the innate healer within others utilizing practices of meditation, gratitude, self-approval, and self-motivation, to develop genuine self-love. Therefore, it is important to rescue and preserve oral teachings in books, films, videos, and other media, to reclaim our ancestral teachings to avoid losing them forever. Shamanic teachings can help us come to terms with our history, heal our past, and reclaim our Indigenous, animistic, and earth-based teachings so the shaman within can emerge anew—complex, resolved, united, and ready to forge a new way of life in integrity.

Novels like Alice Walker's *The Color Purple* remind us of the many women who have healed sexual trauma by calling on their innate divinity which in turn helps them find the courage and self-worth to live a life where their sexuality is an important part of their being. Celie, a fourteen-year-old girl was raped by her stepfather and gives birth to two children who are taken away from her at birth. Celie, at first, finds an outlet for her sorrow in writing letters to God: "I have always been a good girl. Maybe you can give me a sign letting me know what is happening to me."[29] Celie is voicing for millions of young girls the question of not knowing why horrible things happen to good people. We must remember that being raped by a stepfather is a common occurrence across nationalities and race. Celie represents the helplessness and invisibility of the victim of such families. After escaping her rapist, but being forced to marry a cruel man, Celie finds her courage and self-worth through the support and love of women, and particularly that of Shug. At first Shug treated Celie "like [she]was a servant,"[30] but being nursed back to health by Celie allowed Shug to become the first person to see Celie as a woman. One day Celie stops writing to God because "the God [she] was praying and writing to is a man,"[31] and the men she knew had brought her nothing but painful experiences. She feels her prayers are not heard, as she says: "if he ever listened to poor colored women the world would be a different place, I can tell you."[32] Yet it is Shug who reminds her that "man corrupt everything . . . he try to make you think he everywhere. Soon as you think he everywhere, you think he God. But he ain't."[33] Instead Shug shows Celie that God is love manifested in us and in everything around us, caressing her legs she shows her that God also created our sexuality to enjoy being loved, unlike rape. Celie asks if loving her is not a sin, Shug keeps "rubbing high up on [her] thigh"[34] telling her to "just relax, go with everything that's going, and praise God by liking what [she] likes."[35] She shows her lovingly that they are part of the "flowers, wind, water, a big rock,"[36] and the stars that shine above us. Being loved and finding pleasure in her sexuality liberates Celie's creativity to see herself somewhere else creating a new life for herself. Stories like this inspire women who have also been sexually traumatized to find self-love, respect, and to cultivate friendships that are a life support. This is particularly true for women who live in exile, away from their families and community.

Exile is not only a physical location; it can also be a soulless place within for people who suffer from soul loss. Soul loss can cause "identity confusion, depression, loss of self-esteem, internal racism, always feeling divided as if something inside is missing, and a questioning of one's purpose in the world."[37] Soul loss is a self-protecting mechanism that Spirit devised so children and people who are vulnerable could remove the parts that are traumatized until a time when the person is strong enough to reunite with the missing parts of her or his soul. Soul loss is healed via ceremonies, chants, dance, death, and rebirth rituals, and canceling contracts that we enter consciously or unconsciously at any time of our eternal spiritual life. The soul is a central component of our being, and anything we do in this life has an echo in our eternal life, which is why it is paramount to heal all the traumas of our being *when we are ready to face them* to then retrieve the healthy parts of ourselves.[38] We can heal in the present traumas that are recorded in our genes. Indigenous practices from all cultures help open doors for the incorporation of our missing parts through practices like soul-retrieval to help de-pathologize our understanding of how we approach the healing of such deep and vulnerable wounds to bring balance to our five bodies and humanity.

Women are half of the population and mothers of all of humanity. It is thanks to the sexuality of women that humanity exists and must be cherished, respected, and valued, mainly by women. Understanding the sexual connection women have to the brain, uterus, vulva, that in turn is connected to Spirit is vital. Women must learn how the sex organs are intimately connected to spirit through the nervous system, because it is through the energy created by our sexual expression that we get to experience the bliss of being love. This is how we know women's sexual organs are not for reproduction only; first and foremost, they are for women's pleasure, enjoyment, and to connect to the spirit world. Therefore, it is so important to heal sexual traumas and learn how our sexuality is manifested, for even though sexuality is part of being human, how it is manifested depends on our environment and cultural norms of machismo and marianismo that are linked to the religious contexts of sexuality.

We must take ownership of our sexuality and remember that when we get into a car, for example, the car does not drive us wherever it wants—we must drive it, clean it, maintain it, and choose who rides with us. If we do not take the responsibility to choose whose energy to welcome to be part of our energy, we might end up repeating old painful paradigms. Women must learn how our biology connects to our spirituality. It is through self-exploration and the development of our sexual expression that women achieve greater freedom to experience different forms of orgasms which can lead to experiencing a cosmic energetic flow so powerful that women can bring from the spiritual world beings to have a human experience, and which can help enter the spiritual world where the potential for self-healing, self-empowerment, and self-creation exists.

Patriarchal religions treat the sexuality of women as if it exists solely for the pleasure of men. In contrast, most shamanic practices hold women as equal and their sexuality as sacred. The Aymara culture, for example, does not believe there is a creator of any kind. Instead, the belief of a god and the sacred are a loving energy that is manifested in everything and everyone devoid of both heaven and hell. According to the Aymara, the cycles of life are never-ending, and the many different life-forms started with a cosmic wind that no one could hear or see, yet the energetic ripples continue indefinitely in a vibrational spiral that is not linear. Their philosophy of *Ayñi* (reciprocity) guides their lives, knowing their spiritual life is eternal; however, everything we do in this life has an echo in the evolution of our being. This way of being is very healthy, particularly to women who have had painful experiences due to men and patriarchal religions that condemn women to subservient roles away from places of power.

Despite their divergence from, and possible conflict with, Catholicism, Indigenous belief systems, like those of the animist Aymara, can provide support, from everyday practices—*lo cotidiano*—all the way to understandings of our expansive universe. Women since birth are in synchronicity with Pacha Mama, the moon, and the universe through menstruation, intuition, and healing. Consequently, we find the healing needed in practices that are nature-based. We can use matter from our hair to our breath to complete rituals of soul-retrieval, death, rebirth, and canceling contract practices to help us heal and reunite with all the lost parts of our self to lead a healthy life.

Women who seek healing find solace in nature and the support of other women who are a source of knowledge, kinship, and support. The Indigenous women Qnas Soñi of Bolivia have their hair braided by two other women who represent their past, present, and future. Braiding their hair is a joyful practice to remember their connection to Sirius A, B, C, in honor of their Sirius sisters as their ancestors. Hair is the continuation of our thoughts, memories, and a record of our daily living, and we can use hair rituals to let go of painful memories.

Other healing rituals include realignment with the cosmos. Twice a year, during solstices, in Tiwanaku (Bolivia), people from all over the world gather to recalibrate or reset their circadian rhythm also known as internal clocks. To the Aymara, solstices mark the change of seasons and by calibrating their pineal gland with the birth of the new sun, the locals align their being with the new season.

Other Aymaran spiritual practices for when one is going through an arduous challenge are to be in nature and reconnect with the Spirit. This ritual includes connecting with the mountains (Apus), or the spirit of the water (Uma), or the spirit of animals, and/or the spirit of the trees, rocks, crystals, and others (elementals). Nature is always ready to assist us in our search for answers, as well as spiritual allies to help traverse any difficulties. The animistic practices are linked with our animal spiritual guides. If you cannot concentrate and feel as if you are ethereal, you can connect to an Apu. Apus are great to help you let go of traumas because as long as you hold pain, anger, shame, or self-violence, you keep giving power to those who have hurt you. Letting go means being free of their energy because you deserve to be free of anything that does not help you be at peace, happy, and loving to yourself so you can be loving with others, for everything begins with us. We need to be loyal to our divinity, remembering that loyalty is a luxury that must be given in integrity and reciprocity.

If you cry without knowing why, you can connect with the energy of Uma by soaking in water either in a bathtub, ocean, creek, or under the shower or rain. When our eyes release the pain, frustration, and trauma of the soul, Uma helps us remember who we are in essence. Tears are healing. Allow your tears to flow and Uma will connect with your inner magic to spark the healing from within. Every day cells die so that new ones can emerge because death is a part of life, and as such we also go through many energetic deaths to be reborn anew. If you need to let part of you die, fill a bathtub with water and pour Epsom salts, white flowers without thorns, and take a long soothing bath. While soaking ask Uma, the salt, and the flowers to take that part of you that you no longer need. When you are ready, let go of that water, shower, and rinse with some honey to sweeten your new self. Uma will recycle that energy and remind us that the past is only a point of reference, not a life sentence.

If you need answers from Spirit, you could sit next to a tree, rest your back on the tree then connect your root energy to the roots of the tree. Press your head crown to the crown of the tree and ask your question, the tree will answer you with complete ideas as if you just came up with that answer. You may ask the energy of that tree to be with you from that moment on because trees are wise ancient souls. Hug a tree and feel its energy connect to your heart to free yourself from judgment, fear, shame, hatred, rage, and forgive yourself for allowing your spirit to forget your divinity.

Whatever happened to you is not your fault; therefore, you have the right to give that pain, rage, shame, and anything that does not allow you to be Love, back to those who have hurt you. You can also write a letter to them and let them know everything you feel and that they no longer have a hold on you and then burn it. You can do this as many times as you need, until one day you no longer carry your pain. You can liberate yourself.

I urge you to learn from the elemental energy of the plants to help yourself because they can heal anything. We must remember to look for allies in nature, particularly if you do not trust the pharmaceutical and medical fields. It is only fair to reciprocate and not just take. We must reciprocate our spiritual guides and allies by sharing seeds, fruits, and if you do not have anything, then offer your heartfelt thanks and a lock of your hair.

It is important to embody our spirituality knowing we are perfectly imperfect, to not negate our beautiful humanity. Many religions expect humans to strive to be like angels and regard their humanity as faulty, while negating their feelings and desires. However, humans need to understand that perfection is not needed to be a source of healing, sisterhood, and love. Being imperfect helps us to develop our divinity that is free of self-servitude, self-sacrifice, judgment, and self-violence. Being human helps us to love ourselves with all our faults, so we can also love others by accepting their journey as their own. We must learn to clean our lives from the toxic behaviors we inherit, as well as from those who want to use us for their benefit at the expense of our mental, emotional, spiritual, sexual, or biological self. We are here to remember our divinity and to give our best in integrity to our divinity and not to please, rescue, or control others.

Validation of the spiritual and sexual aspects of immigrant Latinas' lives through Indigenous cultural practices rooted in earth-based wisdom provides the support needed to heal from the many colonialist, patriarchal traumas. Spiritual activism that includes Indigenous practices calls us to offer cross-group dialogue among women of all walks of life to heal from soul loss that is a risk factor for depression, self-alienation, and sexual repression. This allows all members of our society to witness our sorrow, celebrate our triumphs, and heal our wounds to rekindle our creative energies to resurrect our dreams of becoming once again the healers we have always been—incognito.

Notes

1 The Aymara are the Indigenous people from Tiwanaku, Bolivia, who hold women not only as equal but as sacred, because god is the energy of creation, and as such women are closer to the divine. The Aymara do not believe they were created by anyone because everything started with a cosmic wind that was inaudible and invisible to human senses, yet the vibration of that wind continues to create from the dark matter. The Tiwanaku culture had many languages from Quellca (cuneiform and hieroglyph), a knot system based on zero and one (chusu and maya) similar to the abacus called Quipu, and various spoken languages, and the one that survived colonization is Aymara. Women are represented like chusu (0) because she is the ovum of creation and also the key to the infinite. In Aymara, all numbers start from left to right, so the numeric system starts with chusu and ends in chusu, as chusu is the source to infinite numbers.
2 I define soul as the energetic flow or spirit that brings all of existence into self-expression. It is the presence of awareness that imparts a sense of identity, connection, and purpose to and within the universe. It is the fundamental essence of who we are—what makes us who we are and not someone else (there are no *things* or *objects* within animistic worldviews, only interconnected *beings*). Soul is the energy through which our identity is expressed to the Other, and also the means by which the soul-expression of the Other may be seen and understood in its interconnected Otherness. [Sandra Saucedo, *A Narrative Inquiry of the Spiritual and Sexual Metamorphosis of Latina Women Through Migration to the United States* (PhD diss., California Institute of Integral Studies, San Francisco, 2019) abstract in ProQuest (2019): 26.]
3 Earth, Pacha, is not just a mother, which is why it is not one word. She is barren like the desserts, fierce like a tsunami, deadly as a volcano, and fecund as the forests.
4 María Pilar Aquino, "Latina Feminist Theology: Central Features" in *A Reader in Latina Feminist Theology: Religion and Justice*, ed. María Pilar Aquino, Daisy L. Machado, and Jeannette Rodriguez (Austin: University of Texas Press, 2002), 140.

5 J. Mayone Stycos, "Sterilization in Latin America: Its Past and Future." *International Family Planning Perspectives*, Vol. 10, No 2 (June 1984); 58–64.
6 Serena Nanda, *Gender Diversity: Crosscultural Variations*, 2nd ed., "Multiple Genders Among North American Indians," (Long Grove, IL: Waveland Press, 2014), 11.
7 Maria G. Murguia, "Machismo, Marianismo, and Hembrismo, and Their Relationship to Acculturation as Predictors of Psychological Well-being in a Mexican and Chicano Population" (PhD diss., University of Wisconsin-Madison, 2001) abstract in *Dissertation Abstracts International*, 62–11 (2001): 6.
8 Ibid., 8.
9 Ibid., 7.
10 Ibid., 9.
11 Ibid., 12.
12 Ibid., 13.
13 Ibid., 11.
14 Ibid., 11.
15 Jeannette Rodriguez, *Our Lady of Guadalupe: Faith and Empowerment Among Mexican-American Women* (Chicago: University of Chicago Press, 1994), 3.
16 Ibid., 3.
17 Ibid., 3.
18 Roberto Segundo Goizueta as cited by Michelle A. González, "Seeing Beauty within Torment: Sor Juana Ines de la Cruz and the Baroque in New Spain" in *A Reader in Latina Feminist Theology: Religion and Justice*, 23.
19 Nancy Pineda-Madrid, "Latinas Writing Theology at the Threshold of the 21st Century" in Women-Centered Theologies for the 21st Century, Rosemary Radford Ruether, ed. (Minneapolis: Fortress, 2007), 57.
20 Ada María Isasi-Diaz, *Mujerista Theology: A Theology for the Twenty-First Century* (Maryknoll, NY: Orbis Books, 1996), 2.
21 Ibid., 68.
22 Ibid., 66.
23 In response to this reality, I developed Reconciliatory methodology to help us come to terms with hundreds of years of colonization that cannot be undone, but we can learn from the mistakes of the past to forge a new life for ourselves and our communities. This methodology helps us to remember that no liberation of the soul can happen at the expense of another. When we reconcile our past, we embrace the liberation of our soul, which challenges us to keep growing, while healing in the present to embrace our differences as women and men. Men are mirrors of ourselves (and we of them), and reconciling our past helps us to build a new life for all our cultures without allowing any one culture to dominate to the detriment of the others.
24 Ibid., 81.
25 Sandra Cisneros, *The House on Mango Street* (New York: Vintage Books, first published by Arte Publico Press, 1984).
26 Maya L. Kapoor, "12 Books Expelled from Tucson Schools" *High Country News*, June 17, 2017, 79. www.hcn.org/articles/education-tucsons-mexican-american-studies-ban-goes-back-to-court.
27 Marshall University Libraries, "Banned Books 2009: *Bless Me, Ultima*". www.marshall.edu/library/bannedbooks/bless-me-ultima/.
28 Rudolfo Anaya, *Bless Me, Ultima* (New York: Warner Books, 1994), 48.
29 Alice Walker, *The Color Purple* (New York: Harcourt Brace Jovanovich, 1982), 2.

30 Ibid., 122.
31 Ibid., 122.
32 Ibid., 192.
33 Ibid., 197.
34 Ibid., 196.
35 Ibid., 196.
36 Ibid., 197.
37 Saucedo, 26.
38 Soul-retrieval can be done in dream work, astral flight, plant medicine, and other ways.

Bibliography

Anaya, Rudolfo. *Bless Me, Ultima*. New York: Warner Books, 1994.

Cisneros, Sandra. *The House on Mango Street*. New York: Vintage Books, 1984.

Goizueta, Roberto Segundo as cited by Michelle A. González. "Seeing Beauty within Torment: Sor Juana Ines de la Cruz and the Baroque in New Spain." In *A Reader in Latina Feminist Theology: Religion and Justice*. Edited by Maria Pilar Aquino, Daisy L. Machado, and Jeannette Rodriguez. Austin: University of Texas Press, 2002.

Isasi-Diaz, Ada María. *Mujerista Theology: A Theology for the Twenty-First Century*. Maryknoll, NY: Orbis Books, 1996.

Kapoor, Maya L. "12 Books Expelled from Tucson Schools." In *High Country News*, June 17, 2017. www.hcn.org/articles/education-tucsons-mexican-american-studies-ban-goes-back-to-court.

Marshall University Libraries. "Banned Books: *Bless Me, Ultima*." Last updated July 18, 2014. www.marshall.edu/library/bannedbooks/bless-me-ultima/.

Murguia, Maria G. "Machismo, Marianismo, and Hembrismo, and Their Relationship to Acculturation as Predictors of Psychological Well-being in a Mexican and Chicano Population." PhD diss., University of Wisconsin-Madison, 2001. Abstract in *Dissertation Abstracts International* (2001): 62–11B.

Nanda, Serena. "Multiple Genders Among North American Indians." In *Gender Diversity: Crosscultural Variations*, 2nd ed. Long Grove, IL: Waveland Press, 2014.

Pilar Aquino, María. "Latina Feminist Theology: Central Features." In *A Reader in Latina Feminist Theology: Religion and Justice*. Edited by María Pilar Aquino, Daisy L. Machado, and Jeannette Rodriguez. Austin: University of Texas Press, 2002.

Pineda-Madrid, Nancy. "Latinas Writing Theology at the Threshold of the Twenty-First Century." In *Women-Centered Theologies for the 21st Century*. Edited by Rosemary Radford Ruether. Minneapolis: Fortress, 2007.

Rodriguez, Jeannette. *Our Lady of Guadalupe: Faith and Empowerment Among Mexican-American Women*. Chicago: University of Chicago Press, 1994.

Saucedo, Sandra. *A Narrative Inquiry of the Spiritual and Sexual Metamorphosis of Latina Women Through Migration to the United States*. PhD diss., California Institute of Integral Studies, San Francisco, 2019. Abstract in ProQuest (2019).

Scrimshaw, S. C. "The Demand for Female Sterilization in Spanish Harlem: Experiences of Puerto Ricans in New York." Paper presented at the 69th annual meeting of the American Anthropological Association, San Diego, November 1970. www.popline.org/node/469137.

Stycos, J. Mayone. "Sterilization in Latin America: Its Past and Future." *International Family Planning Perspectives*, Vol. 10, No 2 (June 1984): 58–64.

Walker, Alice. *The Color Purple*. New York: Harcourt Brace Jovanovich, 1982.

Chapter 9

Healing with Maa

A Shakti Bhaktic Approach

Rachelle Elizabeth

Healing with Maa: A Shakti Bhaktic Approach to Healing

I understand. These words echoed resoundingly in my mind during an experience of *darshan*, in which the awakened eyes of Mahadevi, or the Great Goddess, meet the eyes of the practitioner.[1] In this moment, I felt heard, seen, and believed by the Divine Mother, initiating a new approach to my own healing and the exploration of the ways in which an intimately devotional relationship with the Divine Mother facilitates a unique opportunity for healing after trauma. While the psychological impact of devotional or *bhaktic* worship, especially in relation to trauma, has not been fully explored, my own practice, experience, and study have made a substantially pivotal impact on my own experience as a survivor. In this chapter, I speak from the situatedness of a survivor and scholar-practitioner of Shakti Bhakti in order to illustrate three essential aspects of this tradition that supports the healing process and, through dialogue, may contribute to a greater understanding of the role of spirituality in this particular type of healing.

The Shakti Bhakti tradition approaches devotion through the paradigm of the mother-child relationship, wherein the suffering of the bhakta (devotee/child) may be received with utmost patience, love, and support, even in the context of our least patient and loving moments. First, this chapter explores the theology of identification, wherein the bhakta sees themselves reflected in the Divine and comes to identify those aspects within themselves, supporting the bhakta's need to recover a sense of power and selfhood. Second, the Shakti Bhakti tradition is rooted in tantric theology,[2] which approaches the body as the field of experience, especially for identification, facilitating a deep sense of bodily connection and empowerment. Third, this chapter explores devotional expressions of suffering as a means through which to cultivate identification more truly via authentic connection with the Divine Mother. Finally, I turn to interfaith dialogue as the vehicle through which this chapter constitutes a contribution toward the shared goal of supporting survivors while also honoring the unique heritage of this tradition.

Importantly, the Shakti Bhakti tradition is not systematized, and as such there are myriad ways it can be practiced and experienced by devotees depending on their context, needs, and personal relationship with the Divine Mother. Yet, all are strongly rooted in the theology, philosophy, and aesthetics of the Indian subcontinent, and so also share porous boundaries with other Hindu traditions. This chapter, therefore, serves to illustrate one such perspective and leaves room for the diversity inherent to this tradition while not presenting a monolith that might limit or contest the experiences of other devotees.

A Note on Dialogue

The theology of identification is alive beyond the borders of Hindu traditions. Whenever someone finds inspiration in the strength, power, and beauty of the Great Goddess in any of Her forms, they are experiencing a sort of identification. Unfortunately, this often results in the misappropriation of Hindu themes and practices that generally insult, rather than respect, that heritage through practices like *drunk yoga* or oversimplified tantric sex retreats. Such misappropriation generally ignores the power imbalance present, as those misappropriating fail to examine their situatedness as inheritors of the colonial legacy that treated the bodies, land, and philosophies of India as products to be *mined* while simultaneously dehumanizing the lived heritage from which those philosophies come. To negate this situatedness is akin to self-abandonment, I argue, as it further disconnects the inheritors of that legacy from this history, from which they can learn in order to prevent its repetition. This is especially true in the American context, as the symbols, rituals, and practices of the historically colonized, including Indigenous peoples, are often treated as commodities resulting in perpetuated oppression and the erasure of those peoples and their heritages.

An intersectional book such as this one, may be thought of as a sort of interfaith dialogue. It is from dialogue that I suggest a rubric of ethical engagement may be found, through which we may engage each other's traditions toward the shared goal of supporting survivors of sexual trauma. For example, concepts like meditation and divine-human love are not unique to Hindu traditions, but practices like *nyasa* are and should not be taken out of the theology they are purposefully embedded in. Through dialogue, we can communicate about that which inspires and confuses us, explore, experience together, and cultivate a deeper interpersonal connection that guides us toward the realization that our diversity is a divine gift, because diversity promotes creativity.

Interfaith/interreligious dialogue assumes transformation and encourages critical and creative thinking. In order for dialogue to be fruitful, a few key tenets must be observed: humility, commitment, interconnection, hospitality, and empathy.[3] This framework provides an ethical means through which the tradition and practices described above may be explored by inspired individuals outside of this tradition. In humility we find the necessary openness to change, to fearlessly pursuing self-inquiry including one's motivations and expectations, and perhaps especially one's biases and prejudices. Commitment refers to the connection one has to their *home tradition*, which does not mean a commitment that results in inflexibility or exclusion. This is especially true given that it can be difficult to bring the fruits of dialogue to a home tradition that may be unwilling to explore or expand. The emphasis here is not on a duty to transform those who may be uninterested or unwilling, but instead on the "willingness to openly and humbly engage the larger tradition with the fruits of the dialogue."[4] When considering misappropriation, commitment may be understood as a refusal to abandon one's own background, highlighting the responsibility to engage it. Even those of us who might think of ourselves as converts cannot negate our heritage without negating an enormous part of ourselves, and so I argue that commitment here may be additionally interpreted as a commitment to engaging one's heritage and situatedness, even as they may embark on a new spiritual journey.

Interconnection speaks to the need to intentionally prioritize intersubjective engagement, meaning that when we dialogue, we are not approaching the *Other* like an object to be studied, but instead as a human being with a unique history and perspective. Further, interconnection lends itself to the shared human experience. This volume exists because the suffering felt by those it addresses does not reside in just one tradition or context; we share human experience that connects us. By being hospitable, we make room and hold space for the Other in their full authenticity. We open ourselves to their differences just as much as their similarities, and approached intersubjectively and with humility, understand those differences to be a necessary aspect of our connection even when they bring about difficult moments, such as a core ethical dispute. In such cases, dialogue is a tool through which we can courageously explore these differences and the ways they promote critical thinking and reflection. The goal of dialogue is not to create an amalgamation or to influence the Other, but to become transformed ourselves.

Finally, we both bring empathy to this encounter and facilitate empathy through it, connecting us as human beings in all our diverse wonder. When we are connected through empathy, we perceive the complexity at the heart of our shared problems and through our dialogue may approach them creatively and innovatively. Indeed, such complexity reasonably requires a practically infinite creativity, which humanity is certainly capable of. From my own Shakta perspective, we frequently underestimate humanity's capacity for innovation and creativity, especially on an individual level, qualities which reflect the Divine Mother's immanence.

Shakti Bhakti

A full review of the underlying theology and history of this tradition is far beyond the scope of this chapter, yet in order to move forward, it is first necessary to review some basic tenets of Shakti Bhakti. Before creation, the Ultimate Divine is comprehended as *nirguna Brahman*, the transcendental divine beyond human conceptions of time, space, and causation, or any aspect of material reality.[5] In this *nirguna* state, Brahman, The Absolute, has no attributes or personhood, and is sometimes described only as *Sat-Chit-Ananda*. Or, as the great eighth-century Hindu sage Shankaracharya explained, "Brahman is Eternal Existence, Absolute Knowledge and Infinite Bliss," all of which offer barely a glimpse into the true experience of the Ultimate Divine.[6] In sum, *shakti* is power, capability, or energy, ultimately referring to the infinite creative capacity of the Divine. Outside Shakta theology, *shakti*, as a feminine principle, refers to the feminine creative aspect of a *deva*, who is the *saktimat* or *holder of energy*. For example, Krishna's *shakti* is Radha, demonstrating that the *shakti* of a *deva*, masculine divine being, appears as his feminine counterpart, but they are not truly separate.[7] This is so because, ultimately *shakti* is identical with Brahman, demonstrating the Hindu principle of biunity. With a capital S, Shakti is envisioned as the Supreme Reality identical with Brahman, viewed through the lens of the feminine principle. For Shaktas, *Shakti* refers both to the *nirguna* Brahman as ultimate Being-Consciousness-Bliss, and *saguna* Brahman as the Divine Mother in any of Her incarnations, elucidated below.

The key foundational text of the Shakti Bhakti tradition is the *Devi Mahatmyam* (DM), a sixth-century text from the Markendeya Purana containing the crystallization of previously oral, colloquial, and philosophical traditions of the Great Goddess wherein Her power, love, and forms are illustrated. Other texts, such as various *tantras*[8] and the *Devi Gita*, and the *Shyama Sangeet*, a genre of bhaktic poetry and song hailing from Bengal, offer further clarification and expression while the tantric influence interwoven into the theology and praxis facilitates a deep sense of identification that shall be explored below. In her exceptional work *Offering Flowers, Feeding Skulls: Popular Goddess Worship in West Bengal*, June McDaniel illustrates the diverse array of this bhaktic expression. Of particular note here is her description of *emotional Shakti bhakti*, characterized by the intense love of the bhakta for their Mother that sometimes creates elation, as She is immanent throughout creation, and depression when separateness is more greatly perceived.[9]

This situates us in our present discussion and highlights a key feature of this tradition: the mother-child relationship requires some level of duality in which the child is understood to be separate from the mother, allowing for a relationship between the two. At the same time, the underlying theology is decidedly nondualistic, perceiving Shakti as both the transcendent Divine and immanent throughout creation as Her material manifestation, resulting in a valorization of material reality.[10] Through *sadhana*, praxis, that deeply connects one with the Divine Mother, the bhakta both enjoys the dualistic experience of maternal love while also releasing all that prevents them from realizing their absolute unity with Her, such as the attachments of one's ego. This identification creates a path to True Realization, partly through the cultivation of such qualities as compassion, justice, and knowledge harkening to a verse from the DM: "Oh queen of all, you protect all; having all for your very soul, you are said to support all . . . those who bow down in devotion to you, they become the refuge of all." (11.33)[11] In other words, sadhana that emphasizes identification, refers not to the identification of the Mother with one's ego, but to their True Self.

A key tool in this process is discernment, wherein one who is aligned with the values and principles of the tradition embarks on a continual journey of reflection and inquiry that helps to separate one from the false identities of the ego and unite them with their True Nature as Brahman. This requires the releasing of (negative) labels and limiting beliefs that prevent one from this knowledge, such as an overidentification with one's accomplishments or with one's victimization. This results in *moksha* or Unity with the Divine Mother, perhaps better understood as an uncovering of the unity already present by transcending and releasing all perception of separateness. The verse above implies that such Unity brings about the evolution of the bhakta, transforming them into a vehicle of the Mother's love and protection. However, the deepest meaning of such verses can only be truly understood when experienced. The "deepest meanings of [the DM] make themselves known only through direct experience" which can only come from within.[12] This is why the *Shyama Sangeet*, which includes the poetry of such notable bhakti saints as Ramprasad Sen (d. 1775) and Kamalakanta Bhattacharya (d. 1821), is considered somewhat canonical, as this poetry is the expression of such experience.

Tools and Practices Facilitating Healing

In this section, I review three key aspects of the Shakti Bhakti tradition that, in my experience, create a powerful foundation from which to approach healing. They are the theology of identification, the body as the field of experience, and the practice of *ninda bhakti*, or the bhakti of complaint.

The Theology of Identification

Many individuals, especially women and feminine-presenting people, have found the images of Hindu goddesses like Durga and Kali to be powerful inspiration. For the Shakti bhakta, this means of relating speaks to the theology of identification in which the bhakta seeks various ritual and devotional means through which to deeply identify with Shakti, often in a specific form such as Maa (Mother) Durga.[13] These forms constitute examples of *saguna Brahman*, referring to Brahman *with* qualities or form, effectively creating a relational bridge with the formless *nirguna*, without qualities, Brahman. In Shakta thought and praxis, the forms of the Goddess called upon generally come from the nine forms of the Goddess in the Bengali tradition or the South Indian Sri Vidya tradition wherein the Goddess has ten forms known as the Mahavidyas or Great Wisdoms, in addition to innumerable localized folk traditions. The form one identifies with usually speaks in some way to what the identification accomplishes, such as identifying the courage of Durga within oneself. This identification is not the identification of the ego, but the identification of the Mother as Brahman with one's True Self, which is also Brahman (demonstrating nonduality). Sadhana such as ritual engagement with the senses or sonic means such as mantra further identification toward the progressive goal of true Self Realization or *moksha*. It is identification that is the goal of such practices, rather than the pleasing of a deity or the seeking of blessings.[14]

This is an interesting approach since a relationship in which one cultivates their connection to the Divine internally, without centering it around the expectation of give-and-take, constitutes a relationship of unconditional love that is not dependent on such expectations. This highlights the implicit understanding that the bhakta need not earn the Mother's love, but rather explores all that prevents them from fully knowing and experiencing what is already there. In other words, we are already worthy of love by virtue of our existence alone and we have access to this love as it pervades the fabric of all being. It is our *belief* that we are unworthy that prevents us from accessing it. Identification is therefore a project of focusing within and not beyond oneself.

In my experience of *darshan* mentioned earlier, the words *I understand* created fertile ground for this identification. In that moment, there was no need to explain, justify, defend, or indeed, do anything other than simply be present in the moment—a moment in which the Divine Mother acknowledged everything I had fought for as well as the healing process still underway. The loss of selfhood and humanity that is often experienced in the aftermath of sexual trauma is immediately addressed here, as one identifies as not just fully human, but also inherently divine, worthy, and loved.

Often the theology of identification is considered through the bodies of child-bearing women, who in the carrying and birthing of new life reflect the Divine Mother's capacity for creation and nurturance of that creation. As this identification immediately associates such women with the sacred power of creation, women are uplifted as special incarnations of the Divine Mother. This sentiment is echoed throughout such texts as the *Kaulavali Tantra* and *Nila Tantra*, that both demand that "one should desert one's parents, guru, and even the deities before insulting a woman."[15] In other words, this identification is so strong that to insult a woman is to insult the Divine Mother, but it goes deeper than this. Tantra overall turns the common purity-pollution dichotomy found throughout Hindu traditions on its head, sometimes emphasizing the role of the traditionally impure through ritual in order to fully experience and realize Shakti's true immanence. In the DM, Shakti is identified with all women: "Oh Goddess, all that is knowable are your various distinctions, and all women in the world reflect your capacity entirely."[16] The physical nature of rituals and principles that honor not just a mythic femininity or principle, but the actual bodies of women, speaks to the belief that the Divine Mother is "least concealed" in the bodies of women, including in her physiological functions and bodily fluids, which in many Tantric sects are the "material manifestation of the power of the Goddess."[17]

Here, one may rightly ask how this might apply beyond the scope of a child-bearing woman, whose fluids and functions speak to fertility and birthing. It is important to remember that what is described above is often set against Brahmanical standards of purity and gendered norms that understand events like menstruation to be inherently impure. Yet from a Shakta perspective, to identify with Shakti is to see Her everywhere, including in traditionally impure roles and spaces, such as graveyards. Yet, identification can take us further than that. We may note above that the DM referred to a *reflection* of the Divine Mother, who is actually immanent in all. I suggest that this may be taken to mean that such identification does not imply that child-bearing women are more divine than others, but that this reflection brings our attention to an innate trait found throughout humanity—the ability to create. Indeed, birth is not the only way humans create something, as even in the writing of this chapter I may be thought of as *birthing* it. Further, birthing is followed by the nurturance of what has come into being toward its full becoming or realization. This leads to the understanding that what is reflected in the bodies of women capable of bearing children is *clearer*, but not necessarily more present, as the ability to bring something into being and nurture it appropriately is not specific to such women.

I refer to this as the *principle of nurturance*, wherein what is revealed is a core aspect of what it means to be human; to imagine, bring into being, and manifest, experience it fully, cultivate growth, and participate in evolution and involution as the overarching cycles of life. Understood in this way, identification begins with the bodies of child-bearing women but actually guides us toward the discovery of that quality within ourselves, in all bodies. This principle may then be approached as inspiration for exploring how that reflection might exist within each individual, allowing for the abundantly diverse ways in which that reflection may manifest as all humanity are unique expressions of the Divine Mother. Evidently, there is room here to explore identification beyond the idea of womanhood or femininity, as identification creates a path inward allowing one to explore their unique being as an expression of divinity rather than becoming dehumanized by narratives that argue the body of a trans woman, for example, is less capable of this reflection than others. Speaking directly to the suffering experienced in the aftermath of sexual trauma, a perspective rooted in Shakti Bhakti begins with the belief in one's inherent worth and potential, regardless of the actions of others.

In addition to roughly four thousand years of heritage, an interesting contemporary approach to exploring identification may be found in Kavitha M. Chinnaiyan's book *Shakti Rising: Embracing Shadow and Light on the Goddess Path to Wholeness*. Chinnaiyan's method begins with her own situatedness as a practitioner of Sri Vidya and includes offering illustrative summaries on the forms of the Great Goddess known as the Mahavidyas, mentioned above. These ten forms, including Chinnamasta, Bhairavi, and Tara, speak to different aspects of the Divine Mother, such as Her maternal love and ferocity against ignorance and injustice. Chinnaiyan offers the reader exercises for each form, inviting them to explore the reflection of that form within themselves. In her chapter on Tara, for example, Chinnaiyan guides the reader into a reflection of their own experiences relating to a sense of lack or self-deception.[18] In another, the reader explores Bhuvaneshwari's presence in our bodies and how we might closely examine the labels we apply to ourselves in order to see beyond them.[19] Such tools, relatively unique in the modern era, provide a means through which the practitioner may approach their own identification and reflection through multiple forms of the Divine Mother, each with a different lesson and opportunity for identification.

The Body as the Field of Experience

As the Shakti Bhakti tradition is one of world-embracing immanence, identification is not a matter of transcending the body, but of wholly engaging it. Like tantric practices that intentionally incorporate traditionally impure substances in order to emphasize the Mother's true nonduality, the body is engaged in order to experience identification in all creation. This is true in part because engaging the body, and by extension the world, guides the bhakta toward the full experience of their interconnectedness and the glorious diversity of the Mother in cycles of continual becoming. By beginning with a spiritually focused identification, the bhakta creates an encouraging foundation and can provide valuable support for the body work to come. As a survivor, to say the task of connecting with the body after sexual trauma is an understatement, especially as the body holds our trauma as explained by authors such as Bessel van der Kolk and Peter Levine.[20] Understanding our inherent divinity through immanence supports this work and identifying with the Divine Mother creates a sense of purpose rooted in a goal that exists beyond the task of recovery, helping one see a future that may elicit curiosity and hope.

In Tantra the body is the microcosm of the cosmic macrocosm, as demonstrated above in the way that some birth-giving bodies reflect the power of the Divine Mother that exists in all of us. "As the basis of individual identity, one who knows the truth of the body can know the truth of the universe."[21] The body is the link between the terrestrial and the cosmic where the "psycho-cosmic drama is enacted."[22] Tantra envisions the body as being composed of an assemblage of five *koshas* (sheaths—protective coverings) briefly described below. Rooted in the *Taittiriya Upanishad*, composed some three thousand years ago, these sheaths are briefly described thus:

1. *Annamaya Kosha*: "sheath composed of food," constituting our physical bodies.
2. *Pranamaya Kosha*: "sheath composed of life force," the energy field that connects the physical body and the mind.
3. *Manomaya Kosha*: "sheath composed of the mind," refers to the mind, *manas*, as the processor of sensory experience navigating the relationship between the externalization of our consciousness and the withdrawing into one's imagination.
4. *Vijnanamaya Kosha*: "sheath composed of intelligence," wherein the higher mind (*buddhi*) functions as the vehicle of discernment that helps facilitate certainty and faith.
5. *Anandamaya Kosha*: "sheath composed of bliss," referring not to the emotional experience of bliss but to the True Self that is Brahman.[23]

This way of approaching the body creates a useful structure through which one can perceive their experiences and the processing of them in alignment with specific goals, utilizing the body as a laboratory through which each of these sheaths may be engaged. With each sheath, we explore a new realm of our existence and examine the ways in which that existence interacts with other life-forms. Experience then is both a reference to the experience of the bhakta in relation to themselves and the experience of the bhakta in relation to the world that is the Mother, connecting internal identification and evolution to external ways of being and acting in the world. Our bodies constitute this sphere of connection, linking our inner self with the outer world.

From a bhaktic perspective, the experience of sexual trauma is a violent disruption of this connection. Identification then constitutes a beginning point for the repairing of this connection, aided by the understanding that the inherent divinity of the body cannot be obstructed or negated regardless of what it experiences. What becomes disrupted is, in fact, our knowledge of and connection with that truth.

Through our senses, we connect the immanent divinity of all creation to the inherent divinity of our True Selves. Likewise, through such sense perceptions we come to know the Divine Mother more clearly as She exists in the wild diversity of creation. This perception appears in approaches to eco-theology and social justice that emphasize connection and interdependence. A variety of means are employed, including visualization, meditation, ritual, music, and food that create opportunities for the intentional and focused engagement of one or more senses toward this goal.

The exercises briefly described below are some examples wherein focused visualization, gentle touching, breath, and mantra are variously engaged in order to deepen identification by connecting the internal (mind) and external (body) spheres, with special attention paid to how they might contribute to the healing of a survivor.

Trataka

Trataka is a meditation technique of which the main intention is to further expediate a deep sense of connectedness and divine immanence, or identification. In the Hatha Yoga Pradipika, a 15th century Sanskrit manual on hatha yoga, trataka is believed to aid in the healing of eye diseases and difficulties with focus, and is performed by gazing steadily at a small mark until the eyes are filled with tears.[24] Meaning to gaze steadily, trataka helps develop concentration and memory by holding a steady gaze directed at an image or element, such as the flame of a candle, a *yantra*[25], or a *murti*.[26] This constitutes the external or *bahir* trataka, in which the focus of meditation is outside oneself, and ultimately leads the aspirant to the *antar* or inner trataka, bringing the object of focus within oneself.[27] This focus also helps deepen identification since it naturally encourages a beyond-physical connection with the object of one's focus. In other words, for the survivor the trataka is a meditation in which they may focus on an object that speaks to them of their healing which, when turned inward, creates the opportunity to perceive and nurture those qualities within themselves.

Nyasa

Nyasa (placing) is a ritual technique in which the fingertips and palms of the right hand are placed on various bodily sensory awareness zones in company with a mantra, allowing the power of the mantra to resonate with the body of the devotee.[28] While a mantra is commonly thought to be the repetition of a word or phrase, this is only partly correct. Mantras is a "chant formula composed of words and syllables in the Sanskrit language."[29] More than this, mantra is the sonic expression and form of the Divine and as such has an intrinsic connection with that which it signifies, and therefore with reality.[30] A *bija* or seed mantra, for example, is a single syllable that "is considered to contain the entire potentiality of full significance of a doctrine."[31] Sound is a dimension of immanence like any other. Nyasa is therefore a sonic means of identification with the body wherein "the flesh must be 'awakened' from its dormancy," by situating the power of various forms of the divine, through mantra, in the body's organs.[32] In the *sadanga-nyasa* ritual, thought to be the most popular, the heart center, forehead, top of the head, upper arms, closed eyes, and hands themselves are all touched in a specific order while *bija* mantras are recited.[33]

Pranayama

Pranayama or yogic breathing is a systematic technique that emphasizes the location, duration, speed, depth, and rhythm of breathing.[34] Utilizing the breath, pranayama techniques seek to make the involuntary process of breathing into a voluntary one through the induction of mindfulness, sometimes involving a mantra or physical movements.[35] "It is possible to attain mastery over the breathing process and harmonize the flow of *prana* [rising vital energy] and *apana* [descending vital energy], the two principle flows of energy in the body, through breath awareness and control, coordination of the breath with the mantra, and awareness of the pranic movement within the body."[36] To facilitate this, a 1:4:2 rhythm is employed wherein a beginner inhales (*puraka*) for a count of four seconds, retains the breath (*kumbhaka*) for sixteen, and exhales (*rechaka*) for eight seconds.[37] One cycle constitutes one round, which may be repeated anywhere from 10 to 30 or more times. After completing a round of this technique, the devotee is advised to lie flat on their back in *savasana*, or corpse pose in yoga, to relax the body and mind.[38] The calming effects of such breathing practices are well documented, and for the survivor such practices serve to create a space of peace and protection while also helping them to engage with their bodies as active participants rather than passive recipients, creating a sense of self-affirming authority over one's body.

These three tools constitute a means of gentle connecting beginning with meditation and visualization, moving to gentle touching, and finally the mindful connection with breath as *prana*. None of these tools are specific to the Shakti Bhakti tradition, yet the tradition serves to orient them in relation to the bhakta within the devotional mother-child paradigm. Such orientation keeps the focus of identification and the role of the body at the forefront of the bhaktas mind and intentions, clearly positioned (in this case) toward the goal of healing from sexual trauma. Other tools, such as trauma-informed yoga, continue to utilize Hindu knowledge and philosophy for the sake of healing and are powerful tools in doing so. However, these tools are often utilized without appropriate homage toward the tradition from which they come. This will be addressed further below.

Ninda Bhakti

So far, bhakti has been discussed as a means by which one may come to identify with the Divine Mother, especially in Her qualities of nurturance, compassion, and mercy. But if we understand bhakti as the devotional expression of human emotion directed toward engagement with the Divine Mother, and this expression is limited to a view of the Mother that acknowledges only those qualities that are most like an earthly image of *the perfect mother*, we limit our understanding of Her due to a denial of Her immanence in all aspects of life, including suffering. In my experience, this orientation also tends to create the belief that this image is the only appropriate way to identify with Her, consequently requiring *the perfect child*. However, this is not reflective of true human experience, nor is it reflective of how *mother* is understood in this context. The Great Goddess is not simply the earthly mother—She is the *metaphysical* Mother, "simultaneously a principle of the inner and outer realms," that frequently exceeds what is allowed by traditional conceptions.[39] The Divine Mother's immanence throughout material reality teaches us that She is also *prakrti*, the material substance of creation or nature: "The mad Goddess is now wild, unpredictable, and capricious *nature*, the 'storm-cloud' that can cause floods."[40] She is therefore Nature from all sides: birth and death, light and dark, evolution and involution.

For the survivor, the important thing to understand is that our experiences of suffering are not the result of divine punishment or abandonment. Instead, She is immanently present throughout our suffering, experiencing it with us. At times, this manifests in bhakti as a sort of push and pull between earthly and ethereal realms of identification, sometimes expressed not as love but as anger, frustration, or complaint. In the intimate world of the bhakta, this understanding of immanence does not necessarily assume that we are limited to expressing only that which is beautiful or grateful as this is a dishonest engagement of the mother-child paradigm. There, the child swallows their suffering in order to approach Her *correctly*, betraying the authenticity She calls us to cultivate in order to identify with Her, and perhaps denying Her immanence in all that we tend to think of as *not beautiful* in the world as well as in ourselves. Rather than facilitate connection, this creates disconnection and a relationship built on fear, rather than love, and wherein the bhakta may feel alone and unworthy in their suffering, unable to *appropriately* approach the Divine Mother. Through immanence, we may understand that to love Her is to love ourselves, and as true love requires surrender, authenticity, and vulnerability, the bhakta sometimes finds themselves in a position where their anger may be directed *toward* the Divine Mother, known as *ninda bhakti*.

Ninda bhakti is commonly referred to as the bhakti of complaint. In Sanskrit, *ninda* refers to blame, and ninda bhakti can be found in various Hindu traditions in the form of *stutis*, or devotional compositions. In the words of William Jackson, this bhakti constitutes a "song of praise by way of sarcasm."[41] At times this complaint may be humorous while at others it may appear to be a song of hatred toward the Divine, especially when it is the Divine that is the subject of such a work. In her book *Singing to the Goddess: Poems to Kali and Uma from Bengal*, Rachel Fell McDermott examines this concept in the context of Shakti Bhakti. Considering the experience of suffering, especially the suffering of Her devotees, McDermott explains that the tradition of such bhakti here expresses the anger one might expect when they are lured into a false sense of comfort, concluding with "bitterness and sarcasm" because "no one would worship this Goddess if there were an alternative."[42] The poets in question, however, do not abandon the Goddess. Instead, the expression of their suffering in the form of poetry focused on complaint serves to deepen that connection. Ramprasad writes lines like, "You called and called me, took me on Your lap, and then dashed my heart, on the ground!"[43] Kamalakanta Bhattacarya also wrote of his experience as the Divine Mother's child: "But what kind of behavior is this between Mother and son? Who can understand it?"[44] McDermott notes that the historical evidence is unclear as to whether the suffering expressed is that of the poet or the poet's reflection of the world at large, depicting "spiritual doubts and yearnings."[45]

This would seem to suggest that the suffering one struggles through, and is poetically expressed here, does not necessarily have to happen directly. This expression would seem to reflect a sense of empathy and awareness at the suffering of others or frustration that suffering exists in the world at all. To some, speaking to the Divine with such anger and frustration is akin to blasphemy, but here it is a means of worship because underlying both complaint and adoration is a sense of *trust*. The trust that evolves in the bhaktic relationship between Divine Mother and child may not align with the subjective experience of earthly mothers, but it does align with the understanding that the Divine Mother is beyond all such descriptions, and ultimately facilitates deeper connection via identification. Bhakti, including ninda bhakti, therefore comprises a safe space for authentic expression. The bhakta is not necessarily asked to endure life's difficulties, small or large, with a false sense of patience and adoration amid perhaps the biggest question of all: How could a loving Mother let this happen to me?

In the bhakta's trust there is space for true processing of suffering in the safety of the Divine Mother's company, especially in the flourishing possible after trauma. In my own ninda bhakti, the ability to authentically express such emotions, particularly through poetry or prayer, furthers the work of identification by cultivating authentic love that leads me to the fuller realization of Her pervading goodness and care beyond the experience of suffering. Such an interaction might be imagined as the wise, loving Mother holding Her screaming child with patience, understanding that to limit their expression by means of punishment or judgment is to deprioritize and devalue Her child's genuine experience, which can only be transformed into wisdom when it is expressed and processed. It is worth mentioning here that the poetry quoted is the outward expression of bhakti, while bhakti itself is intimate and often private. Whatever form ninda bhakti takes in the individual is not something that needs to be shared or performed in order to be valid.

This expression can be tumultuous, and afterward the bhakta's spiritual path is intensified rather than dulled, bringing us full circle. When we deny the wholeness and true immanence of the Mother, we deny a part of ourselves. The love, beauty, and bliss we seek cannot be found by negating our grief and suffering, but by walking through and processing it, creating a seemingly paradoxical result. It is authenticity that creates loving connection, even if that authenticity is expressive of emotions that seem to disrupt it. Once again, the situating of ninda bhakti in a paradigm of trust is key, as it creates a paradigm founded on the safety necessary for authenticity. Speaking from my perspective as a practitioner, the sensation of worship after this kind of expression was not one of anger or displeasure, but of a sweet, smiling calmness that received my grief and suffering with unconditional love. In the project of nurturance, this experience lends itself to the appreciation that to hold space for others is perhaps one of the most powerful things we can do, just as She holds space for us.

Conclusion

In this chapter, I have sought to provide a basic outline of theology in the Shakti Bhakti tradition, illustrated through key aspects of praxis that contribute to the healing of survivors by addressing core concepts of identity, one's relationship with the body, and the expression of our suffering. Situated in the context of a nondualistic theology that understands the Divine as the Great Goddess or Divine Mother, the Shakti Bhakti tradition might be thought of as one wherein the bhakta, devotee, strives for union with the Mother by processing and releasing all that might prevent them from it. Through such processing, the bhakta is able to find their inherent worth beyond their trauma and locate that worth in the connection with their bodies thereby furthering their own empowerment. Through ninda bhakti, bhaktas have the space to creatively express their suffering without fear of punishment or judgment and focus instead on strengthening their sense of safety and trust with the Divine Mother toward greater Realization. Recalling verse 11.33 of the DM, through our own healing and inner work we become a means of healing for others, and through dialogue, join hands across boundaries in order to address those shared challenges and protect the flourishing of all life.

Notes

1 For instance, one might meet the eyes of the practitioner through a *murti*, statue or artistic rendition of the Divine Mother.
2 It must be acknowledged that the term religion, as well as theology, is subject to scrutiny as a term that generally carries a Judeo-Christian connotation that at times reflects a colonial mentality. In this instance, the term should be understood loosely to refer to a set of ontological and cosmological beliefs. For more, please see Rita Sherma and Arvind Sharma, *Hermeneutics and Hindu Thought* (Springer, 2008), in Sharma's chapter "The Hermeneutics of the Word 'Religion' and Its Implications for the World of Indian Religions," pp. 19–32.
3 Catherine Cornille. "Conditions for Inter-Religious Dialogue." In *The Wiley-Blackwell Companion to Inter-Religious Dialogue*, edited by Catherine Cornille, 20–33.
4 Cornille, "Conditions for Inter-Religious Dialogue," 24.
5 Swami Bhaskarananda, *The Essentials of Hinduism*. 2nd ed. (Seattle, WA: Viveka Press, 2002) 66–68.
6 Bhaskarananda, *The Essentials of Hinduism*, 68.
7 Gavin D. Flood, *An Introduction to Hinduism*. (New York, NY: Cambridge University Press, 1996) 140.
8 Tantra, from the Sanskrit root *tan*, means to weave or compose. Here it is a set of esoteric practices, beliefs, and principles that adhere to the tantras, a collection of numerous and varied scripture that often take the form of dialogues between Shiva and Parvati, and incarnation of Shakti, describing the pathways to true self-realization. Like Hindu traditions, tantric sects can be diverse with porous boundaries, with some tantric texts and practices being far more well-known and accessible than others.
9 June McDaniel, *Offering Flowers, Feeding Skulls: Popular Goddess Worship in West Bengal*. (New York: Oxford University Press, 2004) 11.
10 Rita Sherma, "Sacred Immanence: Reflections of Ecofeminism in Hindu Tantra." In *Purifying the Earthly Body of God*, 89–131. (New York, NY: State University of New York Press, 1998) 105.

11 Thomas B. Coburn, *Encountering the Goddess: A Translation of the Devī-Māhātmya and a Study of Its Interpretation*. SUNY Series in Hindu Studies. (Albany, N.Y: State University of New York Press, 1991) 77.
12 Devadatta Kāl, ed. *Devīmāhātmyam: In Praise of the Goddess: The Devīmahā tmaya and Its Meaning*. (Berwick, Me: Nicolas-Hays, 2003) 31.
13 Rita Sherma, "'Sa Ham – I Am She': Woman as Goddess." In *Is the Goddess a Feminist? The Politics of South Asian Goddesses*, edited by Alf Hiltebeitel and Kathleen M. Erndl. (New York: New York University Press, 2000) 47–49.
14 Sherma, "'Sa Ham – I Am She': Woman as Goddess," 48.
15 David R. Kinsley, *Tantric Visions of the Divine Feminine: The Ten Mahāvidyās*. (Berkeley, Calif.: University of California Press, 1997) 246.
16 Swami Satyananda Saraswati, trans. *Chandi Path*. 6th ed. (Napa, California: Devi Mandir Publications, 2010) 270.
17 Sherma, "'Sa Ham – I Am She': Woman as Goddess," 43–45.
18 Kavitha M. Chinnaiyan, *Shakti Rising: Embracing Shadow and Light on the Goddess Path to Wholeness*. (Oakland, CA: Non-Duality Press, 2017) 54–55.
19 Chinnaiyan, *Shakti Rising*, 89–90.
20 Bessel A. van der Kolk, *The Body Keeps the Score: Brain, Mind and Body in the Healing of Trauma* (New York, NY: Penguin Books, 2015) and Peter Levine, *In an Unspoken Voice: How the Body Releases Trauma and Restores Goodness* (Berkeley: North Atlantic Books, 2010).
21 Ajit Mookerjee and Madhu Khanna. *The Tantric Way: Art, Science, Ritual: With 148 Illustrations, 18 in Color and 80 Line Drawings*. (New York: Thames and Hudson, 1996) 135.
22 Mookerjee and Khanna, *The Tantric Way*, 136.
23 Georg Feuerstein, *Tantra: The Path of Ecstasy*. (Boston: [New York]: Shambhala; Distributed in the USA by Random House, 1998) 141–42.
24 Swatmarama Swami, *The Hatha Yoga Pradipika*. (CreateSpace, 2011) 29.
25 Geometric form of the divine, such as the Sri Chakra.
26 Satyananda Saraswati, *Meditations from the Tantras*, (Prakash Publishers and Exports, 2013) 254–56.
27 Satyananda Saraswati, *Meditations from the Tantras*, 254.
28 Mookerjee and Khanna, *The Tantric Way*, 136.
29 Guy Beck, *Sonic Theology: Hinduism and Sacred Sound*. (Columbia: University of South Carolina Press, 1993) 31.
30 Beck, *Sonic Theology: Hinduism and Sacred Sound*, 32.
31 Mookerjee and Khanna, *The Tantric Way*, 133.
32 Mookerjee and Khanna, *The Tantric Way*, 136.
33 Mookerjee and Khanna, *The Tantric Way*, 140–41.
34 Mookerjee and Khanna, *The Tantric Way*, 144.
35 Niranjanananda Saraswati, *Prana and Pranayama*. (Repr. Munger, Bihar, India: Yoga Publication Trust, 2010) 106.
36 Niranjanananda Saraswati, *Prana and Pranayama*, 107.
37 Mookerjee and Khanna, *The Tantric Way*, 146.
38 Mookerjee and Khanna, *The Tantric Way*, 146.
39 Vrinda Dalmiya, "Loving Paradoxes: A Feminist Reclamation of the Goddess Kali." *Hypatia* 15, no. 1 (Winter 2000): 133.
40 Dalmiya, "Loving Paradoxes: A Feminist Reclamation of the Goddess Kali," 134.
41 William J. Jackson and Tyāgarāja. *Tyāgarāja: Life and Lyrics*. 4. impr. (Oxford India Paperbacks. New Delhi: Oxford Univ. Press, 2002) 367.

42 Rachel Fell McDermott, *Singing to the Goddess: Poems to Kālī and Umā from Bengal.* (Oxford; New York: Oxford University Press, 2001) 52.
43 McDermott, *Singing to the Goddess*, 53.
44 McDermott, *Singing to the Goddess*, 56.
45 McDermott, *Singing to the Goddess*, 52.

Bibliography

Beck, Guy. *Sonic Theology: Hinduism and Sacred Sound.* Columbia: University of South Carolina Press, 1993.

Bhaskarananda, Swami. *The Essentials of Hinduism.* 2nd ed. Seattle, WA: Viveka Press, 2002.

Chinnaiyan, Kavitha M. *Shakti Rising: Embracing Shadow and Light on the Goddess Path to Wholeness.* Oakland, CA: Non-Duality Press, 2017.

Coburn, Thomas B. *Encountering the Goddess: A Translation of the Devī-Māhā tmya and a Study of Its Interpretation.* SUNY Series in Hindu Studies. Albany, N.Y: State University of New York Press, 1991.

Cornille, Catherine. "Conditions for Inter-Religious Dialogue." In *The Wiley-Blackwell Companion to Inter-Religious Dialogue,* edited by Catherine Cornille, 20–33. The Wiley-Blackwell Companions to Religion. Hoboken: Wiley, 2013.

Dalmiya, Vrinda. "Loving Paradoxes: A Feminist Reclamation of the Goddess Kali." *Hypatia* 15, no. 1 (Winter 2000): 125–50.

Devadatta Kālī, ed. *Devīmāhātmyam: In Praise of the Goddess: The Devīmahā tmaya and Its Meaning.* Berwick, Me: Nicolas-Hays, 2003.

Feuerstein, Georg. *Tantra: The Path of Ecstasy.* Boston: [New York]: Shambhala; Distributed in the USA by Random House, 1998.

Flood, Gavin D. *An Introduction to Hinduism.* New York, NY: Cambridge University Press, 1996.

Jackson, William J., and Tyāgarāja. *Tyāgarāja: Life and Lyrics.* 4. impr. Oxford India Paperbacks. New Delhi: Oxford Univ. Press, 2002.

Kinsley, David R. *Tantric Visions of the Divine Feminine: The Ten Mahāvidyās.* Berkeley, Calif.: University of California Press, 1997.

Levine, Peter. *In an Unspoken Voice: How the Body Releases Trauma and Restores Goodness* (Berkeley: North Atlantic Books, 2010).

McDaniel, June. *Offering Flowers, Feeding Skulls: Popular Goddess Worship in West Bengal.* New York: Oxford University Press, 2004.

McDermott, Rachel Fell. *Singing to the Goddess: Poems to Kālī and Umā from Bengal.* Oxford; New York: Oxford University Press, 2001.

Mookerjee, Ajit, and Madhu Khanna. *The Tantric Way: Art, Science, Ritual: With 148 Illustrations, 18 in Color and 80 Line Drawings.* New York: Thames and Hudson, 1996.

Niranjanananda Saraswati. *Prana and Pranayama.* Repr. Munger, Bihar, India: Yoga Publication Trust, 2010.

Saraswati, Swami Satyananda, trans. *Chandi Path.* 6th ed. Napa, California: Devi Mandir Publications, 2010.

Satyananda Saraswati. *Meditations from the Tantras,* Prakash Publishers and Exports, 2013.

Sherma, Rita. "'Sa Ham – I Am She': Woman as Goddess." In *Is the Goddess a Feminist? The Politics of South Asian Goddesses*, edited by Alf Hiltebeitel and Kathleen M. Erndl, 24–51. New York: New York University Press, 2000.

Sherma, Rita "Sacred Immanence: Reflections of Ecofeminism in Hindu Tantra." In *Purifying the Earthly Body of God*, 89–131. New York, NY: State University of New York Press, 1998.

Swami, Swatmarama. *The Hatha Yoga Pradipika*. CreateSpace, 2011.

Van der Kolk, Bessel A. *The Body Keeps the Score: Brain, Mind and Body in the Healing of Trauma* (New York, NY: Penguin Books, 2015).

Chapter 10

Nature as Muse

Marion Gail Dumont

Introduction

I anticipate that many reading this book have experienced sexual violence, either personally or indirectly. The experience of trauma can leave us feeling shattered and off-center. It is possible to reclaim the fragments of our lives and restore a sense of balance. The task is to nurture life within us so that we can rediscover a sense of pleasure, joy, and trust in our self, in others, and in life. The path of healing takes many forms, and it is my purpose here to share with you some of the insights, experiences, and practices that have nurtured my own journey. It is at the intersection of nature, art, and dreams that I'm able to fill the void created by trauma and grief. I have chosen to fill that void with beauty, awe, love, and spiritual meaning.

My academic training began with a Bachelor of Science and a specialization in maternal-child nursing. Over the years I studied other healing modalities including Therapeutic Touch and Reiki. In 2013 I graduated from the California Institute of Integral Studies with a doctorate degree in Philosophy and Religion with a specialization in women's spirituality and a focus on women's mysteries,[1] sacred arts,[2] and healing. There is substantial evidence that when humans engage with the natural world and participate in creative activities, they experience important health benefits such as reduced stress, the alleviation of depression and anxiety as well as an increased sense of self-worth. In the following pages I will share some of the practices that have helped me to recover a sense of wholeness and well-being.

Nature

Growing up, my siblings and I spent a great deal of time outdoors. In nature I felt free to be me, no judgment, no alienation, no awkwardness, just adventure and pure joy. The smell of the earth and the wind in the trees were our familiars and the creatures of field, forest, and shore our delight. Outdoors, in nature is where I developed a sense of belonging and connection and it continues to be my refuge and place of contemplation. Engagement with the natural world is my healing strength. It's where I find balance, emotional regulation, and confidence. Additionally, my engagement with the natural world informs my everyday life through creative expression—in the clothes that I wear, the arrangement of my household, my writings, photographs, and art forms.

Philosophers, poets, scientists, and artists define nature in unique ways. When I use the word *nature* it is simply a reference to the natural world, that physical world commonly perceived as being outside, as a state that has not been humanly constructed. *Biophilia* is a term used to describe our desire to commune with nature. Socio-biologist and author E.O. Wilson believes that "our existence depends on this propensity, our spirit is woven from it, hope rises on its currents."[3] Engagement with life in the natural world enhances our mental, emotional, and spiritual development.

I credit my love to wander and explore off the beaten path to a childhood lived outdoors. Who I am today was shaped by the liberty and self-determination granted us as children. I don't harbor the fear and timidity that I often hear others express in relation to the natural world. My growing-up could be described as religiously barren yet spiritually rich in the practice of engaging with the natural world. There was a freedom to get dirty, to walk barefoot on the earth, and to breathe fresh, clean air. We swam in streams and hiked in the woods; we broke off chunks of salt set out for livestock and sat hidden in the tall, dry grasses of summer that grew well above our heads; we caught bees in jars and cradled sleepy garter snakes in our shirt pockets. Our playgrounds offered mud slides and ponds. They were shaped by the ebb and flow of the tides that washed away hermit-crab cities built of sand and jetsam. I treasure these memories of childhood—the smell of soft-packed earth after a summer rain and the serenity of nestling in uncut fields outside a small, French village.

Wandering and walking have characterized my engagement with the natural world since a very early age. These practices have enabled me to develop self-confidence and a sense of well-being that sustain me even in the most stressful of circumstances. I have wandered the landscapes of such diverse places as Kodiak Island, western Montana, San Juan Islands, Olympic Peninsula, and Appalachia here in the United States. I've had the good fortune of exploring various rural areas in France and the United Kingdom including places in Normandy, Alsace-Lorraine, Aquitaine, Auvergne, the Pyrenees, parts of Ireland, and the Scottish Highlands.

The thing I loved most about being in France and the United Kingdom was the easy access to walking paths. In North America our culture has been built around roadways instead of walking trails. Today, our society is discovering the profound benefits of walking and I enjoy learning about the ways people are incorporating this simple yet powerful practice into their lives. Daniel Maté of *Take a Walk with Daniel* uses a technique that he calls "mental chiropractor."[4] Because we no longer rely on our feet to get us from point A to point B in our fast-paced lives, walking is something that we must intentionally schedule into our day. Developing a personal practice of what I like to call *walking medicine* has many benefits and can be done whether you are in a city, a suburb, or a rural environment. When practiced outdoors with intention, *walking medicine* will foster an engagement with the natural world that leads to greater self-confidence and a sense of well-being.

This practice is designed to inspire individuals to develop a personal practice of engaging with the natural world for the purpose of building self-confidence and a sense of well-being. One of the ways we can achieve this is simply to develop an awareness of the natural world while walking outdoors. What I'm offering here is one suggestion based on my own practice of engaging with the natural world and is intended to encourage you to develop your own, one that feels right for you. Wear comfortable shoes and dress for the weather. Pack a water bottle with you and any other items you feel you might need. A small daypack or a waist pack is useful. Choose an outdoor environment to walk where you feel safe and relaxed.

After you have arrived at your outdoor location look around. Take note of the weather, the presence or absence of others, and any other details of the place where you will walk. Focus your awareness of your body in relationship to the environment. Engage all six of your senses. I sometimes squat down and touch the earth as a means to ground and center myself. Taking a drink of water or taking a few deep breaths are also ways to ground and center yourself. Take three deep breaths, slow and easy. Through our gestures and attitude, we honor the spirit of place and give gratitude to the land.

Next, set your intention. At the onset of my walks, I often recite the following verse to myself: *Listen to the spirit. Listen to the land. Listen to the spirit listen to the land.* When you are grounded and have set your intention, step forward into that sacred space that you have created—you are ready to engage with your whole self—mind, heart, body, and spirit. Depending on the day and my level of stress, I sometimes simply begin walking and think of nothing else, simply walk until I reach a quiet place within myself. As I relax and the tension leaves my body, I'm more able to focus my attention on my body and become more acutely aware of my surroundings.

When you have fallen into a comfortable pace and quieted your mind, bring your attention to your body. How does your body feel in this moment? Bring your awareness to the muscle and joint movements of your body in your hips, knees, ankles, and toes. Concentrate your awareness on your back and shoulders. Breathe in and out while dropping your shoulders and allowing the release of tension with each exhale. Continue along your intended path, as you place your feet on the earth, say to yourself *Thank you for this mind, body, and soul.* As you continue to walk and enjoy the movement of your body in the outdoors take a few long, slow breaths and allow your mind to wander across the landscape. Walk slowly with intention. For a few steps, each time you place your foot on the earth say to yourself, *yes,* yes to the welcoming Earth.

If your mind becomes cluttered by painful emotions or thoughts that threaten to derail your walk, bring your attention back to your breath, to your body, and to nature. You can return again to the first steps outlined above or to the point at which you left off. Remember to be kind to yourself. This is not a race or a competition but time for you to be self-centered.

Continue to walk and breathe your way along your intended path. Enjoy these moments of peaceful attention. For a few more steps, each time you place your foot on the earth, say to yourself, *thank you,* thank you to the earth for the life that it gives. Reflect on the abundance of the earth and the beauty that surrounds you. Relax into the moment and walk on. As you come to the end of your walk, stand still, reach your arms up towards the sky, stretch your spine and take some cleansing breaths. Take some time to reflect on your experience. How do you feel? What was it about your experience that was beneficial? Is there anything that you would do differently next time? Center on the positive peacefulness of your walk with nature. Pledge to return to this experience often. These intimate nature walks can begin to supplant the grief we feel after sexual assault.

To be heard and to be witnessed during times of grief is critical for healing to occur. Friends and family are often the ones we turn to during this time of crisis. However, for various reasons we may be unable to share our experience with others or be comforted by them. Perhaps their comfort doesn't feel as if it is enough. For grief to unwind itself one must become self-centered for a time. It is important to find what works best for you as you process your experience. The ebb and flow of emotions and the transformative process of healing require grace and flexibility. Busy lives can make it difficult to find the time and space to do what you need to in order to care for yourself. The practice of taking quiet walks in nature is how I meet these needs. Wherever I am, even if it's only for a short visit,

I make it a priority to orient myself to the area and find safe and pleasurable places to go for walks. It has been my experience, whether these walks are through the streets of an unfamiliar city, the outskirts of a small town, or the neighborhood near my apartment, that nature never disappoints but continually astounds me with its wisdom and support.

During a monumental transition in my life, I found that being outdoors and walking enabled me to manage feelings of unimaginable grief. On one occasion, I chose to walk a trail I'd never been on before. Halfway through my walk I sat down and began to weep uncontrollably. As I sat on the damp earth a raven passed overhead calling to a fellow raven who responded in kind. I blew my nose, wiped my eyes, and looked towards the sky. Seeing nothing I turned my gaze to the ground in front of me. It was littered with hundreds of delicate, pink rose petals against the damp earth. I was especially astonished because it was mid-winter, not the typical time of year that the local, wild Nootka Rosa is found. It felt as if the raven and the rose witnessed my sorrow. This experience filled me with comfort and courage. The wisdom of nature, manifest in the vocalizations of the raven (Corvus corax) and the medicinal properties of the rose, were deeply meaningful to me.

According to Scott Kloos, author of *Pacific Northwest Medicinal Plants*, a tea made from the aromatic flowers or from the hips of the Nootka Rose act to soothe sore, bloodshot eyes as well as reduce respiratory inflammation.[5] The crying that accompanied the episode of grief lasted for days, weeks, and ebbed into months. My sinuses ached as I cried. Nature in its wisdom knew just what were needed, rose petals and a comfort song from a raven.

This was not the only time that the presence of a raven comforted me in my grief. It was January 2017 and my granddaughter Mathilde had come for a weekend visit. Mathilde and I had grown very close having shared the same house from the time she was born until she moved away just before her sixth birthday. When she lived with me, we often took long walks in the woods. Today we chose a familiar trail and we walked unhurried. As we reached the midpoint we stopped to rest. As Mathilde and I sat in the middle of the trail, sharing an orange, we heard an unusual bird song, one I'd never heard before that reminded me of tropical bird calls. We got up and walked towards the tree it seemed to be coming from. We looked in astonishment as a raven flew up out of the tree. Several days later, curious about the raven's song we'd heard, I made a web search for raven vocalizations and discovered a recording that sounded very similar to that which we had heard on our walk. The author described this vocalization of the raven as *comfort sounds*. It felt as if the Raven had tapped into our sorrow and gave to us the gift of comfort in song.

Figure 10.1 Raven and the Rose: Pyrography on fungus

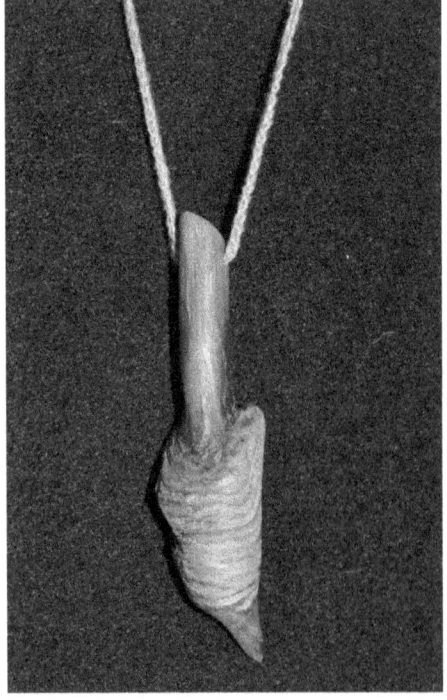

Figure 10.2 Woodland Talisman Pendant: Red Cedar

Art

Toko-pa Turner reminds us that "Art removes the misery of inertia. It is an act of overcoming."[6] We engage in creative acts for different reasons; sometimes these are for practical purposes such as innovation while at other times we create art for the pure pleasure of it. Humans are inherently creative—you do not need to be an *artist* to be creative. Art is a very broad term that encompasses a wide array of creative expression, including crafts, which I believe holds equal value to the arts. The making of two-dimensional and three-dimensional objects, writing, storytelling, music, dance, and theater are just some of the forms of artistic expression. We humans engage our hands and our bodies in creative art for various reasons and benefits including pleasure, distraction, emotional regulation, joy, and comfort.

The creative art process engages the whole self—our physical, mental, emotional, and spiritual selves. I believe that when an individual engages in the creative process that there is the potential to improve well-being, reduce stress, promote self-discovery, and build self-esteem. Over the years I've engaged in many different creative arts. I don't consider myself an artist, but I am creative. My creativity includes fiber arts like hand spinning, knitting, felting, and sewing. It includes drawing, print blocking, watercolors, wood carving, sculpture, cooking, gardening, and beekeeping. I have found that when I engage in creative activities my mind calms, my depression lifts, and my anxiety diminishes. The possibilities of being creative are endless and you don't need a lot of money so don't let a lack of resources be an obstacle. At times, my life was circumscribed by a lack of resources but not of imagination or inspiration. Determination and a creative spirit helped me to engage in new and rewarding activities.

In September of 2018, I left for France with the intention of working on collaborative research and writing with two French scholars whom I'd met earlier that year. When these plans went awry, I was forced to utilize my creative problem-solving skills and craft an alternative plan that took me into Ireland and Scotland. By January I was back in France and working as a live-in elder companion for a woman whose husband was a woodcutter. Caring for a person who is no longer able to ambulate or speak more than a word or two presented a challenge and I found that my days were filled with hours of sitting quietly with little to occupy my mind or my hands. After a few days, I took stock of the available resources and decided to try my hand at whittling. My woodcutter host gave me a French pocketknife and I collected pieces of wood on my walks through the woodlands as well as from the woodpile in the basement.

Additionally, I'd wanted to learn the skill of making netting. Making use of my mobile phone I was able to find several online videos with instructions and images of the items needed for netmaking. With small pieces of wood and the pocketknife I was able to carve the necessary tools needed to create a net, but I needed a source of fiber. The only store within walking distance was a small grocery store. When my day off coincided with my host's weekly trip into the nearest town with a feed supply store, I was able to purchase a large ball of well-made flax fiber. Once I learned the technique of netmaking I found the process therapeutic, and it was an activity that I could engage in while sitting with my client. In the meantime, I'd discovered a fiber store in another nearby village where I purchased some locally sourced yarn and set about carving a pair of knitting needles from a couple of equally sized branches that I'd found on one of my walks. Over the next five months, I whiled away many quiet hours knitting and whittling.

For me, learning to do arts and crafts is not so much about becoming an artist or a craftswoman, but about engaging with the creative process for the purpose of well-being. My creative process has become an integral part of my therapy. Shaun McNiff writes in his book, *Art Heals*, that "Art and creativity are the soul's medicines—what the soul uses to minister to itself, cure its maladies, and restore its vitality."[7] And that's why I do arts and crafts and hope that in sharing my experiences, you are inspired to take up some form of creative activity for your own pleasure and well-being.

I view my engagement with nature and creative expression as a form of spiritual practice that has the potential to heal my soul. And, it brings me tremendous joy and satisfaction—what better medicine is there?

For six years I served as co-chair for an Arts and Religion unit in the Pacific Northwest region. It was a great opportunity to learn from others about the importance of art and spirituality as well as an opportunity to share some of my own work. In May 2017 at the annual meeting in Calgary, Alberta I gave a presentation of an art project titled, *The Wounded Healer: Art, Healing & Spirituality*. This project had been inspired by a sculpture I'd seen in 2016 at a local art gallery. The sculpture, created by a Seattle artist, was in the shape of a small vessel and made of barbed wire and cloth. I was awestruck by its simple construction and the unusual use of barbed wire to create a thing of beauty. I felt an irresistible urge to make a vessel of my own. The result was a series of eleven vessels made from mostly reclaimed or wild-crafted materials each carrying a specific reference or meaning to an experience or phase in my life. As I reflect on this particular creative process in the writing of this chapter, I am reminded of the transformative potential and the meaning derived from our engagement with the creative process.

My wounded healer project was a soul-retrieval of sorts, creating objects that represented aspects of my soul that emerged out of the fragments of past experiences that often involved physical and/or emotional trauma. The idea of the wounded healer comes from the Greco-Roman mythology about Chiron, the centaur, one of the lesser gods in the Greek pantheon. Myth and story have played an important role in several of my creative projects, including the vessel series. Discovering a connection between the theme, the characters, and the context of a story with your creative activities can lend support and depth to your healing work.

My vessel series serves as an example of the relationship between the healing process and creative expression. It's difficult to put into words what this project meant to me at a time in my life when I was struggling to navigate a new life stage. It was the anchor that held me in place, my grounding rod and the compass of my days. As a woman, mother, and nurse I have spent a good deal of my life caring for others. At age sixty I found myself living alone for the first time in my life after my youngest daughter left home. For the first time in my life, I wasn't needed—I had no one to care for but myself. My children were grown, and my granddaughter no longer lived with me. It was a time of letting go and a moving into a new phase of life. This change overwhelmed me, and I sometimes felt as if I were breaking apart. It was a monumental transition, a movement away from the care of others—as a daughter, sister, mother, and grandmother.

The spring before I began work on the vessel series, I created a ritual ceremony that was made into a short film by my talented friend and colleague, videographer, and artist Natasha O. Redina. The purpose of this ritual was to honor the crossing of a threshold in my life and the film served as the creative expression of this important rite of passage. Performing this ceremony and capturing it on film helped me move into something new and unfamiliar.[8] Author Ronald Grimes writes, "Rites of passage are stylized and condensed actions intended to acknowledge or effect a transformation. A transformation is not just any sort of change but a momentous metamorphosis, a moment after which one is never again the same."[9]

A rite of passage signifies movement from one state to another. During the period I was working on the vessel series I occupied a liminal space, a borderland to whatever it was I was becoming, and it was frightening. I was in transition, and it cracked me wide open! I came face to face with myself and the life I'd lived until that moment. When thoughts and emotions of past traumas, loss and grief threatened to derail me, I would immerse myself in my art project. *The project itself became the vessel that held me and gave me comfort.*

It was during my research for my doctoral dissertation that I discovered that my paternal ancestors came from the British Isles including regions in England, Ireland, and Scotland. One ancestor, Peter Garland was a shipbuilder who immigrated to North America from England in 1690. This ancestral connection inspired the design of one of the vessels for the wounded healer series titled, *Ancestors*, a mock-up of a traditional Irish boat known as a currach. The currach is a functional watercraft built for a specific purpose and not for beauty. Similarly, I crafted mine from a worn-out leather boot and branches pruned from the trees on my property. I cherish it for what it represents, a connection with my ancestral past.

In your creative pursuits as you navigate your own healing journey, I encourage you to listen to your heart and your mind. Even the smallest inspirations hold the potential to open you into wide spaces rich with meaning and healing. If you see something—a box of colored pencils, a carving tool, or someone else's artwork, and it moves you to want to create then listen to your heart and do something with that inspiration welling up inside of you. We're not looking for perfection, for sales, for performance; we're looking for the unique expression of life that comes from within and manifests through your hands and heart. This is art for you and your spiritual healing.

Figure 10.3 Drawings and Watercolor

Figure 10.4 Madness of Mis Shawl: Wool fiber, rabbit fur, and turkey feathers

Figure 10.5 Betrayal: Vessel made of copper and silk taffeta

Figure 10.6 Changing Tides: Oyster shell, gold leaf, Moonstone, and Douglas fir

Dreams

Human spiritual practices vary widely and the terms, spirit, spiritual, and spirituality mean different things to different people. Many individuals choose to follow a particular spiritual practice while others view life in purely physical terms. I believe that the element of spirit is inherent to our being and inseparable from the mental, emotional, and physical parts of our selves.[10] When I speak of spirituality, I'm not referring to religion but rather to that which gives our lives meaning. For me, living life is my spiritual practice—living it with integrity and in all of its fullness. Authors Ronald Grimes and Wilfred McSherry describe spirituality as something personal that arises out of our everyday life.[11] This concluding section on dreams is intended for everyone, whether you believe in spirit or not—whether you follow a particular spiritual path or not. Outside of organized religion today, spirituality and the sacred arts expand and become more rich and diverse encompassing dream work, astrology, tarot, intuitive readings, and certain use of plant medicine.

Dreams are sometimes disturbing, sometimes insightful, often elusive, but almost always interesting and self-revelatory. When we pay attention to our dream life and work with the material given to us, they can serve as guides and avenues for healing and self-development. You will find that the more you work with your dreams, the more you dream.

I work with my dreams using a simple process of dream incubation that I created for myself. Dream incubation is not a new concept within Western culture. It was a key element in the healing practices of Asclepius and Hygeia, the Greco-Roman god and goddess of medicine.[12] Temples and sacred healing centers, known as *Asclepieia*, served as places where people would go to engage in various rites and practices including dream incubation. The word incubate comes from the Latin verb *incubare* (to lie upon). Mabel Lang describes these dream centers in her book, *Cure and Cult in Ancient Corinth*. In describing the ritual of incubation Lang draws a connection between nature and dreaming when she ascribes dreams to Sacred Mother Earth.

Dream incubation, ancient mythology, the earth, and nature come together as part of a creative healing practice. For instance, there is a deep and abiding affiliation between Asclepius, Hygeia, and serpents/snakes. Kate Campbell Hurd-Mead writes in *A History of Women in Medicine*, "It is interesting to note that the snake has always been associated with the gods of healing, whether among the American Indians, or the early Greeks, or the rebellious Hebrews in the time of Moses. Apollo's wand and modern medical insignia have coiled serpents on the staff—Aesculapius and Hygeia were never seen without such a wand."[13] According to authors Monica Sjoo and Barbara Mor the symbol of the ouroboros is seen as the "dream-circle of sleep."[14] Oroboros is the ancient symbol of a snake curled around with its tail in its mouth, forming a circle—the cycle of life.

I will share a simple technique that I developed for myself and that I've found very effective in cultivating active dreaming. The first step, *setting an intention*, is meant to guide and nurture one's dream life. At bedtime choose one thing that you would like to know more about or gain insight into; it can be written in the form of a question or a request. For example, *I want to know more about the work I should undertake* or, *show me how to heal my relationship with . . .* Write down your intention in a notebook or dream journal. Set this same intention three nights in a row.

The next step in the process of dream incubation is to work with the content of your dream. This process begins upon awakening. How you work with your dream can take on many different forms. I like to ask myself if the dream has anything to do with my everyday reality and if so, what might the connection be. Connections are those liminal spaces in-between things. Pay attention to any words or phrases that may have been said in the dream and any colors or objects that stand out or grab your attention.

It's best to keep a notebook and a pen beside your bed so that you can write down any dreams as soon as you awaken, making note of any details that you may recall or any sensations that you experience, even if they seem irrelevant. Take a few minutes before rising to 'lie upon' your dream, to reflect on details, feelings, associations. Try not to censure your dreams or your reflections. In other words, don't disregard those dreams that come across as fearful, disturbing, or that contain elements that are culturally taboo. As an example, my *Spring Fertility Dream: Sex with a Talking Rabbit*.

In 2019, I dreamed I had sex with a talking rabbit. In my dream I wanted to get pregnant, but I didn't have a partner, so I mated with a talking rabbit. He was a large, soft-brown furry rabbit. Even though it could speak as a human, it looked exactly like a regular rabbit. The two of us couldn't figure out what best position to assume and we initially tried like bunnies, from the back but that didn't work so I positioned the rabbit at the front of me. All the while the rabbit, with an unabated sense of urgency yelled, *It's coming out, it's coming out! Open up, open up!* The rabbit's wee penis was long and pointed. Whether or not this is what a real one looks like I couldn't say, but in the dream, I thought it looked as a real one should. I *opened up* and the rabbit penetrated quickly and briefly, I orgasmed and it was over. And even though there was a sense of pleasure I felt a lingering sense of guilt as I'd just had sex with a rabbit. There was also a feeling of accomplishment and of having done the ordinary.

Toko-pa writes, "I believe every dream has a secret longing, and to work well with our dreams is to discover what that longing is. Longing is the vital impulse at the center of every living being which inclines it to wholeness. Our job is to come into conversation with that longing, uncomfortable as it may be, so we can hear how it's calling us homeward."[15] Thus we must treat our dreams as if they are above suspicion. Consider the characters in your dream as irreproachable, after all they are ethereal. The details of dreams have a tendency to evaporate like mist in the morning sun. If you had a dream and can't recall any of the details, take note of how you felt either while dreaming or after you've woken up. As you gain practice in working with your dreams you will come to understand that even the briefest of dreams can reveal a wealth of meaning and intrigue. Sometimes, the meaning of a dream may not reveal itself until years later. This is why keeping a dream journal can be important. An event or an experience may trigger a memory of a long-forgotten dream. Being able to review the details of a dream can be not only fun but insightful.

Occasionally, I pull out journals and review old dreams. Here is a dream I recently came across, dated October 27, 2016. I have no recollection of this dream, but I love the imagery, especially, after many years of wanting to keep bees, I recently set up my first hives. I wrote in my journal:

> Last night I inhabited the body of a honey bee
> Warm, soft and woolly

I rubbed my legs together
And stared into the dark with my large eyes
Deep down inside the earth
Perfectly fitted inside the chamber
Each side of the hexagon painted with fragrant wax
I rest my head and dream of a better world.

I hope that my words have inspired you to embrace nature as your muse and to engage in creative activities that empower you to dream a life of wholeness. May you create your own path of spiritual healing through nature, art, and dreams.

Notes

1 Simply put, women's mysteries are the embodied experience of being human in a woman's body. It is a reference to a person's experience across the lifespan: birth, childhood, adolescence, adulthood, and elderhood.
2 Fundamentally, sacred arts speak to the relationship between human creativity and spirituality. Artistic expression can be found in the rituals and traditions of every religious practice. Within Western culture and outside of organized religion these include dream work, astrology, tarot, intuitive readings, and plant medicine.
3 E. O. Wilson, *Biophilia: The human bond with other species*. (Harvard University Press, 1984) 1.
4 Daniel Maté, www.walkwithdaniel.com/.
5 Scott Kloos. *Pacific Northwest Medicinal Plants: Identify, Harvest, and Use 120 Wild Herbs for Health and Wellness*. (Portland: Timber Press, 2017) 94.
6 Toko-pa Turner. "The Knower in You: An Animist Approach to Dreamwork," Lecture, Comox Valley C. G. Jung Society, April 22, 2022, www.comoxjung.com/.
7 Shaun McNiff. *Art Heal: How Creativity Cures the Soul*. (Boston: Shambhala Press, 2004) xii-xiii.
8 You can view my film on *Vimeo* at this link https://vimeo.com/165080650 or on my website at https://mariondumont.com An unintended outcome of the making of this film was that Natasha was invited to show it at several public venues in London, Venice, and San Francisco.
9 Ronald Grimes. *Deeply Into the Bone: Re-Inventing Rites of Passage*. (Berkeley: University of California Press, 2000) 6.
10 What I consider to be the most important treatise on the human spirit available today is a book by Russian physicist and healer, Nicolai Levashov, *Spirit and Mind*, a pdf version is available online at www.levashov.info/English/index-eng.html. Levashov writes, "The spirit (or soul) comprises a system of bodies which living matter evolves in the process of adapting to the environment . . . Each body of the spirit is a structural copy of the physical body on a corresponding planetary level." (25)
11 Wilfrend McSherry. *Spirituality in Nursing Practice: An Interactive Approach*. (Edinburgh: Churchill Livingstone, 2000).
12 Even older than the cult of Asclepius and Hygeia were the Eleusinian Mysteries also known as The Greater Mysteries, a celebration of Demeter and Persephone, mother and daughter goddesses of ancient Greece. The rites of

Demeter and Persephone had been celebrated for hundreds of years prior to the establishment of the cult of Asclepius and Hygeia which began in Athens around 420 B.C. [C. A. Meier, *Ancient Incubation and Modern Psychotherapy*. Trans. Monica Curtis. (Evanston: Northwestern University Press, 1967) 16.

13 Kate C. Hurd-Mead, *A History of Women in Medicine: From the Earliest Times to the Beginning of the Nineteenth Century*, (Connecticut: Haddam Press, 1938) 5. Available online https://wellcomecollection.org/works/daym3nxy/items?canvas=9 accessed July 24, 2022.

14 Monica Sjoo and Barbara Mor, *The Great Cosmic Mother, Rediscovering the Religion of the Earth*, (San Francisco: HarperSanFrancisco, Second edition, 1991) 62.

15 Toko-pa Turner, "Courting the Dream: The Sacred Practice of Dreamwork," online course enrolled in July 2022.

Bibliography

Grimes, Ronald. *Deeply Into the Bone: Re-Inventing Rites of Passage*. (Berkeley: University of California Press, 2000).

Hurd-Mead, Kate C. *A History of Women in Medicine: From the Earliest Times to the Beginning of the Nineteenth Century*. (Connecticut: Haddam Press, 1938).

Kloos, Scott. *Pacific Northwest Medicinal Plants: Identify, Harvest, and Use 120 Wild Herbs for Health and Wellness*. (Portland: Timber Press, 2017).

Langlands, Alexander. *Craeft: An Inquiry into the Origins and True Meaning of Traditional Crafts*. (New York: W. W. Norton & Company, Inc, 2017).

Maté, Daniel. www.walkwithdaniel.com, accessed July 2022.

Meier, C.A. *Ancient Incubation and Modern Psychotherapy*. Trans. Monica Curtis. (Evanston: Northwestern University Press, 1967).

McNiff, Shaun. *Art Heal: How Creativity Cures the Soul*. (Boston: Shambhala Press, 2004).

McSherry, Wilfred. *Spirituality in Nursing Practice: An Interactive Approach*. (Edinburgh: Churchill Livingstone, 2000).

Sjoo, Monica and Mor, Barbara. *The Great Cosmic Mother, Rediscovering the Religion of the Earth*. (San Francisco: HarperSanFrancisco, Second edition, 1991).

Turner, Toko-pa. "Courting the Dream: The Sacred Practice of Dreamwork," online course, enrolled in July 2022.

Turner, Toko-pa "The Knower in You: An Animist Approach to Dreamwork," Lecture, Comox Valley C. G. Jung Society, April 22, 2022, www.comoxjung.com

Wilson, E.O. *Biophilia: The human bond with other species*. (Boston: Harvard University Press, 1984).

Chapter 11

The Healing Power of Divine Intimacy

Mary Sue Barnett

Background

At age 19, I was drugged and raped on a university campus. An acquaintance handed me a red solo cup of beer and after a few of sips I was unable to stand. Perpetrators took me from the party to the backseat of a car where for several hours, while in and out of consciousness, they sexually assaulted me. Men violated my body, my mind, and my spirit. Healing has been a long journey of attending to nightmares, anxiety, and depression, while also paying close attention to supportive dreams and sacred images that have risen from contemplative silence. My ongoing contemplative centering has provided spiritual richness that is often difficult to express in words.

I begin this chapter with one of the useful dreams that reveals a vision of profound beauty residing within. Despite the trauma of sexual violence carried in a woman's body, soul, and psyche, the power of new life and love may surely rise from within her vast and wonderful depths to speak to her and to heal her. This life and love can be named as God Herself.

My Dream

In my dream I am watching a little girl enjoying a bath. She is between three and four years old and experiencing the deepest delight that seems humanly possible. She is on her back, her body stretched out; I notice her sweet self from head to toe. Her head is submerged in shallow water with only her nose above the water. Her drenched hair floating in a wispy fashion, her eyes and lips squinched up. The water covers her whole body, but barely so. I see her legs and feet. I watch as she paddles her little hands in the water like she is swimming on her back. She is beautiful, perfect, safe, contented, and completely accepting of her current state. And yet, she seems too authentic, too little, too unassuming to be kept there or anywhere. I watch her lovingly. I don't know if the joy emanates from her or from me, but most likely the joy comes from the loving beholding itself. The joy stems from the Divine indwelling that is an ever so quiet but steady preciousness rising from her squinched eyes and nose, from her paddling hands. She is blessed and held in safe, pure water. My eye, my soul, my heart, my body resonate with a most delicate, electric energy. The joy makes me smile in a way that feels eternal, stretching beyond the sky. I call in a loved one to see her beauty, to glimpse the few and fleeting moments of her so as not to miss it. The loved one gets there in time to glimpse her, the vision of her as I see her and experience her—the beholding infused with divine presence, with original sublime wholeness. The child who is she. The child who is joy. The child who is eternal. The child who can never be disturbed or disdained.

This dream exudes the earthly, transcendent light of a female child, safe and free, cherished beyond measure by a female adult. This is a dream of supreme spiritual significance as femaleness is experienced with profound worth and respect. The *well-being* of both female child and female adult creates a spiritual state of wholeness and joy. This dream arose from the deepest center of my soul where the Divine dwells and intermingles with the whole of my life. It is this innermost within-ness of my soul where I am rooted, where my naked life stands in accessibility to the Holy, and where numerous visions of the Divine Feminine have arisen over my lifetime. It is a place of intimate relationship with the Divine and sacred solidarity with girls and women. This inner ground of the Holy in all of us, as a locus of hope and healing, bears revelatory power for girls and women in a world in which we experience violence at the hands of others.

"I found god in myself and I loved her/I loved her fiercely."[1]

Episcopal priest Cynthia Bourgeault describes *point vierge* as "the divine ground itself," within a person's inner depths that "manifests in and through one's individual form . . . where something of our being presses deep into the heart of God." It is the ground of one's own arising where the unfathomably deep presence of God within a person inspires hope.[2] Thomas Merton described it as an inner place where one "shares not only the likeness, but even the substance of God's own being," an innermost place where a person is *found* by God through the person's openness to enter the unknown.[3] This beautiful language describing *point vierge* is foundational to this chapter as I explore this place where the Divine Feminine makes Herself known, perhaps especially in women traumatized by male dominance and violence. *Point vierge of the Divine Feminine*, as I will call it, is a profound source of healing where the Divine in female form sustains a woman through the violent event/s, and stays with her always, as a constant Holy *indwelling*. Thus, I began with my dream of a girl child and woman dwelling in love and safety as a glorious expression of healing made possible with the Divine Feminine as the foundation of a woman's soul.

Spiritual healing can be difficult for women within their male-dominant Christian churches that perpetuate notions of God as a powerful male controlling women's bodies that mirror women's assailants. The misogynist attitudes within most religious organizations prevent women survivors from recognizing the healing presence of the Holy in themselves. This spiritual violence further dehumanizes her, exacerbating the sexual violence. This environment threatens to cut women off from a potentially deep, intimate healing source—the Divine Feminine in whose image women are made. The Divine Feminine holds women tenderly and brings healing light to the open wounds.

My personal evolving consciousness of *point vierge of the Divine Feminine*—using dreams, visions, words, and profound silence—has transformed and healed me. The three contemplative pieces I have written—*Woman God*, *Woman Christ*, and *Sophia's Healing Tent*—demonstrate the intimate, healing dynamism of the Divine Feminine. And to contextualize this transformative process, I include insights from feminist theologians, mystics, and poets who validate women's deepest spiritual intuitions about their darkest nights; a validation that is another crucial spiritual gift. Thus, I seek to encourage women survivors of sexual violence seeking spiritual healing to listen to their own souls for the intimate stirrings of the Divine in female form in their search for beautiful, spacious new horizons of healing and flourishing.

Woman God

My poem *Woman God* expresses the experience of the Divine Feminine visiting me in a dream when I was suffering. She, a spiritual power surpassing anything I had known before, eclipsed the distant, punishing male god of my childhood. This beautiful Deity that rose from the depths of trauma during a night's sleep called me to Herself with stunning nearness and inexplicable kindness.

> Woman God, She appears
> at darkest night,
> in solemn silence,
> softly emerging from
> millennia of hiddenness
>
> Woman God, She arrives
> from celestial realms,
> on the echoes of prayers
> from ancient tongues,
> and from my own body

Woman God, She uncloaks
Herself to meet me in
the depths of sleep
to awaken me to Her

Woman God, She shows
Her countenance,
a gold luminosity
opening my being

Woman God, She unbosoms
Her reassurance, as Creatix of
my healing, summoning me
into Her presence

Woman God, She lives
at my center, authoring
the unveiling of truth, that
makes me whole

Woman God, She reveals
Her graciousness, sweet as honey,
certain as a swallow's song,
to comfort my weariness

Woman God, She beholds
my face in wordless peace
a radiant mother's kiss
imprinted in my heart

Woman God, She rouses
my soul to see Her
Holiness, that defies evil
and commands love

Woman God, She smiles
before me, imbuing
my body with safety,
my spirit with joy

Woman God, She feeds
me Her bread of intimacy,
that my heart is availed
to the violated

Woman God, She enfleshes
divinity at my core
that I pour out
my life in courage.

This poem expresses a profound truth of the Divine Feminine. She flings open a door to a woman's inner self, a path of spiritual safety, a path lined with jewels of hope and strength, shimmering in the darkness, proclaiming from the depths of a woman's body and soul, *I am within you.*

Emily Dickinson's words, "After great pain . . . This is the Hour of Lead . . . As Freezing persons, recollect the Snow,"[4] aptly described for me the visceral pain and deathly stillness after rape. As a young woman, I would often lie motionless on the bed or sofa, groaning with the spiritual pain I endured. As I breathed, I could hear in my throat a primal moaning. Sexual assault is an extreme form of personal violation that rips into the core of one's being. The weight of the suffering is so deep, it can feel unreachable. And yet it wasn't. A dream created the trajectory of my inner healing, a dream that can best be described as luminous kindness. In my dream a voice says, *Remember the identity of God.* A woman's beautiful, radiant face, very close to my face, gazed at me. I felt light of heart in the brightness emanating from Her countenance. The dream was an experience of sustained seeing and being seen with untold, deep respect. The scared energy vivified my suffering heart. Upon waking, I felt joy.

I understood this feminine radiance-filled presence as Divine Wisdom. I had already encountered Her as *Chokhmah* in the Hebrew Bible and as *Sophia* in the Apocrypha and Christian scripture. The dream, in its profundity, called me into a deeper relationship with Her. As a young adult carrying a grievous trauma in my being, Holy Sophia, the Divine Feminine, became the center of my study, the energy of my prayer, the focus of my heart, and the holiness at the depth of my pain. In the Book of Wisdom, a mystical biblical text that emerged from ancient Israel's Babylonian Exile, Holy Sophia is described as "a reflection of eternal light," and "compared with light she is found to be superior."[5] Bourgeault describes Sophia as one who "dances and weaves her way between the created and uncreated realms in her role as primordial, pristine awareness."[6] Though patriarchal churches have long neglected biblical wisdom literature, women of the 20th and 21st centuries have been turning their attention to Holy Sophia. Feminist theologian Elizabeth Johnson describes Sophia as "the mother of the universe, the unoriginate, living source of all that exists," who carries and comforts while at the same time, "seeks to overcome whatever destroys beloved creation."[7] Johnson points out that vast numbers of women around the world are having conversion experiences of God as female. She explains, "this profound conversion to the goodness of what is female brings in its wake a new sense of God as beneficent toward women."[8] And she echoes Martin Buber in her assertion that *great images of the divine* do not come about as simple projections of the imagination, "but are awakened from the deep abyss of human existence in real encounter with divine power and glory."[9] Carmelite sister Constance Fitzgerald writes: "I now find myself asking if possibly this *is* the time, the age, for Sophia: God experienced in feminine categories from the ground up."[10] The Hebrew Sophia invites us all to form an intimate relationship with her:

> Come to me, you who desire me,
> and eat your fill of my fruits.
> For the memory of me is sweeter than honey,
> and the possession of me sweeter than the honeycomb.
> Those who eat of me will hunger for more,
> and those who drink of me will thirst for more.[11]

Holy Sophia reached me not through church doctrine or traditional church services, but through the innermost center of my own being. God as She, rising to my consciousness from within, flung open a door into a benevolent, safe, and spacious place; myself. In the wake of sexual trauma, She set me on a gracious path that would necessarily supersede the male dominant god of my childhood and youth, a god inadequate to the complexity of trauma healing.

This dawning of the Divine Feminine at *point vierge* within, imprinted an awareness of feminine sacred energy as freely, generously given. Elizabeth Johnson writes, "seeking the female face of God releases divine mystery from its age-old patriarchal cage so that God can be truly God."[12] Holy Sophia plants seeds of yearning to summon growth and to deepen peace through the long night of healing sexual trauma. She is in conversation with the ever-unfolding mystery of one's own heart. Holy Wisdom, says Johnson, is "indwelling spirit, the ground of our being, the beyond in our midst, the absolute future, being itself, matrix, mother, lover, friend, infinite love, the truly incomprehensible mystery that surrounds and supports the world."[13] This Divine One, freed from the patriarchal cage, whispers today into the souls of women Her loving messages about their human, holy beauty.

On a particularly difficult day as a young woman, I covered myself in a blanket, rolled over to my side, and groaned as I breathed. My breath going in and out of my inner wound caused pain. As I began to relax and go to sleep, I saw an eye. It was one eye. It looked at me. As I breathed, the eye felt nearer and nearer to the center of me. So attentive was the eye—so present to my wound—it joined me in that wound—in the center, so near, so open, so clear, so steady. I went deeply into restful sleep.

I awakened with renewed energy. This Divine presence is kind, gentle, inexplicably intimate, and insistent that Her love sustains. Not merely is the healing process under Her watchful eye, She *is* the healing process. Wisdom, writes Rabbi Rami Shapiro, "doesn't change anything. She illumines everything. She is right seeing. She is the center that holds the periphery."[14]

During a Holy Week service in preparation for Easter, my body was suddenly overcome with a coldness, and I trembled uncontrollably. I was standing in the back of the church listening to a male priest preach about the Passion, which triggered waves of turbulence in my body. A friend noticing my distress, put her arm around me and I closed my eyes in private prayer. A vision came to me of Holy Sophia outside in the night's darkness moving around the church with love and power and hovering above like Ruach moving over the primordial waters. It took many years for me to truly appreciate what was happening in my own depths that night. The violence that marked my own female self and the Divine Feminine within was outside the scope of male religious leadership, their theological understanding, and their compassion. A male priest preaching about a patriarchal god requiring masculine violence against a male Jesus, his male voice reverberating from the pulpit, male clerical bodies clustered at the center, the sight and aroma of incense in the air, and music creating an ethereal feel, assailing me at my deepest vulnerability. My body was telling me I was spiritually unsafe. Absent was a woman's strength of presence leading the church service. Silent was a woman's voice to speak a theologically sophisticated message that the patriarchal violence in the Passion narrative does not save anyone, that masculine violence ubiquitous in today's world is evil and destructive. Silent and invisible in the Holy Week liturgy are the women in the pews who carry the marks of masculine violence in their female bodies and souls. And forbidden from the sanctuary by male clergy is receptiveness to the protective presence of Woman God Who knows this suffering intimately.

I am not alone in these feelings. Theologian Serene Jones writes of her friend Leah, a rape survivor, who was retraumatized during worship. In Leah's words, "it was the part about Jesus' blood and body. There was a flash in my head, and I couldn't tell the difference between Jesus and me, and then I saw blood everywhere."[15] Afraid, confused and disoriented, she raced to the restroom. Jones' witness to her friend's pain had a profound effect on her. Describing it in terms of a mystical experience, she writes of a powerful vison in which, "A new world appeared before me. In it, we were still in the sanctuary, but Leah's cold, ice-white tiled bathroom had expanded to hold a whole congregation of shivering souls."[16] In the vision, she saw the sanctuary erupt in violence; "At times the words spoken, sung, or prayed struck violently against the fragile, traumatized people that gathered there, deepening the terror."[17] In the vision she wants to shield Leah from the *assaultive force of the broken church* and its history of violence. As a feminist theologian and ordained pastor focused on how liturgy and preaching retraumatizes trauma survivors, Jones asks, "How can we make theological sense of what happened on the cross in a way that speaks to the experience of traumatized victims without glorifying violence?"[18] Feminist theologian Shelly Rambo says that trauma is the suffering that does not go away, that something of the violence remains, "and its remaining is a continuous encounter with the enigma of suffering."[19]

Woman Christ

My poem *Woman Christ* expresses the experience of the indwelling Christ in female form, sacred aliveness stirring in my sinew, flowing through my bloodstream, breathing through my lungs, during the assault in the backseat. This Divine Feminine energy is not mere presence during a bad time, not simply God *with* me and *in* me. The deeper truth is that She and I are *one* through the violation, crying out in protest with one voice, being sustained in love with one heart. She leads the way through the darkness.

> Christ, She indwells me
> In the deathly hours
> When bent by evil
> Young men take siege of me
>
> Christ, Her Word
> Commands my self-love
> While they strip from me
> All clothing and agency
>
> Christ, Her light
> Races through my veins
> Illuminating the shadows
> While they devour my flesh
>
> Christ, Her fire
> Blazes through my blood
> Igniting my strength
> While they violate my depths
>
> Christ, Her lament
> Shrieks through my pain
> "Why do you desecrate?"
> While they spill their filth

Christ, Her power
Seizes my spirit
My soft breathing self
Away from the rhythmic throb

Christ, Her love
Burns in my being
Divinity taking hold
Through the abysmal night

Christ, Her waters
Pour into my soul
Washing my vulnerable self
Of the torrid trauma

Christ, Her voice
Speaks through my body
"We are one heart"
In time and eternity
Against the humiliations

Christ, Her justice
Lives through my flesh
Irrevocably established
To prevail against evil

Christ, Her wisdom
Hails my soul
With healing tidings
Of Woman Christ in the world

Christ, Her silence
A universal cathedral
Expands through my being
For safety and peace.

Woman Christ is a poem that expresses the inexpressible—the inseparability of me and Christ as Woman. And not merely my individual self, but my profound connection to countless traumatized women of the vast and transcendent spiritual Body of Woman Christ.

Christ crucified *is the power and the wisdom [Sofia] of God* (1 Corinthians 1:24). It is only by way of Holy Sophia[20] within, that I can safely and lovingly know Christ crucified at the center of my trauma. It is in the sanctity of solitude where I have come to know Divine Wisdom's indwelling as Woman Christ. Sophia's luminous face and Her watchful eye becoming divine pathos in my innermost being—Christ in female form. In the private, vulnerable places of my female self, Christ was woman enduring it with me. In the brutal hours there was sacred sustenance, my breath, Her breath, my body, Her body. Her light holding my body, bearing the death of it all. Sophia says, *You are alive. You live in Me*. My own heart became the new sanctuary of my survival and my long healing. My heart is my safest spiritual dwelling place. At *point vierge* of the Divine Feminine, Woman Christ rises continually to cloak my being, as if with the golden rays of a soft summer morning. She is protector. Her divine power, like an ever-greening vine, wrapping lovingly around the core of my soul, calls me into brighter and brighter light, with each year, with each decade.

Several years after the campus sexual assault, a female pastor gave me a photograph of *Christa*, the bronze sculpture of a female crucified Christ created by artist Edwina Sandys. An immediate, profound inner stirring occurred. My viscera felt to quiver with sacred significance as I was able to see with my physical eyes the invisible truth of the female cruciform of my dreams and private contemplative prayer in the years following the attack. Female crucified Christ, the passion and power at the center of my deepest suffering, was suddenly freed from hiddenness and silence. A woman-to-woman pastoral moment opened breathing space for my female-centered spiritual truth; in a male dominated church that rejects it. Not only did the art speak directly to the divine in my solitary trauma, but it also pulled me into the universality of Woman Christ; into women's collective sexual trauma, forging a fierce connection, primordial yet brand new, with violated, crucified women and girls the world over.

Edwina Sandys' *Christa* was created in 1974 for the United Nations Decade for Women: Equality, Development, and Peace (1976–1985) and was placed at the side of the main altar in the Episcopal Church of St. John the Divine in New York City during Holy Week in 1984. The sculpture portrays "a slumped female nude wearing a crown of thorns with outstretched arms depicting the cross."[21] The broken body of Sandys' *Christa* "naked upon the cross, gives voice to ways in which the bodies of women have been abandoned and alienated from the Body of Christ," and has the power to bring women's experiences of violent abuse out of silence and into speech."[22] Upon seeing *Christa* Edwina Hunter described the experience as a "visual sermon," and "a sermon of hope," moving her to experience oneness with all her "crucified sisters everywhere."[23] Another sculpture also created in 1974, *Crucified Woman* by Almuth Lutkenhause-Lackey, portrays a naked young woman in cruciform. It was placed in the chancel of Bloor St. United Church, Toronto in 1979 during Lent, including a Good Friday service devoted to battered women, and throughout Eastertide. Lutkenhause-Lackey said she was deeply touched by all the women who told her that "for the first time they had felt close to Christ seeing suffering expressed in a female body."[24] And in 1986, *Crucified Woman* was installed in the grounds of Emmanuel College, Toronto, a theological college of the United Church of Canada. The sculpture then became a shrine to the memory of the victims of the 1989 Ecole Polytechnique misogynist massacre in Montreal in which twenty-seven women were shot.

Bosnian Christa was created by Margaret Argyle during a personal Lenten meditation on the systemic rapes of women in 1993 in the former Yugoslavia. The art features a black wool backdrop split down the center. A bold red opening is framed by red velvet and standing inside the opening of the vulva is a naked female cruciform. Megan Clay writes, "there is a paradoxical dignity rather than degradation in the scene, for the cross can also be understood to be standing guard at the mouth of the vulnerable exposed vulva, quietly repelling the aggressor."[25]

Bosnian Christa was featured prominently in the "Coming Out of the Shadows: Women Against Violence" ecumenical service of the World Council of Churches Decade for Churches in Solidarity with Women (1988–1998) in the Anglican Cathedral in England in 1993.

In her book *Seeking the Risen Christa*, Nicola Slee writes that the idea of Christ as female has very ancient roots in the biblical tradition of Wisdom (*Chokhmah, Sophia*). In earliest Christian thought, Christ was understood in terms of female Wisdom's divine light, cosmic power, and dynamic presence among humanity. In her quest for a feminist language of prayer, Slee has her on eye on Christa as the "heart of the public prayer of the church."[26] In this profound collection of poems, prayers, and reflections, Slee unveils for readers her love and passion for Christa. The introduction opens with a pressing, creative question about the risen Christa, *where is she?* "Why is the Christa always suffering, broken, dying?"[27] In her poem "Christa Crucified," she answers, we need "her dead and dying," "bleeding and gasping," her body spread open, "to stand for all that has split women open."[28] In her poem "Christa sister," she makes pleas to Christa; "do not hide your face from me," "come out of the shadows," "show me your wounds," "let me find you."[29] She says that Christa is the girl trafficked, the woman with bruises, the woman sleeping in the underpass, and the anorexic teenager. Slee prays, "Christa, God's beloved, show your face, where we have not wanted to see it, where we resist your presence among us."[30] It is only in seeing and embracing the oppressed women and girls in our midst and afar that we can hope to see Christa in risen form. When women defy the many marks of violence and suffering in their bodies and souls, Slee proclaims about the risen Christa, "Look at her! Though the forces of death that tried to pull her back were legion, her resistance is awesome. She flings herself full tilt into living."[31]

Several years after the campus attack, I dreamt of a light, fiercely bright. The light was engulfing me with the swiftness of a lightning strike and I felt a rising upward, within and beyond myself. Instantaneously, its power and love marked me indelibly. It was only after this dream that the female cruciform began to rise in my consciousness. In the eternal Wisdom of Woman God, only with the light and power of *divine love* given as a startling burst through my being, was I ready to understand suffering Woman Christ. Images of female cruciform came into my awareness through dreams and deep prayer and with this came a long,

Figure 11.1 Woman Christ, Raped on Campus by Julie Tallent

strenuous self-emptying of the internalized maleness of Christ insisted upon by patriarchal clergy. The Divine Feminine met me in the ashes and ruins of sexual assault and initiated a profound rebuilding in my soul. As if from an unfathomable abyss, Christ in female form gradually became the heart of my existence. My soul and its healing became a holy ground anew, inhospitable to any misogynist Christian doctrine. This apophasis, a Divine-initiated self-emptying of misogynist spirituality, opened my soul to the understanding that the cross is a site of patriarchal violence,[32] but that Christ's love in female form is a power far greater than the evil of male domination and sexual violence—a healing power of resistance to the violence.[33] Experiencing Christ in female form in my body and soul at the deep center of personal violation became the abiding light at the core of my being. *Woman Christ, Raped on Campus*, a pen, and ink drawing created by artist Julie Tallent, depicts this inner truth of the inseparability of Christ and my nineteen-year-old self. Furthermore, it expresses my connection with all girls and women violated by men, in the mystical Body of Woman Christ.

Sophia's Healing Tent

I co-wrote the poem *Sophia's Healing Tent* with my therapist to plumb new depths within myself where my spirituality of the Divine Feminine was given creative freedom to interact with therapeutic knowledge of trauma care. In this poem, we unveil tender truths about the tentative steps of rape victims in need of divine care that is gentle enough to meet them in the depths of personal violation. The writing process was profound for me as a survivor as the fullness of my being and the fullness of my power poured out onto the page in dialogue with a compassionate caregiver. And as a clergywoman who is caregiver to female survivors of sexual violence, I was strengthened by the joining of voices to speak into existence a safe, spacious place for trauma care beyond myself. This space that we describe poetically as a *tent* is filled with Holy hospitality. Even so, the trauma victim may well meet it with fear and hesitancy. The pain and vulnerability can prevent victims from entering the threshold. A victim's trauma makes her fragile and she may want to hide or run away. She may connect, then disconnect, enter in, then leave, or peer in from a distance. But when she can stay in a healing spot under the tent, the trauma can begin to *burn* away allowing the ashes of suffering to fall while the Divine guides her through each moment of healing.

> From the highest heavens
> She draws near
> Her Divine Heart breaking
> for Her daughters

Her stars shine for you
She appears on earth
settling in the desert
in the holy tent
where She ministers
She wants joy for you
While Christ as Mother
invites, "Come to me
all you who are weary
and I will give you rest."
She wants you to love your life
Gentleness of heart
you will find here
where you will know
"rest for your souls."
She helps you
St. Joan of Arc,
guardian against evil,
offers lavender balm
a tender anointing
at the tent's entrance
That you may flourish
Wings of the dove
touch gently to the ground
providing cover from
the searing heat
of the daylight.
You can trust Her
Ashes litter the ground
from previous occupants
a purified blanket of
so many past wounds
She pervades all things
The next person
arrives eviscerated by
the unspeakable menace
She bears your rape, struck down and afflicted
Ducking into the tent
unsure of who is trustworthy
but needing protection
needing to heal
She is breath that will help you breathe
Even within these
confines trust evades

promises are useless
for one so injured
She makes things well
She sets Her table
But need surpasses reason
pain overwhelms fear
relief is all that can sustain
the humanness within
the broken pieces
She offers you sweet bread
Come under the wings
drink fully from the
breast of healing
stay little or long
there is no cost
Your healing is sweeter than the honeycomb
Ashes fall and litter the ground
the tent warms without burn
fear evaporates with the slowness of death
yet sanctity abides, abounds
She sees your light
Come to the river
wash yourself clean
wounded and marred
your beauty is eternal
Excelling every constellation of the stars.

In *Sophia's Healing Tent*, the Divine Feminine summons rape victims to find refuge under Her care. For much of my life, I have experienced Holy Sophia as a summoning power to an ever-deepening interiority and self-transcendence. Sophia ministering from Her tent is not mere borrowed metaphor. It is an aliveness, a presence, a palpable love, a spiritual space inwardly and outwardly that stretches my being unceasingly with healing and hope. It is contemplation itself. In *Sophia's Healing Tent*, the *tent* is a truly safe place for trauma care.

With the expert care and tender accompaniment of my therapist, it is a spiritual and therapeutic place to be, to breathe, to process pain, to feel my wholeness as a sentient person, to sit in the quiet for love to stir and to allow love to sound through my being for others who are traumatized by rape. Judith Herman, in her classic *Trauma and Recovery*, writes that rape is essentially "the physical, psychological, and moral violation of the person" where the intent of the rapist is to "terrorize, dominate, and humiliate his victim."[34] Sexual violence is pernicious to a woman's sense of self and to her sense of connection with others. Herman states that while trauma isolates, shames, stigmatizes, degrades, and dehumanizes victims, forming a community recreates belonging, bears witness, and affirms, exalts, and restores humanity. As such, the *tent* is a state of heart, it is my presence, my loving agency where from my healing I welcome other girls and women who need safety and tender accompaniment to be, to breathe, to process pain, to lean with hope into the wide horizon of their unique beauty and purpose. The *tent* is of supreme spiritual significance that femaleness is experienced with profound worth and respect.

The Divine Feminine is vast and mysterious. It is the essence of Her to reveal Herself in myriad ways to diverse women everywhere, accessible to women in their most intimate selves so that they heal and flourish. Kaia Tingley writes that the Divine Feminine calls us back to beauty as the one who is "the ground under our bare feet and the wind in our hair. Do you hear her singing?"[35] She is also one who offers us a cup of calming tea, "Do we dare to allow her softness again? I take the cup of tea."[36] Arlene Bailey writes that she has "screamed guttural prayers to the Mother of All that enough is enough," and this *Mother of All* assures her that "the light always returns," and "while grief and trauma shift and morph, you will survive and even prosper."[37] And she writes of a shape-shifting divine feminine who brings healing. First as Wolf, she howls and awakens her soul and "sits beside me holding a space for the ineffable to be felt and the insidious to be silenced," and in this space she is safe. She is then a Woman holding "a thousand candles with flames as bright as the sun."[38]

Elizabeth A. Johnson describes the limitlessness and incomprehensibility of the Divine as the "ineffable mystery beyond all telling," and "unspeakably Other."[39] It can be profoundly encouraging and freeing for survivors to be reminded of this by feminist theologians as sexual trauma may send women into new inner depths where the soul thirsts beyond old notions of god, where the heart longs for true relationship with the Divine. This new yearning rising from the debris of trauma exposes a patriarchal god, hyperfocused on sin and judgment, for what it is, a dead metaphor. When women listen to their own souls and when women listen to other women who listen to their own souls, the incomprehensible Other can appear wondrously within her as She Who is bent on healing—fiercely, lovingly so. Mystic Mechthild of Magdeburg describes wonderfully her experience of the Divine One Who longs for closeness, "It is my nature that makes me love you often, for I am love itself. It is my longing that makes me love you intensely, for I yearn to be loved from the heart. It is my eternity that makes me love you long, for I have no end."[40]

The Divine Feminine, Architect of love and compassion, longs to be revealed in the hidden, holy depths (*point vierge*) of women. If a woman feels within herself a stirring, a longing, for the Divine Feminine, she should breathe slowly. Breathe deeply. Be still. Enter the quiet. Listen attentively and know that she can love and trust herself. She should consider these loving affirmations:

- Her life is a wondrous gift.
- Her life is safe with the Divine Feminine.
- Her female body is suffused with the splendor of Her Divine love.
- Her inner depths are her sanctuary.
- Her trauma healing work is sacred.
- Her darkness will give way to new luminosity through her struggle.
- Her desert of suffering will bring forth vibrant bloom.
- Her joy will be returned to her.
- Her beauty and power are connected to the beauty and power of survivors all around the world.

Remember, "You are being held in Shekhinah's arms and protected by her wings . . . you are becoming lighter and lighter. Now, you let the light of Shekhinah transport you to an inner palace of warmth and love, light and peace."[41]

Notes

1 From Ntozake Shange's choreopoem and Broadway show *for coloured girls who have considered suicide/when the rainbow is enuf* (San Lorenzo: Shameless Hussy Press, 1975), 63. Daphne Hampson writes, "At the conclusion a Black woman, dressed strikingly in red, and standing centre stage, declares: "i found god in myself & i loved her/ i loved her fiercely. What a comment on what western culture has done to those who are both female and Black!" *Theology and Feminism* (Cambridge: Basil Blackwell, 1990), 111.
2 Cynthia Bourgeault, *Mystical Hope: Trusting in the Mercy of God* (Lanham: A Cowley Publications Book, 2001), 39, 40.
3 Bourgeault, *Mystical Hope*, 38.
4 Adrienne Rich, *On Lies, Secrets, And Silence: Selected Prose* (New York: W. W. Norton & Company, 1979), 179.
5 The Wisdom of Solomon 7: 26, 29, (New Revised Standard Version).
6 Cynthia Bourgeault, *The Wisdom Way of Knowing: Reclaiming an Ancient Tradition to Awaken the Heart*, (San Francisco: Jossey-Bass, 2003), 12.
7 Elizabeth A. Johnson, *She Who Is: The Mystery of God in Feminist Theological Discourse*, (New York: Crossroad, 1992), 179, 180.
8 Elizabeth A. Johnson, *Abounding in Kindness: Writings for the People of God*, (Maryknoll, New York: Orbis Books, 2015), 128, 129.
9 Johnson, *Abounding in Kindness*, 129.
10 Constance Fitzgerald, "Transformation in Wisdom: The Subversive Character and Educative Power of Sophia in Contemplation," ed. Kevin Culligan and Regis Jordan, (Washington, DC: ICS Publications, 2000), 283.

11 Sirach 24: 19–21, (New Revised Standard Version).
12 Johnson, "Naming God She: The Theological Implications," 5.
13 Ibid., 11.
14 Rabbi Rami Shapiro, *The Divine Feminine in Biblical Wisdom Literature: Selections Annotated and Explained*, (Woodstock: Skylight Paths Publishing, 2010), xxii, 16.
15 Serene Jones, *Trauma and Grace: Theology in a Ruptured World*, (Louisville: Westminster John Knox Press, 2019), 7.
16 Jones, *Trauma and Grace*, 9.
17 Ibid., 10.
18 Ibid., 85.
19 Shelly Rambo, *Spirit and Trauma: A Theology of Remaining*, (Louisville: Westminster John Knox Press, 2010), 18.
20 Johnson, *She Who Is*, 266.
21 Julie Clague, "The Christa: Symbolizing My Humanity and My Pain," Sage Publications, (2005), 85, https://journals.sagepub.com/doi/abs/10.1177/0966735005057803.
22 Elisabeth Vasko, "Redeeming Beauty? *Christa* and the Displacement of Women's Bodies in Theological Aesthetic Discourses," Sage Journals, (2013), 200, sagepub.com.
23 Clague, "The Christa Symbolizing My Humanity and My Pain," 87.
24 Ibid., 89.
25 Ibid., 97.
26 Nicola Slee, *Seeking the Risen Christa*, (Great Britain: SPCK, 2011), xii.
27 Slee, *Seeking the Risen Christa*, 1.
28 Ibid., 79.
29 Ibid., 78.
30 Ibid., 76.
31 Ibid., 132.
32 Elizabeth Johnson says the cross "stands as a poignant symbol of the 'kenosis of patriarchy,' the self-emptying of male dominating power in favor of the new humanity of compassionate service and mutual empowerment." [Johnson, *She Who Is*, 161]
33 Elizabeth A. Johnson writes that in the mystery of divine sorrow, God, in unimaginable compassion, suffers with beloved creation. Moreover, "Holy Wisdom keeps vigil through endless hours of pain, while her grief awakens protest." God not only consoles but strengthens "those bowed by sorrow to hope and to resist." [Johnson, *She Who Is*, 260, 261]
34 Judith Herman, *Trauma and Recovery: The Aftermath of Violence—From Domestic Abuse to Political Terror*, (New York: Basic Books, 1992), 58.
35 Ibid., 51.
36 Ibid., 51.
37 Ibid., 63, 64, 65.
38 Ibid., 93.
39 Elizabeth A. Johnson, *Quest for The Living God: Mapping Frontiers in the Theology of God*, (New York: Continuum, 2008) 17.
40 Janet K. Ruffing, R.S.M., *Spiritual Direction: Beyond the Beginnings*, (New York: Paulist Press, 2000), 10.
41 Rabbi Leah Novick writes that she began to experience the Divine Feminine (Shekhinah) "in the hills, the ocean, the landscape." [Novick, *On the Wings of Shekhinah: Rediscovering Judaism's Divine Feminine* (Wheaton: Theosophical Publishing House, 2008) 1]

Bibliography

Aldred, Louise, Daly, Pat, and Hendren, Trista eds. *Remembering with Goddess: Healing the Patriarchal Perpetuation of Trauma*, Girl God Books (2022).
Bourgeault, Cynthia, *Mystical Hope: Trusting in the Mercy of God*, Cowley Publications (2001).
Bourgeault, Cynthia, *The Wisdom Way of Knowing: Reclaiming an Ancient Tradition to Awaken the Heart*, Jossey-Bass (2003).
Clague, Julie, "The Christa Symbolizing My Humanity and My Pain," Sage Publications https://journals.sagepub.com/doi/abs/10.1177/0966735005057803 (2005).
Doehring, Carrie, "Spiritual Care After Violence: Growing from Trauma with Lived Theology," https://cct.biola.edu/spiritual-care-violence-growing-trauma-lived-theology/ (2014).
Doehring, Carrie, *The Practice of Pastoral Care: A Postmodern Approach*, Westminster John Knox Press (2015).
FitzGerald, Constance, "Transformation in Wisdom: The Subversive Character and Educative Power of Sophia in Contemplation," in *Carmel and Contemplation: Transforming Human Consciousness*, eds. Kevin Culligan and Regis Jordan, ICS Publications (2000).
Fortune, Marie, *Sexual Violence: The Sin Revisited*, The Pilgrim Press (2005).
Giles, Mary E. ed., *The Feminist Mystic: And Other Essays on Women and Spirituality*, Crossroad (1982).
Hampson, Daphne, *Theology and Feminism*, Basil Blackwell (1990).
Herman, Judith, *Trauma and Recovery: The Aftermath of Violence—From Domestic Abuse to Political Terror*, Basic Books (1997).
Johnson, Elizabeth A., *Abounding in Kindness: Writings for the People of God*, Orbis Books (2015).
Johnson, Elizabeth A., *Quest for the Living God: Mapping Frontiers in the Theology of God*, Continuum (2007).
Johnson, Elizabeth A., *She Who Is: The Mystery of God in Feminist Theological Discourse*, Crossroad (1992).
Johnson, Elizabeth A., "Naming God She: The Theological Implications," Scholarly Commons, https://repository.upenn.edu/boardman/5/ (2000).
Jones, Serene, *Trauma and Recovery: Theology in a Ruptured World*, Westminster John Knox Press (2019).
Knight, Jennie S., *Feminist Mysticism and Images of God: A Practical Theology*, Chalice Press (2011).
Lanzetta, Beverly J., *Radical Wisdom: A Feminist Mystical Theology*, Fortress Press (2005).
Meehan, Bridget Mary, *Exploring the Feminine Face of God*, Sheed & Ward (1991).
Novick, Rabbi Leah, *On the Wings of Shekhinah: Rediscovering Judaism's Divine Feminine*, Quest Books (2008).
O'Donnell, Karen and Cross, Katie, eds. *Feminist Trauma Theologies: Body, Scripture and Church in Critical Perspective*, SCM Press (2020).
Rambo, Shelly, *Spirit and Trauma: A Theology of Remaining*, Westminster John Know Press (2010).

Rambo, Shelly, *Resurrecting Wounds: Living in the Aftermath of Trauma*, Baylor University Press (2017).
Rich, Adrienne, *On Lies, Secrets, and Silence: Selected Prose*, W. W. Norton & Company (1979).
Ruffing, Janet K., *Spiritual Direction: Beyond the Beginnings*, Paulist Press (2000).
Shapiro, Rabbi Rami, *The Divine Feminine in Biblical Wisdom Literature: Selections Annotated and Explained*, Skylight Paths Publishing (2010).
Slee, Nicola, *Seeking the Risen Christa*, SPCK (2011).
Slee, Nicola, "Visualizing, Conceptualizing, Imagining and Praying the Christa: In Search of Her Risen Forms Sage Publications," sagepub.com (2012).
Van Deusen Hunsinger, Deborah, *Bearing the Unbearable: Trauma, Gospel, and Pastoral Care*, William B. Eerdmans Publishing Company (2015).
Vasko, Elizabeth, "Redeeming Beauty? *Christa* and the Displacement of Women's Bodies in Theological Aesthetic Discourses," Sage Journals, sagepub.com (2013).
Weber, Christin Lore, *Woman Christ: A New Vision of Feminist Spirituality*, Harper and Row (1987).
Winter, Miriam Therese, *WomanWisdom: A Feminist Lectionary and Psalter Women of the Hebrew Scriptures: Part One*, Crossroad (1991).

Chapter 12

Reclaiming the Divine on the Road to Recovery

Debra Meyers

The Roots of Religious Subjugation

Biblical scholars have not adhered to a literal view of the Bible for more than two hundred years based on overwhelming evidence. For instance, we know that the oldest extant version of the Bible—the Sinai Bible (c. 350 CE) housed at the British Library—differs from the King James translation (c. 1611 CE) in nearly 15,000 instances. And we know that the King James version (KJV) has undergone *dozens* of revisions over time, often at the hands of printers. Significant revisions to the KJV include the total omission of the Book of Wisdom by the Puritans after settling in colonial New England. Moreover, scholars know that the Bible is a collection of books written over roughly a thousand-year time span and none of the books were written by an eyewitness. Additionally, many of these books were revised at different times—in some cases nearly 500 years separated the revisions. Furthermore, a quick examination of any gospel parallels book provides numerous examples of *irreconcilable* differences in the gospels of Mark, Matthew, Luke, and John. Some examples of these differences include Jesus's genealogy, the geography and timespan of Jesus's ministry, as well as the timing and details of Jesus's passion story.[1] Biblical scholars know that the Bible should not be understood as the literal word of God or as a historical document of facts.

Despite considerable research to the contrary, many Protestants and Catholics in the United States adhere to a literal interpretation of the Bible imposing significant damage on women, men, nonbinary, and genderqueer humans.[2] Texts such as the *household codes* contained in Paul's letter to the Ephesians emphasize liminal groups' subordinate position to males in power. This toxic scripture—particularly Ephesians 5—has created collateral damage for nearly two thousand years. It is worth reviewing some of the text at length from the King James version since many literal interpreters of the Bible employ this particular translation to support their positions.

DOI: 10.4324/9781003323631-13

Ephesians 5:21–33 (KJV)
21 Submitting yourselves one to another in the fear of God.
22 Wives, submit yourselves unto your own husbands, as unto the Lord.
23 For the husband is the head of the wife, even as Christ is the head of the church: and he is the saviour of the body.
24 Therefore as the church is subject unto Christ, so let the wives be to their own husbands in everything.
25 Husbands, love your wives, even as Christ also loved the church, and gave himself for it;
26 That he might sanctify and cleanse it with the washing of water by the word,
27 That he might present it to himself a glorious church, not having spot, or wrinkle, or any such thing; but that it should be holy and without blemish.
28 So ought men to love their wives as their own bodies. He that loveth his wife loveth himself.
29 For no man ever yet hated his own flesh; but nourisheth and cherisheth it, even as the Lord the church:
30 For we are members of his body, of his flesh, and of his bones.
31 For this cause shall a man leave his father and mother, and shall be joined unto his wife, and they two shall be one flesh.
32 This is a great mystery: but I speak concerning Christ and the church.
33 Nevertheless let every one of you in particular so love his wife even as himself; and the wife see that she reverence her husband.

Additional texts of domination and subjugation include, but are not limited to, "Let women keep silent" (1 Cor 14) and "Women not to teach" (1 Tim 2: 9–15). It is important to investigate how and why these toxic texts—and others like them—were adopted as sacred scripture and then used to control oppressed people.

Paul of Tarsus in Cilicia (Asia Minor) was a Jewish Christian and, some would argue, founder of the Christian mission to the gentiles in the immediate years following the death of Jesus. Scholars date Paul's portion of the New Testament as the oldest and closest in time to Jesus's ministry.[3] Before being executed by the Romans (c. 64 CE), Paul wrote letters to his scattered Christian communities in Rome, Corinth, Galatia, Philippi, and Thessalonica establishing some of the earliest Christian doctrine; even though Paul never had contact with Jesus during his earthly ministry. Disciples of Jesus who had intimate contact with Jesus during his ministry, also provided leadership to their own large communities, such as those led by Jesus's brother James and Jesus's apostle, Mary Magdala. In contrast to other early Christian community leaders,

Paul felt compelled to write letters—particularly while incarcerated—largely because of his desire to unite disparate Jewish and gentile followers faced with seemingly irreconcilable differences including whether gentiles would have to be circumcised to join Paul's community of Jesus followers.

As important as Paul's letters are to Christians today, scholars have identified numerous difficulties with these documents in the New Testament. For instance, most scholars attribute Paul's letters to the Ephesians and Colossians to Paul's followers at least a generation or two after Paul's death. Scholars base their assertions on specific literary, historical, and theological differences among the disputed letters as compared to the writings that were clearly written by Paul. It is important to recognize this authorship dispute. Elizabeth Johnson states: "Whether or not Paul wrote Ephesians and Colossians (or 2 Thessalonians or the pastoral letters) determines whether or not we can legitimately use the undisputed letters (Romans, 1 and 2 Corinthians, Galatians, Philippians, 1 Thessalonians, and Philemon) to interpret them and vice versa." She adds that if Paul was not the author of Ephesians, Colossians, 2 Thessalonians or the pastoral letters, then "they do not cease to be the church's scripture, but they must be understood in a historical context different from Paul's."[4]

Ephesians and Colossians, in particular, contain distinctly different themes and issues that are never addressed in Paul's undisputed letters. In addition to several key theological issues, they also present two antithetical views of marriage. Both Ephesians and Colossians share a concern with peculiar community problems that reflect the fears of followers *long after Paul's death*.[5] These two documents also share a distinctively different form and style. Instead of using a straightforward standard letter format, the authors of Ephesians and Colossians appear to have created a cover letter to explain and summarize the collection of Paul's epistles with the intention of distributing the writings to many of Paul's communities. This stands in stark contrast to the letters written by Paul that addressed solutions for specific problems for specific communities.[6] On the contrary, the author of Ephesians outlines harsh *household codes* that establish hierarchical relationships with inherent duties and responsibilities as a distinctive Christian community attribute.

Moreover, the imagery in these texts offers *justification* for the subordination and oppression of marginalized people who lack power and authority in the society. For instance, the image of marriage in which 'two shall become one flesh' has been a useful tool employed by religious leaders and male heads of households to control married women through coercion and physical violence. The text has often been used to inculcate fear, not mutual respect.

Significantly, Ephesians and Colossians stand in stark contrast to Paul's undisputed letters regarding patriarchy. Indeed, Galatians 3:28—undeniably written by Paul—proclaimed a new equitable social order for all humans—males and females, gentiles and Jews, enslaved and free—since humans were all made in the image and likeness of God. But Ephesians 5 suggests that this was merely rhetoric. Clearly in the years after Paul's death, Paul's position on social equality did not permeate the household—the microcosm of the entire social structure of the Greco-Roman world. After Paul's death, wives, children, and slaves were to maintain the traditional patriarchal structure of the larger society according to Ephesians 5 with an added Christian twist that aligned the household hierarchy with that of the hierarchy of the Christian community with God.

Subsequently, we are left with disputed Pauline letters of Ephesians and Colossians that strongly state the ideal patriarchal relationship employed to oppress women, children, and slaves. Some theologians would have us declare these household prescriptions anachronistic and therefore better left on the margins, or even ignored entirely. The problem with merely setting aside anachronistic text is that we fail *to acknowledge the significant damage* done by such text over the last two thousand years. Rosemary Radford Ruether and others have recognized the destructive role Church Fathers have played in the perpetuation of the subjugation of women in emphasizing Ephesians 5—and others like it—rather than underscoring the egalitarian society that Paul proposed in Galatians 3:28. Saints Augustine, Thomas Aquinas, John Chrysostom, Jerome, and Gregory of Nyssa—to name just a few—all encouraged women's subjugation based largely on Ephesians 5. For instance, Aquinas often used Ephesians 5—and Aristotle's biological assumptions that women were merely malformed men—to underscore female inferiority. And theologian Mary Shivanandan tells us that when Chrysostom delivered his first homily in 386 CE, he declared that:

> The wife is a second authority; let not her then demand equality, for she is under the head; nor let him despise her as being in subjection, for she is the body; and if the head despise the body, it will itself also perish. But let him bring in love as a counterpoise to obedience.[7]

Chrysostom's position was clear. Patriarchy—as outlined in Ephesians 5—is necessary to ensure peace and tranquility when dealing with weak, childlike women. Most of the Church Fathers have perpetuated this ideology to the point that women often do not even recognize the oppressive nature of the hierarchy within their religious organizations. Their teachings have been used—very effectively—over the last two thousand years to demean, marginalize, control, and exclude liminal people.

One way to counter the subjugation of women perpetuated by church teachings, according to some scholars, is through *special hermeneutics*. Mary Ann Tolbert, for instance, in response to an upsurge in fundamentalist insistence on literal translations, argues that we should view the Bible as *inspirational* rather than as an authoritative historical document of God's will.[8] Viewing the Bible as inspiration rather than God's spoken word, allows Christians to utilize it to encourage a vision of an equitable, just, and diverse society.[9] And while some sects can set aside or selectively impose *special hermeneutics* on anachronistic biblical text, many other groups interpret Ephesians' *household code* as a justification for *complimentary roles* for husbands and wives today.[10] Husbands are to manage the household while wives are to nurture children and abide by their husbands' rules and desires. According to adherents of *complimentary roles* ideology, married couples must submit to each other, but the male head of the household must always be in control. Feminist scholars argue that the concept of *complimentary roles* only reinforces inequity and justifies oppression as the *natural* order of society.

The belief in *complimentary roles* serves to justify fundamentalist positions that accept all scripture as God's sacred word and that there is a natural hierarchy of authority—God rules men and men have authority over everyone else. Carole Bohn suggests that these ideals found in what she calls patriarchy's "theology of ownership," stems from a misinterpretation of Genesis giving men control over every living being.[11] Susan Thistlethwaite also finds patriarchy's theology damaging. Thistlethwaite studied fundamentalist women as victims of their theology in which men are empowered by a *just battering* tradition. According to that tradition, a husband has a *duty* and the *authority* "to punish his wife when, in his judgment, punishment is necessary to maintain his headship."[12] Thistlethwaite argues: "for those who care about violence committed against women and children in their own home, there is no substitute for learning and teaching a liberating interpretation of Eph. 5.21–33 and similar texts." She points out that "frequently, women with strong religious backgrounds have the most difficulty in accepting that the violence against them is wrong."[13]

We need to take seriously the warning that women from these fundamentalist traditions cannot—and will not—trust someone telling them to set aside any scripture that is taken as the "word-for-word-and-God-inspired rulebook for Christian living" regardless of its historical context.[14] Instead, Virginia Ramey Mollenkott asks us to find the *liberating* possibilities in Ephesians 5 in order to challenge the *justified battering* tradition and thus free fundamentalist women from physical and emotional abuse imposed by both the church and their husbands.

Mollenkott argues for several liberating texts in Ephesians 5. First, the husband is "compared to the Christ only in Christ's self-emptying of superior status, taking on voluntary servanthood." Second, "the word 'head' is used not in the sense of 'boss' but in the sense of 'source.'" And finally,

> Christ is identified with the body as well as the head, that the church/body is urged to grow up into the Christ/head, that the human head and body are mutually interdependent, and therefore that the Christian marital structure is depicted as an organic union of mutual subjection and inter-supportiveness.[15]

Mollenkott maintains that by recovering the liberating theology of Ephesians 5, we can assure abused fundamentalist women that they have a *right* to their religious beliefs. But they also have *a right* to their freedom from physical and mental abuse and that they deserve to recover their self-esteem. But does this arduous exercise to find *liberating* theology in scripture really free women and other oppressed groups? Or, do we need to jettison scripture altogether?

Gary Macy reminds us: "Our picture of earlier periods is shaped by what survives, and what survives has been carefully selected and preserved to reflect and support the views of those doing the selecting and preservation."[16] Should we then, dismiss the destructive biblical texts and other oppressive religious dogma and start over? Could this help us to deal with our own oppression *and* move us forward on a pathway to healing and recovery after sexual assault? I argue that it is *essential* to jettison patriarchal texts if we are to create a viable pathway to spiritual healing after sexual assault.

Reclaiming the Divine

Let's begin creating a new pathway to healing and recovery by first retrieving the reason for Jesus's presence on earth. His actions reveal his true purpose—to remind human beings that their existence on earth mandates their continuous work to love one another in an effort to make the world a better place. Jesus's message of love, reciprocity, generosity, and the importance of forgiveness is shared with many other spiritual prophets of the Old Testament as well as prophets outside the Judeo-Christian tradition, including Buddha, Mohammed, Confucius, Krishna, and Shankara. Similarly, these core tenets of love, reciprocity, generosity, and forgiveness can be found in Indigenous spirituality and many other belief systems across time.

Equally important is Jesus's stated purpose when he declares "I have come that they may have life and have it to the full" (John 10:10 NIV). In the King James translation of this verse, Jesus says "I am come that they might have life, and that they might have *it* more abundantly."

If the author of the Gospel of John is correct in the assertion that Jesus pursued his ministry so that humans might live a human existence more abundantly through love, reciprocity, generosity, and forgiveness, then perhaps we might rethink our notions of God and our need for religious dogma and scripture and focus more appropriately on replicating or mirroring Jesus's actions and his way of life. Indeed, the earliest Christians did just that.[17] Early Christians took seriously Jesus's instructions, such as those in the Sermon on the Mount, that prescribed an ethic (what to do and how to be), *not* a belief system established by church doctrine found in the Nicene Creed (325 CE) that only tells people what to believe as a method to control unruly subjects in the Roman Empire.[18]

To begin our journey to healing and recovery after sexual assault, we need to jettison the Bible as the divinely inspired word of God, and as a literal or historical treatise. Instead, we must embrace a more logical and rational way to conceptualize the Divine and our purpose on earth. Our inspiration for this new conceptualization of the Divine can begin with natural laws.

At a young age, we learn a simplification of the earth's ecosystem of water as a continuous cycle of precipitation, evaporation, and condensation in which the essential life-giving compound transitions from solid to liquid and to gas. This multi-billion-year-old water cycle is a *closed system*. When liquid water in a puddle evaporates, transforming into vapor, it may condense to form clouds and when conditions are right, we see precipitation back to the earth's surface as rain, snow, or sleet. Water in liquid form flows across solid surfaces into the ground and percolates through soil, sand, and rock to reside in the water table where ground water fills the space between sediments and rock. Plants can absorb the life-giving compound from this underground water supply. From the plant, the water will then evaporate back into the atmosphere. Water may also accumulate in large bodies, such as ponds, lakes, and oceans. This water can become a solid in freezing environments and remain in this state for extended periods of time. Whether solid or liquid, this water will eventually evaporate joining other particles and condensing into clouds to begin the process anew. At each step of this continuous closed-system process, water particles are transforming from one state to another. Sometimes these particles can be identified as an individual delicate snowflake, while at other times, the particles merge to form a massive tidal wave with the power to destroy human edifices and permanently alter the earth's natural topography.

Regardless of the distinctive features particles may take, the water in this closed system is the same water that has been on earth for at least 3.8 billion years. We drink and swim in the same water that cooled volcanic lava and the same water that quenched the thirst of dinosaurs.

The *law of conservation of matter* determines that the elements of water on earth cannot be created or destroyed. These natural forces, governed by natural laws, are replicated in many forms. For instance, physics tells us that energy also follows natural laws as it transforms from one state to another. Energy, like water, cannot be eliminated, it can only be transformed.

For example, all of the materials that were present at the beginning of our universe during the 'big bang' are still here today. The original sounds, minerals, and elements remain in this closed system. In fact, every lifeform contains the DNA of exploding planets and stars. We now know through DNA research that humans are related to all living things—apes, clams, weeds, cabbages, and even the smallest plankton in the sea. The eighty-four minerals, twenty-three elements, and eight gallons of water that make up the human form are recycled particles from the universe. And when we stop breathing, our essence—our divine spirit, our energy, our light, and the stardust that make up our earthy forms—is transformed, not destroyed. If we apply these natural laws to spirituality, we might rediscover our connection to the Divine as well as the meaning of life as the foundation for healing after sexual assault.

Imagine that all lifeforms—all energy—follow a similar cycle of transformation that the water cycle sustains. In this lifeform cycle, humans and the Divine are merely different molecular states of matter analogous to the solid, gas, and liquid states of water. The eternal energy of all lifeforms that cumulatively makes up the Divine is a state of being that has a consciousness.[19]

The energy in this collective web of awareness, shares information throughout the web of existence; it is a Divine state comparable to that of Artificial Intelligence (AI). The volume of information is incalculable and the possibility for solving problems is limitless. Nevertheless, AI cannot feel anger and love, touch soft or rough surfaces, smell the emergence of spring in the air, or distinguish between sweet and bitter tastes. AI is incomplete.

Similarly, the web of energy that constitutes the Divine is also in a state of incomplete existence. While there is comfort in the collective energy of trillions of life-form particles in this intelligent consciousness, there is a sense that something is missing. The Divine collective of life-form energy yearns to experience feelings, smells, tastes, images, creativity, and the impact of other natural laws including light, sound, gravity, mass, et al. To experience emotions and other human conditions, portions of the web choose to transform energy into life-forms, such as humans. In human form, transformed particles experience human emotions and the senses of touch, sight, sound, and taste. In the words of Jesus, the human lifeforms 'may have life, and have it to the full.' To be sure, we are the Divine having a human experience.

The Divine is not an old Caucasian bearded man sitting on a cloud punishing evil doers and granting wealth and happiness to faithful followers of his whims and laws. And certainly, the Divine does not grant forgiveness of sins—a distinctly human socially constructed concept—for the select group of people who profess to accept Jesus as their savior through a magical incantation. This patriarchal imagery represents "men as more godly and more normative than women." This image of God "as male or father is often a serious spiritual issue for women who have been abused by fathers or male authority figures."[20] The destructive and anachronistic personification of *God* is merely a patriarchal tool employed by those in power to dominate and control people for both benevolent and malevolent purposes.

The Divine is not a being at all, but instead it is the collective state of all energy. The Divine is *being*. When particles are in human form, they covet a return to the Divine state—free from the horrors of human life; namely, physical pain, intense feelings of isolation, emotional anguish, and spiritual uncertainly. The horrors of our human life experience *are never a punishment from God*. This malevolent patriarchal explanation was used for thousands of years to control and oppress us. The very essence of the human experience includes both pleasure and pain, and our pleasure and pain have absolutely nothing to do with divine rewards and punishments. *Nothing*.

The horrors of human existence prompt us to wish for a return to the Divine state manifest unambiguously in the human proclivity to addiction. In other words, the yearning to transcend the negative experiences of human existence via excessive abuse of opioids, alcohol, or sex is an overwhelming desire on the part of humans to rejoin the communal web of existence in the Divine where the collective provided safety, belonging, and peace. It is worth exploring, then, addiction and its relationship to a spiritual recovery process in order to reveal potential pathways to spiritual healing—including the spiritual healing needed after a sexual assault.

Addiction and the Desire to Reconnect with the Divine

Humans seeking the Divine take many different paths. Some join religious organizations for guidance. Some read spiritual tracts or visit sacred spaces. Others connect at regular retreats by isolating themselves from human society while still others commit to daily meditative practices that can include prayer rituals. In all cases, these active seekers hope to reconnect with the Divine to recover a sense of safety, belonging, and peace. But increasing numbers of people attempt to leave behind feelings of isolation, physical pain, emotional anguish, or spiritual uncertainty through excessive use of drugs, alcohol, or sex. Humans longing to return to a sense of safety, belonging, and peace in the Divine realm is so strong that people sometimes find themselves addicted to drugs, alcohol, or sex. Some mental health practitioners advocate beginning with an addict's current spiritual state through storytelling while encouraging spiritual growth and the acceptance of Divine grace as a conduit to recovery. Investigating this process can help us to establish pathways to move forward after sexual assault.

Craig Nakken reminds us that human relationships involving family, the Divine, self, and society "are based on emotionally connecting with others" while "addiction is based on emotional isolation."[21] And Gerald May emphasizes the power of the Divine's grace to this emotional isolation that results in addictive behavior, writing "true addictions are compulsive habitual behaviors that eclipse our concern for God and compromise our freedom, and that they must be characterized by tolerance, withdrawal symptoms, loss of willpower, and distortion of attention."[22] He adds, "it is in failure and helplessness that we can most honestly and completely turn to grace. Grace is our only hope for dealing with addiction, the only power that can truly vanquish its destructiveness."[23] Of course, humility and surrender play an important role in this process as well. He admits that he became "slightly more humble, through a growing appreciation of what I could and could not do to help myself or anyone else ... To be alive is to be addicted, and to be alive and addicted is to stand in need of grace."[24] Similarly, in order to take the first step toward addiction recovery, Ernest Kurtz and Katherine Ketcham argue that we need to reconnect with our spirituality.[25] Indeed, it is this common denominator that should be the focus of every aspect of our lives, not just addictions.

We must also come to appreciate the power and importance of stories in identifying addictions as well as treating them. Kurtz and Ketchum argue convincingly: "We can 'tell' only what we know, but we come to 'know' only in the telling."[26] They add,

> in the long history of spirituality, those recognized as somehow spiritually 'great' have consistently been called 'Teacher'—they help others to learn, to become teachable. Spiritual teachers (who are never 'experts') do three things: First and foremost, they listen. Second, they ask questions. Third, they tell stories. Each practice reflects the acceptance of not having all the answers, and each teaches the essential truth of spirituality's open-endedness.[27]

Storytelling is essential to spiritual growth.

Humility also plays a crucial role. Humility is "the acceptance of being human, the acceptance of one's human being."[28] And while humility is easy to identify and define, it is a very hard concept to own. This is extremely important for recovering addicts because it allows us to acknowledge that we have faults and that the faults are an essential component of being human. "Humility, as A.A. co-founder Bill Wilson understood so well, begins with rejection of the demand to be 'all-or-nothing' . . . Humility involves learning how to live with . . . being both saint and sinner, both beast and angel."[29]

This discussion of addiction reminds us that forgiveness, storytelling, and humility are essential components in any recovery or healing process. Ernest Kurtz and Katherine Ketcham suggest the positive aspects of letting go of the victimization caused by addiction. They argue, "This sense of *shared weakness* creates what is truly a *community*." And they submit that "Spirituality begins with this first insight: We are all imperfect. Such a vision not only invites but requires Tolerance: active appreciation of the richness and variety of human beings on this earth."[30] Recovery for victims forces us to embrace forgiveness, humility, and tolerance while setting aside our desire to control and dominate. Perhaps addiction offers *all of us* an opportunity for spiritual progress.[31] For when we embrace and cultivate the pain, hurt, and injustice in our lives, we become trapped in our victimhood, and we are robbed of our individual strength. Our *victimization becomes our identity*. Therefore, we must embrace forgiveness and humility if we choose to heal our wounds.

Pathway to Spiritual Healing: Forgiveness, Storytelling, and Humility

Ernest Kurtz and Katherine Ketcham suggest that we must embrace forgiveness in order for healing to take place. This does *not* mean that perpetrators should go unpunished. Certainly, a justice system that serves the victims of sexual assault might bring some type of punishment for perpetrators. But we know that this doesn't happen often enough. Many victims cannot testify against their abusers for a variety of reasons. Some victims feel so much responsibility for the attack that they cannot press charges due to successful grooming by the perpetrator or because society tells them that they wore the wrong clothes, drank too much, or engaged in other risky behaviors that were 'asking for it.' Other victims feel the need to suppress and compartmentalize the memory of violation in order to carry out daily functions. And still others know that many perpetrators found guilty in a court of law will never see any jail time. So why is it so important that a sexual assault victim forgives a vile perpetrator? Katherine Schwarzenegger cautions that holding on to our anger and the "traumatic past does nothing but consume your present emotional space." It is akin to "keeping the wound fresh and open; you never give it the chance to heal."[32]

Kurtz and Ketcham maintain, "To forgive, truly to forgive, involves letting go of the feeling of resentment *and* of the vision that underlies that feeling—the vision in which we see ourselves as being offended against, the vision of *self-as-victim*."[33] Similarly, Fred Luskin—co-founder and director of the Stanford University Forgiveness Project—outlines his prescription for an emotionally gratifying life in *Forgive for Good*. Luskin makes a convincing case for his process of *Positive Emotion Refocusing Technique* (PERT) and *HEAL* (Hope, Educate, Affirm, Long Term). Based on long-range studies, these steps *practiced religiously* change the way victims feel about others and themselves in an efficacious and sustainable healing process. Luskin reminds us that *forgiveness is not for the perpetrator*. Rather, it is an essential component of the healing process for victims. Only in this first step of forgiveness can victims begin to really move on to a state of healing.

Positive Emotion Refocusing Technique is a quick strategy for calming ourselves. First sit comfortably and take in mindful breaths. Inhale and exhale slowly and thoughtfully. Once you have grounded yourself in slow and mindful breathing, think about a person or animal you love. While you continue to breathe mindfully, focus your attention on your feelings as you concentrate on a loved one. When you find a sense of peace, begin to explore how you might overcome the violence you have endured. This exploration of the pathway to healing will not be accomplished in one session. We must revisit this process daily. The road to recovery is long.

Luskin's research shows these PERT strategies make people feel much better based, in part, upon his training sessions with Catholics and Protestants in Northern Ireland who lost family members to the brutal political violence. Forgiveness, Luskin explains,

> is a complex experience that changes an offended person's spiritual feelings, emotions, thoughts, actions, and self-confidence level. I believe learning to forgive the hurts and grudges of our life may be an important step for us to feel more hopeful and spiritually connected and less depressed.[34]

The foundation for most of the pain, suffering, and loss in our lives lies in the stories we create to describe our mistreatment and victimization. Luskin calls this process the *grievance story* in which we tend to exaggerate how much we have been offended then we blame this person and cultivate and encourage the pain we feel over time. This storytelling creates more agony and increases feelings of victimization. By dwelling on this pain and victimization, we allow perpetrators to control who we are—they have sustained power over us. Consequently, these *grievance stories* motivate us to create *unenforceable rules* to explain the behavior of others that prevent us from forgiving them. Our *grievance stories* almost always lead to long-term physical, mental, and spiritual anguish.

Instead of replaying these *grievance stories* and *unenforceable rules* over and over in our heads, Luskin counsels us to use forgiveness techniques designed to free us from the burden of victimization by assuming responsibility for *how we feel and behave*. Luskin reminds us that we have the *power to be the hero* or victim in our own life stories.

Luskin's HEAL (Hope, Educate, Affirm, Long Term) strategy can help victims to heal and grow after an assault. This process allows victims to take back their power, own their feelings, and choose to forgive and heal *for their own wellbeing*—not that of the perpetrator—without minimizing or denying the victim's pain and suffering. This process offers a pathway to peace and a means to recover one's hope for the future. The HEAL process asks victims to create *hope* statements to remind them that we can't control the actions of others, but we can aspire to hope for good things in our future. The *educate* step is a welcome reminder that there are limits to what we can control and limits to what we can accomplish. To *affirm*, a victim must learn something about themselves that will lead to a positive outcome in the future. And *long term* refers to our commitment to the healing and growth we desire and deserve. If victims take time each day to identify their grievances for the injustice they experienced, write about their feelings, design a plan for attending to their wellbeing, and create a plan to release the grievances, they can find a way forward as a hero in their personal story rather than as a victim. This process can include support groups or professional therapy if the individual cannot, or chooses not to, do this alone.

Moving beyond grief, hatred, anger, and resentment aligns with spiritual practices honored in monastic communities for centuries. But we all know how difficult it is to really forgive a heinous transgression against us committed with true malice. When we are able to accomplish this immense feat of forgiveness, we can glimpse the great goodness of Divine grace. James Timlin reminds us that we must "love one another. It's not easy; it never was easy to love your enemies, to love your neighbor. It's not ever going to be easy. Yet, that is what we are called to be."[35] An essential component for loving one another is forgiveness.

> You look at yourself. Put yourself up against that kind of great love and forgiveness to see how far we have to go. How much road we have to travel to become people who can be so loving and forgiving under those horrendous circumstances.[36]

Yet, forgiving is not as simple as Kurtz, Ketcham, Luskin, and Timlin suggest. In fact, forgiveness is quite complex. Everett Worthington advocates for two distinct types of forgiveness—decisional and emotional. Decisional forgiveness is a short-term act that requires the offended person to acknowledge the hurt, empathize with the offender, and make a deliberate decision to forgive. Emotional forgiveness, on the other hand, begins when the victim makes a public commitment to forgive and then works on forgiving for an extended period of time.[37] Certainly, committing to a forgiving mindset is not a quick and easy solution. It takes a resolute dedication to daily practices—as in Luskin's PERT and HEAL methods—to genuinely embark on a pathway to healing. Allen Gee warns that "what passes on the surface as forgiveness is not real forgiveness, but mere repression. It only works for so long before the hidden unforgiveness manifests in both subtle and obvious ways, negatively impacting our lives." Gee suggests that we must use language that "speaks to the heart in terms that the heart can hear."[38] However difficult the long process of forgiveness is, the process does offer hope for a peaceful and spiritually satisfying existence after sexual assault.

For me personally, shedding the oppressive religious dogma and scripture of the faith I grew up with and embracing a more holistic spirituality with an emphasis on compassion, love, and forgiveness was the first step toward my recovery after sexual assault. This first step allowed me to leave behind the unwanted baggage of self-loathing and victim blaming justified by these patriarchal texts and teachings. With this step, I felt more open to explore the storytelling, humility, and forgiveness that many practitioners believe can lead to recovery for addicts, and as I argued in this chapter, the recovery path for sexual assault victims as well.

Indeed, my current spiritual life is greatly impacted by my commitment to forgiveness and humility. I identified with the core components of the grievances that have been taking up a lot of space in my own mental warehouse; namely the exaggerated taking of personal offense, blaming the offender for how I feel, and the creation of an expanding grievance story.[39] Examining this issue of forgiveness forced me to recognize the destructive nature of holding onto grievance stories and the enhanced victimization that they produce. I had always struggled with the Christian mandate to forgive and reconciling it with my inclination to abandon unhealthy relationships. But the exploration of forgiveness provided in this chapter, does not require reconciliation with hurtful people, nor does it require me to condone their illegal and immoral actions. My current spiritual life benefits from this recognition in many ways. First, I am living the Divine's mandate to forgive and I'm doing it in a way that is meaningful. I really can forgive without embracing the perpetrator and this allows me to release the anger and free up the space in my mind and soul for love and service. Gerald May reminds us that "Often it is not until this momentum brings us to some point of existential despair, some rock bottom, some impasse, that we become capable of beginning to reclaim our true desire" to be in communion with the Divine.[40]

> *If I develop bad feelings toward those who make me suffer, this will only destroy my own peace of mind. But if I forgive, my mind becomes calm.*
>
> (Dalai Lama)

Notes

1 See for instance, Burton Throckmorton's *Gospel Parallels: A Comparison of the Synoptic Gospels* (1992).
2 For an excellent synthesis of modern biblical scholarship, see John Shelby Spong's *Re-Claiming the Bible for a Non-Religious World* (2013).
3 Biblical scholars agree that the authors of the four gospels in the New Testament were not eyewitnesses to the events they depict.
4 Elizabeth Johnson, "Ephesians" in Newsom and Ringe eds. *The Women's Bible Commentary* (Westminster: John Knox Press, 1992) 338. Some scholars argue that Paul's Epistle to the Hebrews was written by Priscilla, one of Paul's trusted ministers. [See for instance: Ruth Hoppin, *Priscilla's Letter: Finding the Author of the Epistle to the Hebrews* (Lost Coast Press, 2009)]. Paul thought so highly of Priscilla as an equal that it is difficult to imagine that he authored the misogynistic text in Ephesians.
5 Johnson, "Ephesians," 338.
6 Johnson, "Ephesians," 338. The documents addressed to the Ephesians and Colossians were created to dispel heretical teachings that had infected the community and threatened a major schism after Paul's death. Community interlopers appear to foster a systemic threat that only an apostolic letter as a preface for a collection of Paul's letters might subdue. Toward that end, Ephesians and Colossians call on believers—significantly, a *united* group of both Jews and gentiles as "one new humanity" (Eph. 2:15)—to dissociate themselves from these interlopers (Eph. 3–14) and cling to their *unique* Christian fellowship (Eph. 5:15–20).
7 Mary Shivanandan, "Feminism and Marriage: A Reflection on Ephesians 5:21–33" Accessed 10/15/21 www.catholiceducation.org/articles/printarticle.html?id=817.
8 Mary Ann Tolbert, *Sowing the Gospel: Mark's World in Literary Historical Perspective to Multiple Interpretations* (Fortress Press, 1989).
9 Sandy Hack Polaski, *A Feminist Introduction to Paul* (Chalice Press, 2005) 188.
10 John MacArthur Jr., *Divine Design: God's Complimentary Roles for Men and Women* (David Cook, 2011).
11 Carole R. Bohn, "Dominion to Rule: The Roots and Consequences of a Theology of Ownership," in *Christianity, Patriarchy, and Abuse: A Feminist Critique*, ed. Joanne Carlson Brown and Carole R. Bohn (Cleveland: Pilgrim, 1989) 107.
12 Virginia Ramey Mollenkott, "Emancipative Elements in Ephesians 5.21–33: Why Feminist Scholarship has (Often) Left Them Unmentioned, and Why They Should be Emphasized." In Amy-Jill Levine's *A Feminist Companion to the Deutero-Pauline Epistles* (T&T Clark, 2003) 40.
13 Mollenkott, "Emancipative Elements in Ephesians," 41–42.
14 Mollenkott, "Emancipative Elements in Ephesians," 42.
15 Mollenkott, "Emancipative Elements in Ephesians," 55–56.
16 Gary Macy, *The Hidden History of Women's Ordination: Female Clergy in the Medieval West* (Oxford University Press, 2008) 51.
17 Erin Vearncombe, Brandon Scott, Hal Taussig, *After Jesus Before Christianity: A Historical Exploration of the First Two Centuries of Jesus Movements* (HarperOne, 2021).
18 Robin Meyers, *Saving God from Religion: A Minister's Search for Faith in a Skeptical Age* (Convergent Books, 2020).

19 Consciousness is a state of self-awareness that is not biological. Nobel laureate Roger Penrose argues that consciousness is a product of quantum effects. [Penrose, *The Emperor's New Mind* (Oxford University Press, 2016)]. See also Johannes Kleiner and Sean Tull "The Mathematical Structure of Information Integration Theory" (2020). Retrieved 2.19.22 at https://arxiv.org/pdf/2002.07655.pdf.
20 Christie Cozad Neuger, *Counseling Women: A Narrative, Pastoral Approach* (Minneapolis: Fortress Press, 2001) 97.
21 Craig Nakken, *The Addictive Personality* (New York: MJF Books, 1997) 23.
22 Gerald May, *Addiction and Grace: Love and Spirituality in the Healing of Addictions* (New York: Harper, 1991) 37.
23 May, *Addiction and Grace*, 16.
24 May, *Addiction and Grace*, 11.
25 Ernest Kurtz and Katherine Ketcham, *The Spirituality of Imperfection: Storytelling and the Search for Meaning* (New York: Bantam Books, 2002) 199.
26 Kurtz and Ketcham, *The Spirituality of Imperfection*, 89.
27 Kurtz and Ketcham, *The Spirituality of Imperfection*, 142.
28 Kurtz and Ketcham, *The Spirituality of Imperfection*, 186.
29 Kurtz and Ketcham, *The Spirituality of Imperfection*, 190.
30 Kurtz and Ketcham, *The Spirituality of Imperfection*, 199.
31 Theologian Mary Reuter argues "we need to become detached from material gain, second from self-importance and third from the urge to dominate others. Only through this process of stripping away these attachments, she writes, can we lay claim to spiritual progress." [Quoted in Kurtz and Ketcham, 172–173]
32 Katherine Schwarzenegger, *The Gift of Forgiveness: Inspiring Stories from Those Who Have Overcome the Unforgivable* (Penguin Life, 2021).
33 Kurtz and Ketcham, *The Spirituality of Imperfection*, 222.
34 Fred Luskin, *Forgive for Good* (New York: Harper, 2003).
35 James Timlin, "Love One Another" www.catholic.org/featured/headline.php?ID=2950 (accessed June 1, 2021).
36 Timlin, "Love One Another."
37 Everett Worthington, "The Power of Forgiveness" www.thepowerofforgiveness.com/about/peopleinthefilm/worthington.html (accessed June 1, 2021).
38 Allen Gee, *The Language of Deep Forgiveness: Break from Struggling to Accept the Unacceptable* (Purple Dove Press, 2020).
39 Luskin, *Forgive for Good*, xiii.
40 May, *Addiction and Grace*, 95.

Bibliography

Bohn, Carole R. "Dominion to Rule: The Roots and Consequences of a Theology of Ownership," in *Christianity, Patriarchy, and Abuse: A Feminist Critique*, ed. Joanne Carlson Brown and Carole R. Bohn (Cleveland: Pilgrim, 1989).

Carnes, Patrick. *A Gentle Path through the Twelve Steps* (Center City, MN: Hazelden, 1993).

Durken, Daniel ed. *New Collegeville Bible Commentary: New Testament* (Liturgical Press, 2008).

Gee, Allen. *The Language of Deep Forgiveness: Break from Struggling to Accept the Unacceptable* (Purple Dove Press, 2020).

Hoppin, Ruth. *Priscilla's Letter: Finding the Author of the Epistle to the Hebrews* (Lost Coast Press, 2009).

Johnson, Elizabeth. "Ephesians" in Newsom and Ringe eds. *The Women's Bible Commentary* (Westminster: John Knox Press, 1992) 338–342.

Kurtz, Ernest and Ketcham, Katherine. *The Spirituality of Imperfection: Modern Wisdom from Classic Stories* (New York: Bantam, 1992).

Luskin, Fred. *Forgive for Good* (New York: Harper, 2003).

MacArthur Jr., John. *Divine Design: God's Complimentary Roles for Men and Women* (David Cook, 2011).

Macy, Gary. *The Hidden History of Women's Ordination: Female Clergy in the Medieval West* (Oxford University Press, 2008).

May, Gerald. *Addiction and Grace* (New York: Harper and Row, 2007).

Mollenkott, Virginia Ramey. "Emancipative Elements in Ephesians 5.21–33: Why Feminist Scholarship has (Often) Left Them Unmentioned, and Why They Should be Emphasized." In Amy-Jill Levine's *A Feminist Companion to the Deutero-Pauline Epistles* (T&T Clark, 2003) 37–58.

Nakken, Craig. *The Addictive Personality* (New York: MJF Books, 1997).

Neuger, Christie Cozad. *Counseling Women: A Narrative, Pastoral Approach* (Minneapolis: Fortress Press, 2001).

Polaski, Sandra Hack. *A Feminist Introduction to Paul* (Chalice Press, 2005).

Ruether, Rosemary Radford. *Sexism and God-Talk: Toward a Feminist Theology* (Boston: Beacon Press, 1983).

Schwarzenegger, Katherine. *The Gift of Forgiveness: Inspiring Stories from Those Who Have Overcome the Unforgivable* (Penguin Life, 2021).

Shivanandan, Mary. "Feminism and Marriage: A Reflection on Ephesians 5:21–33" Accessed 10/15/21, www.catholiceducation.org/articles/printarticle.html?id=817.

Spong, John Shelby. *Re-Claiming the Bible for a Non-Religious World* (HarperOne, 2013).

Throckmorton, Burton. *Gospel Parallels: A Comparison of the Synoptic Gospels* (Thomas Nelson, 1992).

Tolbert, Mary Ann. *Sowing the Gospel: Mark's World in Literary Historical Perspective to Multiple Interpretations* (Fortress Press, 1989).

Vearncombe, Erin, et al., *After Jesus Before Christianity: A Historical Exploration of the First Two Centuries of Jesus Movements* (HarperOne, 2021).

Worthington, Everett. "The Power of Forgiveness" www.thepowerofforgiveness.com/about/peopleinthefilm/worthington.html (accessed June 1, 2021).

Index

accountability 9, 11, 13, 15, 27, 44, 117
ancestors 121, 125, 131–32, 167
anger 46, 60, 64–65, 67, 73, 109, 126, 135, 152–54, 202, 205, 207–08
Aymara culture 127–132, 134–137

betrayal 7–8, 9–10, 11, 13, 45, 46, 47
Biblical manuscript tradition 195
binary thinking (Dualism) 61, 62, 87–89
Black female sexuality 97, 98, 101–04
bodily autonomy 9, 84, 90

Catholics: 69, 70, 71, 129, 130–32, 195; and the *Baltimore Catechism* 71–72; clergy sexual abuse 42–45, 47–53
Christianity (general): 1, 68–71, 85–87, 89–90
clericalism 44, 45
cognitive dissonance 63, 68, 70
college students *see* university students
colonization 127–30, 142
Common Ground 24–40
compassion 14–15, 26
complexity of God 69–71, 86–87
congregation: 6, 7, 9, 28, 34, 72, 181; case studies involving 8–14
consent 6, 9, 72

dialectical (non-binary, cyclical) thinking 60–61, 62, 70–71
Divine Feminine 175–91

Divine Mother 141–42, 145, 146–48, 152–55
dynamics of power and vulnerability 6–8, 37, 177

empathy 74, 87, 143, 153

faith communities *see* spiritual communities
FaithTrust Institute 5–17
feminism and feminist theory 5, 6, 11, 99, 110, 177, 179, 182, 185, 190, 199
fiduciary responsibility 6–8, 14
forgiveness 2, 13, 17, 86, 116–17, 122, 124, 129, 200–01, 203, 205–08
Fortune, Marie 5, 14, 72

gender identity 11–14, 48, 53
Gnosticism 88–89, 91, 101

healing: through the arts 83–84, 108, 119, 165–70, 177–79, 182–84, 187–89; through dreams 107, 109, 110–11, 170–73, 175–76, 186–87; through empathy 74, 143–44; through interdependence 120, 125; through interfaith dialogue 142–44; through justice 14–16; through listening 24–26, 86–87; through liturgy 27–30, 37, 38–40; through love 71, 73–75, 146–48, 200–1; through nature 135–37, 160–64; through physical (somatic or tantric) therapy 83, 90, 91, 148–50, 151–52, 206; through

play and storytelling 108, 204–5; through prayer 23, 26–37, 38–40; through self-dialogue (or trataka meditation) 107, 150
Hebrew Bible 7
hembrismo (or the exaggerated feminine) 129–30
hermeneutics 199
heuristic paradigm 3, 99–100, 104–09
Hinduism and Shakti Bhakti tradition 141–42, 144–55
Hispanic theology 130
household codes 195–96, 199

imago Dei 84–85, 90
institutional betrayal 6–8, 9–11, 45, 47
intersectional recovery *see* healing

Jehovah's Witnesses 101, 116
Jesuits 24, 25, 47–48, 50
justice-making agenda 5, 14–16

Latin female sexuality 134
LGBTQIA+ community 11–14, 48, 50–51, 53, 60, 63–64, 70, 71, 195
linear (sequential) thinking 61–62, 66, 69–70
liturgy 23–40, 181–82

machismo (and the macho man) 129–30
male gaze 81, 84
marginalized communities 2, 8, 11, 12, 26, 27, 40, 53, 87, 195, 197
marianismo (or mariana woman) 129–30
moral injury 42–53
Myth of the Virgin Mary Survivor 11

natural law 69–70, 201–2
New Testament 29, 33, 67–68, 71, 73, 89, 91, 101, 196–97

Pacha Mama 127–28, 135
patriarchy 2, 84, 99, 101, 128–29, 198–99

Paul of Tarsus 196–98
Pentecost 29
PTSD (post traumatic stress disorder) xiv, 46, 50, 80, 83, 88
prayer 23–40, 44, 66–67, 71, 73, 89, 90
Presbyterian *Book of Order* 27–28
process theology 70
Protestants 26, 49, 69, 195
purity culture 36, 147

racism 11, 133
religious communities *see* spiritual communities
restitution 14, 15–16, 117

self-identity 97, 98
self-objectification 81, 84, 87
sexual abuse *see* sexual assault
sexual assault: 42, 43, 80, 81, 82–85, 87–91; in childhood 43, 97–99, 100, 102, 103–04, 105–06, 109, 116–17; and Christianity 33, 42–53; by clergy 42–45, 63, 72, 73; and exploitation 84–85, 102; and legal system 117–19; and morality 11, 45–47; and rape culture 25, 80, 81, 102, 106
sexual assault victims *see* victim-survivors
sexual harassment 11–14
sexual objectification 80–92
sexual perpetrators 43, 44, 103
sexual violence *see* sexual assault
shame 27, 36, 39, 45, 46, 47, 80, 83, 100, 105, 110, 125, 132, 135, 136, 190
shamanism 127–28, 130–31, 132–33, 134–35
sin 10, 67–70, 72–73, 85–86, 117, 132, 133, 190
slavery 98, 101–02, 120
social media 10, 24, 87
somatic spirituality 88–91, 91–92
soul xv, 71, 73, 84, 88–89, 106, 125, 166, 175, 176–77, 178–79, 181, 183, 184, 185, 187, 188, 190, 208
soul loss 133
soul-retrieval 127–28, 130, 133, 135–37

spiritual communities: case studies involving 8–14, 24–40, 47–53; and justice for victims 14–16; moral responsibility of 5, 13; as protector of sexual predators 5, 10, 15, 42–43; as resource for healing 5, 13, 24, 26, 27, 39–40, 85, 86; as roadblock to healing 5, 9, 13, 27, 43–44, 85, 198–99; safety of 8, 11, 13
spiritual leaders 6; on campus 24–29, 34–35; failure of 8–17, 36, 42–53, 64, 72; power of 6–8, 9, 16, 37, 44, 64, 72; training of 30–37, 44, 45
suicide xii, 84–85, 100
survivors *see* victim-survivors

theology of the cross 86, 91–92
theology of glory 86
theology of identification 146–148
trauma 1, 3, 7–8, 13–14, 15–16, 23, 25, 27–28, 36, 39–40, 42, 45–46, 52, 73, 80, 82–92, 97, 103, 117, 122, 125, 127, 130–31, 132–137, 141, 142, 147, 149–50, 152, 155, 159, 166–67, 176, 177, 180, 181–84, 187, 189–91

trauma-informed care: 85–87; case studies involving 8–14, 27–28, 36
trust xiii, 1, 8, 10, 36–37, 43, 46, 52, 64–65, 73, 131, 153–55, 159, 188, 191, 199
truth-telling 14, 16, 116

university students: 24–40, 47–53; and sexual assault 25, 175

victim-survivors: 25, 39, 72, 84–85, 91–92; case studies involving 8–14, 105–11, 116; and justice 14–16; mistreatment of 45; protection of 15; and race 102, 109; and social media 10, 24, 87; vulnerability of 6–8, 36, 84
vindication 14, 16

West African religion 100, 107
women of color: experiences of 8, 11; Black women 97–111, 116–26; Latina and indigenous women 127–37
worship 23–40

Xavier University 24, 25, 26